Adventures in Hell

Volume 1

Vietnam War Stories

D0880561

Adventures in Hell, Volume I

Vietnam War Stories by Vietnam Vets

Edited by David 'Doc' Andersen

Foreword by John F. Stetter, Director
Texas A&M University Press

Cover art by Gary Spears, Seattle
Photo of editor by Randy Forbes, Spokane

Ritz Publishing
202 West Fifth Avenue, Ritzville Washington 99169

First printing 1990

Although the authors and publisher have ascertained all sources to ensure the accuracy and completeness of the information contained in this book, we assume no responsibility for errors, inaccuracies, omissions or any inconsistency herein. Any slights of people or organizations are unintentional.

This volume contains explicit reference to violence, drugs and profanity, none of which Ritz Publishing endorses. Such references were retained by the editor as a natural part of the stories in which violence, drugs and profanity were an integral part.

Library of Congress Cataloging in Publication Data
Andersen, David Arnold
    Adventures in Hell, Volume I
Library of Congress Catalog Card Number:
90-63442
ISBN 0-9627904-3-5

This collection of stories,
poems and historical, first-person
essays is dedicated
to all those whose lives
were touched and troubled
by the Vietnam War.

Foreword

As with every major conflict preceding it throughout twentieth century history, the Vietnam War has been the source and inspiration for literally thousands of short stories, novels, and essays. The published literature of this war, which ranges from classic examples of reportage like Michael Herr's *Dispatches* to intensely autobiographical fiction such as *The Thirteenth Valley*, has often been written by trained journalists and historians on the one hand and skilled professional writers on the other.

There is a third group of individuals who have recorded the Vietnam War in words: the veterans who have important stories to tell who, in many cases, still struggle with the memories of that war on a daily basis. By publishing the work of Vietnam vets who, in some cases, might otherwise go unpublished, David Andersen is bringing you an uncensored and unadulterated vision of the longest and most controversial war America fought in this century. His volume is a remedying of a situation, putting important stories in the hands of libraries, bookstores, and the American people.

These stories are raw and painful in the same say that combat is, and require that the reader abandon conventional notions of good and evil in the same way that soldiers must in war in order to survive.

The stories that follow here won't be turned into made-for-TV movies of the week, won't turn up as plots for "China Beach." They will provide you with a true and harrowing vision of what the Vietnam War was like for the individuals who actually fought it.

As my publisher/combat medic friend David Andersen would say, "Welcome to Hell . . . "

> John F. Stetter
> Director
> Texas A&M University Press

Table of Contents

Introduction

Twenty-two years ago I began a brief odyssey that was an adventure in hell. When I returned from South Vietnam, I expected a great song to arise from the tumult, a paean of triumph and sorrow. But there was only an uncomfortable silence. Much later, fragmentary images of the war appeared, as novels and movies. Like reflections on a lake, those images created a desire to see the waters at greater depth.

This book, the first volume in a series, taps into reflections and currents that still move in our society. It offers true expressions that often represent long pent-up visions of life in hell. It contains fiction and non-fiction, and sometimes a combination of both. I have touched as little as possible the alchemy of the following words. Each tale contains its own magic, its own unique reflections. These voices are part of a long, great song.

David Andersen

Robert J. Flanagan

Robert J. Flanagan, with seven years in the Marine Corps, retired as a Warrant Officer after sixteen years in Army Intelligence. He served two tours in Vietnam in air and ground units, moved around with intelligence assignments, and saw a lot of country, from "Eye" Corps to the Delta. After the war, and several special assignments, he retired in Virginia, where he completed his work for a degree in Communications, was the first graduate of George Mason University's MFA program in Creative Writing, and went on for a second Masters in Literature.

He taught American Literature and Writing part time, while continuing work on a novel of the war, publishing excerpts from the novel as short fiction. He has published other short stories and poetry, and he has given poetry and fiction readings, while working full-time at a "paying" job. He is still at work on the novel, of which the following story ("Green on Green") is a part. And he still worries that the rush for instant results and spelled-out information/instructions in today's life continues to erode the time and place for poetry.

Says author Flanagan: "I've been at this novel so long, I've seen all the perturbations in attitude toward so-called Vietnam Literature, from anathema, to hysterical and slavish overkill when it became fashionable to suddenly 'discover' the writings of vets, to commercial exploitation, and now to drawdown and forgetfulness as we as a society rush on to new infatuations. That's just us — that's America: attention span and long-term commitment is in the decimal point range. But there's still so much to be said, to be told, to remember, to critique... to learn from.

"In 1981, a major literary agency told me that I should direct my writing to some other area, that everything had been said that needed saying about Vietnam and that no one would buy anymore books on the subject. This was before the flood of increasingly prescient literature of the mid- to late-80s, before The Wall, before *Platoon* and *Hamburger Hill* and *Full Metal Jacket* hit the screen. And still it goes.

"The style, in 'Green on Green' and in much of the novel from which it comes, is perhaps unique. All writers, I think, hope for some of that, but fear it also. In my case, I found nothing else works. The Vietnam War had no continuity. It had no consistency — except for fear, heat, and malaria pills — either in our policies or goals, and I think all who served there intuitively felt that discontinuity, even at the grunt level. A tour in Vietnam was 365 days of vignettes, stand-alone events which may or may not have had correlation with any other event. The events in 'Green on Green' were such a vignette, a minor ripple in the flow, and when it was over, it might never have happened — just a hiccup in a life of indigestion."

GREEN ON GREEN

By Robert J. Flanagan
From a novel in progress

DANTON was stenciled on his gear. DANTON, M., with no middle name. No one in the platoon ever knew his first name either — records showed only an initial. He came to Delta Company from a recovery ward at Cam Ranh-South, and some old timers — elderly nineteen and twenty-two year olds who had come in country with the 133rd and had managed to remain vertical and warm because they looked quicker, moved faster, and learned without question — remembered him from earlier existence of a Charlie Company. Before Charlie Company took Operation Junction City into the Ashau Valley. Before a diet of realism, of hard truths, bad country, and the 391st NVA Battalion had slimmed them down from a hundred sixty-three men to just Danton and two other fragile remnants in the 45-hour doodah that shaped the Brigade forever after.

Back then, in the days of Charlie extant, Danton was just a draftee infantryman, designated sniper. Fashionably hip, strung out on whatever he could find, whenever: beads, peace symbols, numbers on his helmet cover in a descending arrogance as if they were some kind of holy promise of making it all the way down to zero, some kind of magic marker mantra. His record photos showed nothing extraordinary. He was near cross-section height and weight, and his coloring was white or pink or tan, depending upon whether you saw him in the sun, the shade, or the light of flares. Just a kid grunt.

He was competent as a sniper, nothing special, though he joked he suffered because he wasn't a country-bred, squirrel hunting natural like Alvin York of Tennessee. The product of riverfront New Orleans, he'd acquired what skill he had by practice, reasonable dedication to the mystique of the craft, and slightly more than a passing interest in surviving his three-sixty-five in Nam. But that was before.

When he left the burn ward at Cam Ranh, the skin on his hands was still candy pink and glossy and the hair had not come in evenly. But he was total billboard soldier: the sparse hair was high and tight, the patchy skin clean-shaven, decked out in shiny brand new pressed green ripstop jungle fatigues with that quartermaster sheen still on them that marked the wearer as a new guy or some kind of career freak. The spitshine on his boots was a measure of how out of place he was on the firebase. For their sins, Second Platoon got Danton while the battalion was in standdown in a semi-secure zone near a ville without a name, appearing only as a dirty smudge on the tactical map.

Snipers are never run-of-the-mill, since often they're the only ones who have a chance to see who they're killing, the only ones usually who know for sure they *have* killed. The mechanized, depersonalized, managed-rather-than-commanded killing-and-dying-in-a-hail-of-automatic-fire so far removed the average soldier from any identification of moral objectives that personal motivation was not even vigorously sought and was looked upon with surprise and mild cynicism when encountered in a non-career soldier. Still, Danton's second coming was no more than a ripple on the pond that was the 133rd's AO.

Something about him, though — actually everything about him — discouraged familiarity. The new troops, the replacements who were Danton's civilian life contemporaries, the FNGs who stumbled in through the dust of chopper pads wherever in Two Corps they could catch up with the brigade, walked a wide circle about him from the start. Young troops conditioned by a generation of John Wayne filtered through Freudian overlays thought it was merely that Danton was a sniper, thought the personal facing off with verified kills, seeing the faces through the friendliness of the scope, provoked the isolation. Captain Crunch knew the young convert's particular job, albeit a labor of love, had nothing to do with it. *HOW* Danton killed was only incidental to *why*.

It was never complicated. Junction City had been Danton's rite of passage, sterner perhaps than that of most nineteen year olds, and it left him in a somewhat enviable mode vis-a-vis his craft, devoid of the tangential impedimenta of compassion. In the Ashau, he'd left behind not only a lot of friends, but all he had of naivete, innocence, and compassion. The bloods said he had no Soul, but even the humorless skeptics in the Recon Squad knew he had no *soul*. And then there were the eyes.

Black, like marbles, like there was no iris, just a large pupil. And no luster. Writers of hard-core adventure tales would have him with cold eyes. Not Danton. Those flat black shark's eyes burned as if with fever, day and night, happy or sad, little opportunity though there was to see Danton happy. The only time when his eyes did not have that burning, possessed look was when he snuggled into the stock of the Model 70 and found the rim of the scope. Then there was a sort of vagueness about his entire expression, a relaxing of the rigid lines. At least the left eye, the one free of the scope, was blank. Not cold, not burning then, just blank.

But the real kicker, what defined him as the cynosure he became, was the paint. Danton wore LRRP mascara, camouflage grease paint on the face and hands for patrolling and skulking about in someone else's real estate. But Danton wore the camouflage inside the wire, too. At first it was the standard broken pattern of black and brown and green. Later, as his devotion to the world outside the wire grew, there was a subtle shift toward using two or three shades of green. He slept and ate in the anonymity of the mask. He put it on the day he joined Charlie Company and he was never without it after that, a sad, surprisingly green Pagliacci in a bad production.

The first time the platoon watched him at what he did best, they realized it wasn't as if he got any pleasure from it. And that first evening, even as the members of his squad watched and knew he was setting up shop for the first time since the Ashau, they saw nothing that looked like sloppy work.

He came on line in the early dusk, the delineations between shades of green on his face faded to insignificance. He walked bent-over to the corner of the berm where the sandbags projected out over a little draw that ran down into the bush. The sun was already below the jungle crown to the west, and the sky had that fading luminescence that makes scope work tricky. He just stood in the corner, staring off across the ravine for awhile at the hill line behind the village some nine hundred meters away. Then he crawled into a tight corner of the sandbags and pulled from a canvas bag an old, scarred spotting scope, wrapped in Ace bandage. He lay staring through the scope for a long time. He never spoke when he worked.

Dusk was the time, all right. There was a lot of movement in and around the village as the resident farmers shifted gears and became the resident Viet Cong. Through the scope Danton had a clear picture of anyone carrying a weapon or acting compromisingly military. Finally, he slid the Model 70 into place, worked the bolt slowly and silently to load a round, and lay still.

Lieutenant Franconi sat by the command APC and watched Danton for almost an hour. Sergeant Glasgow came and waited with him for awhile, neither speaking, Danton acknowledging neither of them. It was like scrutinizing a still life, waiting for it to declare itself in some unlikely move. Danton just lay, hunkered into the corner of the sandbags. The long taped-up rifle barrel stuck out through the firing enclosure over no-man's land. Everyone on the firebase knew by then, and they waited. Everything slowed down. Stopped.

After more than an hour of increasing tension, just before stark dark, there was a sudden explosion. One shot. Beyond the wire everything was a sameness of deep shadow. Danton lay where he was, hunched into the scope, for another ten minutes. Then he straightened, stood up and stepped carefully back down off the ammo box, slung his piece, and slipped on down the line in the dark.

After that he selected just one target from the vantage point of the firebase in a day's time, never more. Sometimes none at all, as the VC presence went subliminal. Occasionally, a hit was made in the opposite quadrant, into what was supposedly a secure and friendly area, but if it was questionable how valid his target was, no one voiced the query.

When Danton began disappearing from the firebase, it was assumed he was out hunting on his own with no spotter or backup, a violation of sniper orders but within the bounds of acceptable performance. Then a captain visiting from Brigade took a round through the head on the edge of the berm one rainy dawn. The round was from an SKS Soviet sniper's rifle, but the shot came from out of range of the regular VC snipers. The Delta XO remembered afterward that it was while Danton was beyond the wire. By the time he was sought out, Danton was found in his bunker.

No one from the battalion was ever fired on in such circumstances, but when a brigade major on an inspection visit was grazed by a shot as he unexpectedly bent over, the brigade visits stopped. Soldiers began to remember rumors of staff ineptness, brigade waffling, that led to the Ashau Valley disaster. Danton was had before the CO and later some CID people, but he came back to his bunker almost smiling.

That all happened in the first month or so after Danton joined Delta Company, and was distinctly separate from what happened when he began to recognize his targets beyond the wire, his rare comments relating sightings of soldiers known to have bought it on Junction City, people wasted, stuffed in body bags, and rotated.

And then Danton went away.

SURVIVALS

By Robert Flanagan

November
downside of the year . . .
village streets overhung
with bells that will not ring,
red berried wreaths that smell of plastic wrap,
tinsel candles,
obscene Santas in styrofoam. Flamboyant
maple dress in tidy heaps
shadows the base of trees,
swept crisp into pyramids:
fields for burning,
gold and red carnage,
lifestyle of the season.

On a branch
against the autumn sky
persists one cluster, leaves not brown
or red
or even gold;
green, not yet begun to fade.
An anachronism of verdure
perennial in its audacity,
flaunting its perverse indestructibility,
it is so alone!

The first time, there was wonder
a curiosity only: a missed meal
and those found in the rubble
missed the rest of the war.

Continued

The maples, bare
but for the stubborn aberration, sway
in the preparative winds of coming winter.
Unstrung fletches, green against
      the backdrop sky
   where a hawk drifts on the airborne tide.
His wings do not flap; neither does he fly,
but slides, whispering
acrest the bitter drafts,
lazing through altitudes haughty in rule
over domains synthetically ordered.

   The next time I knew an uneasy fear.
   Without playing odds, I sat out the
   mission and Army One-Five-One took out
   three sapping trees in Michelin Tresieme.

Out of the west
down from eight o'clock high, like a MiG
hurled at a BUF, a murderous
deranged starling bold
in his madness dives
   on the hawk who is complacent with ignorance.

Continued

One slashing pass and the interceptor climbs out,
erratic,
a killing urge sated. The hawk staggers
across the cobalt battleground, flounces,
regains what little remains
of a reigning demeanor.

A feather — hawk or starling — spirals
crimson with stain
through the branches of the maple to blend
in the crimson of the fallen leaves.

The third time is when the dreams began:
hooch and bunk, rent by Slavic steel
rotting sandbags against my sweating cheek,
aces and queens, wasted like the chips
across the abandoned floor,
and the rockets walking away through the
silent aircraft crouching in revetments.

Faced with anomalies of the maple
and the audacious starling
I can but marvel on this silly season,
acknowledging my own part
in these pompous grasps for survival.

Down the darkened hallway behind me
away from the militant, feathered avenger
discounting greenness in the sugared bough,
seeing only irregularity, ugly in the burnished
steel shard against blue velvet,
the memory is overplayed.

How dramatic we posture
over mere instinctive survival.
Probably the hawk would understand.

WIRE

By Robert Flanagan

Once as a child on the farm
I tore a berry stained hand on a rusty talon of fencing.
Grandma put kerosene on it —
   a very southern remedy —
but my mother insisted . . .
I cried when I got the shot.

Flat crowned and ten-gallon-hatted outriders,
myth building down the years,
stretched long shimmering bands of two prong
      and Glidden strands
 across the land
along the steady flowing east-west highways.

On the docks at First Log
ugly rolls with hotcross ends
share the Sea-Land space with
  pallets of Lucky Lager
  stacks of C-s
  and empty aluminum boxes.

At Phan Thiet
astride Route 13 on a hill that bears the name
of its prominence
 four-sixty-seven
the sun creeps up, scattering demons
beyond Phan Rang
somewhere in the lOlst's area of operations.
The colonel told me Apollo works for the Screaming Eagle.

Continued

Here the wire,
concertina in stark prickly relief
against the blaze of dawn,
is strung with rags and odd, disjointed puppets
no longer responsive to strings.

Tiny brown commissars who came last night without invite
must stay now
indifferently awaiting the cleanup squad.

The hot season is months away,
the heat of the day hours distant, yet
already yesterday's *nuoc mam* and garlic are blending
    gasses in the few bellies that are whole
filling the dawn with a wretchedness
only scavengers can cure.

The wire will be clean before dark,
long before they come again,
but already the enthusiasm for windchimes is waning.

James M. Mueller Jr.

Says author Mueller: "I volunteered for service in Vietnam. I was assigned to Advisory Team 3 MACV (with the 1st ARVN Division) in Hue. I was clerk-typist, security clerk, OER clerk and awards clerk from May 1967 to May 1968. I was awarded the Army Commendation Medal for meritorious service, and the Bronze Star for valor.

"My Vietnam experiences taught me that when a war is fought, it should be a military action, not political! I also learned that I wanted to do something special with my life when I returned to the 'world,' so I got my BS in elementary education from Penn State, my M.Ed. from Millersville University, and my principal's certificate from Temple. I have devoted the past eighteen years of my life to education.

"I am currently a fifth-grade teacher in Lancaster, Pennsylvania. I have also been involved with teaching students about death and dying. Because of this important work, I have been featured in *KAPPAN* Magazine (Oct. 1978), ABC's '20/20' (Sept. 1990), and the *Philadelphia Inquirer* (Sept. 1990). I have been happily married for over twenty-one years, and am proud of our two beautiful teenage daughters."

A Christmas to Remember

By James M. Mueller Jr.

The weather was cooler, the leaves were changing color and the season of autumn was in the air. The cool breeze of November was a relief from the hot, hazy and humid summer. That was the message that was on the tape recording from State College, Pennsylvania. My family was telling me about what it was like at home. It was Thanksgiving... 1967.

This hour-long tape was recorded for me, Specialist James M. Mueller, Jr. I was a clerk typist assigned to the MACV Advisory Team 3. My duties were to assist the 1st ARVN Division, headquartered in the ancient imperial city of Hue, South Vietnam. My tour of duty was from May 1967 to May 1968.

Little did my family know that I was in the process of volunteering my time, energy and money to help about fifty Vietnamese orphans at the local orphanage that was run by Catholic sisters. Around Thanksgiving a group of officers and enlisted men organized a campaign to collect money to buy gifts for a Christmas party for the children. Everything was purchased and a time for the giving was coordinated with the sisters. What was needed was a person to play Santa Claus.

I did not have the build of a Santa Claus because of my six-foot, one-hundred-and-twenty-pound frame. But that did not stop me from volunteering for the job. Somehow, somewhere in the craziness of the Vietnam War, a Santa suit was found. I dressed the part, with pillows supplying needed cushioning. Cotton from the dispensary aided in the formation of a realistic white beard. When all was said and done, I looked like Saint Nicholas!

That was a very special day. As I came out of my hooch, complete with outfit, cushion and white beard, the officers and men of the MACV compound had a field day taking numerous pictures of Santa so they could mail them home to show their friends, wives and children that Santa Claus was also in Vietnam.

After numerous poses the photo session was over and it was time for Santa to venture out through the streets of Hue to the orphanage that was just a few miles away from the compound. The mission was to visit the orphans and distribute the many gifts that had been purchased and wrapped in order to bring a special meaning to those parentless children. As the Jeep drove through the hot, crowded city streets, amid the young women, the old men, and the young men on bicycles, the locals were amazed to see a crazy American in the passenger seat of a Jeep waving to everyone and saying "Merry Christmas!" and "Chow."

When we arrived at the orphanage, there was a feeling of anticipation that only happens with children and Christmas. These foreign, homeless children had never seen Santa Claus before, but they knew he was something unusual and nice, especially when they saw the huge bag of beautifully wrapped gifts.

The reward for all the work that was done to make this Christmas a special event was written on the faces of the innocent children as each special gift was given to every boy and girl. No one was forgotten! The screaming and excitement of the afternoon made all our efforts worthwhile. Even though we missed being home with our families during that joyous season, we knew that we had done something very unselfish to help others enjoy Christmas.

For everyone involved in that Christmas, it would be a time in our lives that would never be forgotten. The meaning of Christmas was truly felt by everyone involved on that day. For me, Christmas 1967 will always be... A Christmas to Remember.

Postscript: About a month after this joyous event, during Tet 1968, many hundreds of citizens of Hue were killed during one of the worst confrontations of the Vietnam War — The Battle of Hue. Because of tighter restrictions on travel in the ancient imperial city, I never did have a chance to return to the orphanage. So, to this day I do not know what happened to the Catholic sisters and those special children.

Brothers Lost

Author requests anonymity

Brothers lost: I am lost.

I live in thick forest overlooking Benewah Lake in northern Idaho.

I try to get as close to mental homeostasis as I can...

Questions float in my head like reflections on lake waters at twilight. Like the pastel waters that glisten in front of me now, at dusk. Questions spawned by epiphany, by touching up against Pain-Fear, which has no face. The eternal visage, glowering without sight, blind yet omniscient, staring from the pastel waters in front of me.

I watch from old man's eyes, made old at twenty by fear... fear so strong, it rode adrenaline into my veins, but didn't stop at capillaries. It seeped out spiritual pores and became a kind of smell in the jungle air, death seeking a mountain valley echo. And laughing, sneering, that evil face was, haunting me, and coating the silence of last breathings... lost breath. I see it even now, staring ahead at the misty lake of my childhood. The ethereal quiet of dying, like mist hovering on a lake, making old men of boys. Old men of boys, grasping for lost vision.

But that was not beauty, not misty Benewah Lake.

This lake is alive! It was alive while all the dying took place. I am alive, as I was then.

I am soaking up the stillness of the trees, where harsh light seldom hits me. And the calm.

But always afraid that what made the boy an old man, overnight, will surface and strike. Visionless. Faceless. Yet vile, and virile as the pristine forest that shrouds me. How many others — brothers — sit out there, seeking homeostasis, but not trusting it, even when it approaches?

The sun has set beyond the mountains, beyond Benewah Lake. A bed of needles awaits me, with pine cones, for comfort. Distant shadows move slowly in the evergreen mountains. I see the last light, ripples across calm waters. I look up through a spire of trees and see stars. Sparks. Tracers of life.

Is anyone else out there, seeking quiet? Where did they go, brothers with bile in their laughter, in the smoky air, clutching their weapons? Are they here, among the trees?

I can no longer see the ink of this pen. Yet I can still see with the same vision that came to me, the night a boy became an old man.

Did I die too?

I walk ten meters down a deer trail, away from the comfort of forest needles. In the peaceful, pristine forest, I pee. I search the surrounding brush with eyes, ears, and the other sense. Just peeing on another trail, hoping no gook appears — hoping to be quick at the kill if a gook appears.

There is no homeostasis, only the semblance, the visage, of home.

O Benewah Lake. Please love me again.

I need one long second of peace.

I can no longer read the ink, see the ink.

It's time to snuggle in among my bed of needles.

There they are, out there, white dots in the sky.

Brothers, ghosts, followed me into the forest.

They too want to rest.

Stephen T. Banko III

Scholars and sages have long argued the might and merit of the pen versus the sword, but few men have been asked to wield both with such ability as Steve Banko. Having earned every decoration for combat heroism except the Medal of Honor during his two tours of infantry duty in Vietnam, Steve has long since laid aside his sword and taken up his pen to chronicle the Vietnam experience, and to advocate on behalf of Vietnam veterans.

A native of Buffalo, New York, Steve was drafted into the U.S. Army in 1967. During the course of his Vietnam service with the fabled 1st Air Cavalry Division, he endured some of the heaviest fighting of the war, fighting which resulted in his being wounded a total of six times, four by gunshot. In December of 1968, Steve was involved in a savage, five-hour battle along the Song Be River, which resulted in the loss of more than ninety percent of his 125-man company.

Steve began his writing career shortly after discharge in early 1970. He has been a frequent essayist in the *Buffalo News*. His work has also been published in the *Wall Street Journal*, the St. Louis *Post-Dispatch*, and the *San Diego Register*. His first-person accounts of Vietnam combat have appeared in several national magazines. He is a much sought-after speaker on college campuses and at veterans' reunions across the country and, in 1986, he was cited by the Freedom's Foundation at Valley Forge for his achievements in public speaking on Vietnam-related issues.

His advocacy on behalf of Vietnam veterans extends beyond

the written and spoken word. Steve is the annual chairman of the Western New York Vietnam Veterans Scholarship Luncheon. He is a past president and founding director of the Vietnam Veterans Leadership Program of the Niagara Frontier. He is the author of the dedicatory statement on the Western New York and West Seneca, New York Vietnam Veterans Memorials, and is the chairman of the Western New York Vietnam War Museum in Buffalo. In 1989, Steve was chairman of the organizing committee that presented "The Moving Wall" exhibit to nearly a quarter million people in the Buffalo area. His work on behalf of his fellow veterans was recognized by the Erie County Council of AMVETS, which designated him Citizen of the Year for 1989.

Steve has served as principal speechwriter to the Speaker of the New York State Assembly, Manager of Policy Development for the Niagara Frontier Transportation Authority, and Press Secretary to the presidential campaign of Senator Edward M. Kennedy of Massachusetts. He is currently Chief of Staff to New York State Senator Anthony M. Masiello of Buffalo.

His combat awards for heroism and valor include: the nation's second highest combat award, the Distinguished Service Cross; two Silver Stars; four Bronze Stars for Valor; the Air Medal for Valor; the Army Commendation Medal for Valor; four Purple Hearts; the Combat Infantry Badge; the Vietnamese Cross of Gallantry with Palm, and the New York State Conspicuous Service Cross.

THE WISEST KNOW NOTHING

By Stephen T. Banko III

"Sorrow makes us all children again —
destroys all differences of intellect.
The wisest know nothing."
-- Ralph Waldo Emerson

Duffy watched the mottled, gray-brown land leech inch its way up the dirty nylon of his jungle boot. There was much to hate about Vietnam. Duffy had a special loathing for the leeches. He hated them for the way they looked — rheumy and shapeless and ugly. But he hated them most for being sneaky.

They struck swiftly and silently, sinking their suckers without even the decency of inflicting pain. One minute, you were whole, the next, the phlegmy parasites were feasting on your blood.

Duffy had long ago realized that if Vietnam was, indeed, the asshole of the world, leeches were its hemorrhoids.

For five interminable minutes, the leech went its way up Duffy's boot. With every slink of its body, the parasite stopped to feel around for a food source. Not finding one, it continued undaunted. Duffy didn't know how the disgusting suckers navigated, but he raised the leg of his jungle pants to reveal the sickly white flesh of his calf.

"Come on, scum bag, just a little farther," he urged softly.

The leech was poised to drop from the boot to the pale skin when Duffy caught the blob between his thumb and forefinger and squeezed it into a sticky wet mess. His eyes softened and a hint of a grin curled his lips as he added the remains to the three weeks of accumulated filth ground into his pants. Once, even killing the leech might not have been so easy for Duffy. Gloating over it would have been out of the question. But that was an eternity ago, before Vietnam, before he'd learned to kill the enemy. And once he'd killed the enemy, a leech was no sweat.

It was a simple matter of definitions, Holmes had instructed him. You got a few friends and you got a lot of enemies. Keep the friends and grease the enemies.

That's all a war is — nothing complicated. And in that quick and easy lesson, twenty-odd years of ethics and morality dissolved into a single absolute. Duffy glanced down at the smear on his pants. One more enemy gone, he thought, a couple million to go.

His sport ended, Duffy scanned the jungle. When he got his first look at the rain forest, he was instantly reminded of the cathedral where he used to serve Mass. The tallest trees reached a hundred feet toward the light, filtering the sun through their branches much like the stained glass of the church. In the semi-darkness, bamboo and smaller trees formed the second canopy. Beneath them, the underbrush grew, thriving on the decay of the losers of the life struggle. Dead trees, vines and moss grew among the ferns and shrubs in a wild tangle of green. As in the cathedral, the jungle was cluttered rather than ornate — too much competing for too little.

The jungle also taught Duffy a lesson about Vietnam. The winners were the ones who could adapt. The tallest and the strongest got all they wanted. The rest had to compromise, to adjust, to make do. Survival was the name of the game and everything contributed to that end. There were only absolutes, no middle ground, no grays, no transitions. There was either the sweltering heat of the steaming rice paddies or the dark tomb of the jungle, the choking dust of the dry season or the torrential rains of the monsoon, a living being or a misty memory in an overgrown cemetery. But that was long ago, before Duffy learned the high price of daydreams. Duffy's jungle was no longer a classroom. It was a battleground where the score was kept in body counts and there were no medals for second place.

Scattered behind Duffy were the three new guys getting their first taste of the jungle. He laughed out loud when he watched them prowling through the bush with their rifles at the ready, while Duffy and Holmes set out at a brisk pace. If there was anything ever routine about Vietnam, this observation posting was it. But fucking new guys learn. And now that they knew this was Vietnam's equivalent of a walk in the park, they were getting too relaxed. A laugh here, a giggle there. Duffy was getting a case of the ass. He was preparing to go back to the FNGs and do a little verbal ass-kicking when a quick movement in front of him made him forget all about the new guys.

This was definitely not good news. The only one in front of Duffy was Sgt. Holmes and he never moved without a purpose and in the jungle, purpose meant gooks. Instinctively, Duffy slid a little farther behind the tree. He no longer looked for the things Holmes saw. He didn't have to. Holmes was a divining rod for gooks.

And the rod was definitely aroused.

As he watched Holmes tensing, Duffy's thumb moved the selector switch on his rifle to automatic while his body burrowed a little deeper in the loam. At the same time, his heart kicked up a few beats.

Holmes was a deadly professional. Without ever taking his eyes off the jungle, he slipped two grenades from his belt and straightened the pins. Then he pulled a handful of shotgun shells from his sack and put them in his pocket. He'd spotted three bodies moving toward the company's landing zone and if he went about this the right way, he'd kill them all.

Duffy abandoned all hope the alarm might prove false as he watched Holmes curl in behind the teak tree, his 12-gauge at the ready in one hand and a grenade primed in the other. Duffy's skin erupted in a million little hard-ons. His breath came in short gasps. His blood raced, triggered by jets of adrenaline surging through his system. At that terrible, frantic moment, tingling with the narcotic mix of fear and terror and excitement, Duffy was more alive than he'd ever been. That intensity, more than any conscious decision, ordered his fingers to close tightly on the pistol grip of his rifle and his eyes to focus every power of sight on the jungle. The dead jungle air, too impotent to dry sweat, couldn't give his lungs enough air. He started sucking it in through his mouth, terrified the noise would expose him. He could hear the beating of his own heart and prayed they couldn't. And just as the tension was about to chase sanity from his mind, the explosion of the grenade provided the release.

A short scream penetrated the blast as Holmes leapt to his feet, jerking the pump on the 12-gauge. Duffy caught a khaki blur to the right of Holmes and ripped a short burst from his M-16. After a final shotgun blast, the silence recaptured the jungle. The bitter smell of cordite, black powder and blood hung over the area. The low moans of the dead and near dead were punctuated by the sounds of Holmes re-loading the shotgun. Three broken bodies lay bleeding into the spongy earth when Duffy approached and surveyed the damage. One man was dead. His khaki uniform was blotched with large dark stains. One leg was ripped by a huge gouge eaten away by the explosion of the grenade. The raw, red flesh encircled the shiny white of the bone jutting out where his thigh should have been. His two comrades were still alive, if just barely. One lay a few feet from the dead man. His hands were buried in his exposed entrails, trying desperately to stanch the leaking of his life onto the jungle floor. Ten meters away, the third man was lying still and calm with bullet holes in his chest and shoulder. With each breath, a pink foam bubbled from his mouth. Six months ago, Duffy would have begun a frenzied and futile effort to save this man. But long ago, his real life had been replaced with the surreal existence of the jungle. The man was dead, he just hadn't stopped breathing yet. He was suffering a lot. He was bleeding even more. And even if he survived long enough to be evacuated, he'd never survive the helicopter ride to the hospital. There was no need for him to suffer like that. So even before Holmes nodded to him, Duffy was moving to send the gook to Buddha.

He dispatched him with a single shot to the head. Fifty feet away, the shotgun blasted and the third man was officially dead.

Only then did Duffy remember the FNGs. They were shocked

by the instant violence of the ambush and the sudden death. Only when Duffy signalled them forward did they rise from the dirt. As they approached wearily, Duffy tried to remember when his own uniform looked that green and when the devastation around him might have been more shocking. But he couldn't.

Holmes droned the situation report into the radio handset, translating a mad minute of war into a neat line score.

"Heavy Bones Six, this is Bones One-One. We just popped an ambush on zero three November Victor Alpha and capped them all. We have zero -- I say again -- zero friendly casualties. Over."

"One-One, this is Six. Confirm three boogiemen for body bags. Hold your position until we arrive for a look-see. Out."

Holmes tossed the handset to Duffy.

"You know the drill, Duff. Circle up the FNGs for security. We got to wait for Six."

The sergeant pulled a tropical chocolate bar from a pocket and peeled away the wrapper. As the others moved out, he was left alone with his breakfast and the obscene buzzing of the flies feasting on the bloody bodies.

"I don't care if he hears me! I want him to hear me!"

Holmes' head jerked up. Who the fuck could be talking that loud in the jungle? he wondered. Duffy had gone ahead to find spots for the cherries. The three were standing together. One of them was real mad about something.

"What the fuck is the problem, assholes?" Holmes asked. "You guys think you're back on the block, or what?"

Two of the men looked back sheepishly while the angry one took a step toward the sergeant.

"You, Sergeant Holmes... you're the problem. You and your stooge, Duffy."

"Oh, and what exactly is it about my friend and I that troubles you, dickhead?" Holmes returned.

"Murder," the new guy answered. "I saw you and Duffy murder those two wounded Vietnamese and I intend to report you for it."

Duffy was making his way back from his impromptu scouting trip. The mention of his name caught his attention. The mention of murder brought him to the brink of rage.

"You pansy-assed pussy sonofabitch!" he said, clutching the new guy by the shirt. "Who the fuck you accusing of murder?"

"Both of you," the new guy said, pulling away from Duffy's grasp. "We all saw what you did. You just executed those two and that's murder."

"That's war, asshole," Duffy answered. "Those gooks were already dead. They were just suffering through the end is all. One of these days, that might be your ass down in the mud and the blood and it might be them standing over you. What would you do then, cherry? Ask them to do a little open heart surgery for you? I'll tell you what you'll do, asshole — you'll pray for them to kill you."

"Hey, Duff, take it easy," Holmes interrupted, "don't go so hard on the new guy. He's seen a lot today and it's his first day."

"Fuck you, Holmes. You aren't going to bullshit me. I saw what you did and it was murder and that's what I'm telling the captain."

Duffy started to go after the FNG but Holmes stopped him.

"Well, you gotta do what you gotta do," Holmes said. "But right now, you gotta pull some security. So saddle your asses up and get out in the bush."

The three new guys moved off cautiously while Holmes held Duffy back.

"We might have a problem here, amigo," the sergeant said.

"What the fuck kind of problem? We didn't do anything we haven't done ten times before. Who's the Six going to believe, us or some pansy-assed FNG?"

"I don't know, Duffy, who? Don't you get it? If these three guys tell the captain we executed these gooks, who knows what'll happen? The big-mouthed FNG could put our asses in some real hot water."

"Come on, Sarg, this is all bullshit. Those guys were gone. We just put 'em on the express. Who's going to call us on that?"

"That's the point, Duffy. I don't know who's going to call us, and I don't want to find out. I only got three months left and I'm gone. But I ain't like you. I ain't getting out. The Army's my home, man. I get wrapped in some heavy duty shit like this and I got a big problem."

For the first time, Duffy stopped to think about their predicament. Holmes was right. Just the accusation of murder could create big problems for both of them, but especially for Holmes. Duffy had a life to go back to when his tour was over. But Holmes was going to be a lifer, a career man in the military. He'd been in Vietnam for nine months, been wounded twice, saved scores of GIs and wasted gooks in bunches. He was the everything a combat soldier should be. But now, on the word of a fucking new guy with no time in-country, he could wind up in jail at worst, or disgraced and dismissed from the Army he'd chosen to be his life, at best.

Duffy knew he couldn't let that happen. Holmes had once made the choices faced in war starkly simple. Just by applying those basics, Duffy knew what he had to do. Change the names, avoid the faces, don't look in the eyes, forget about the uniforms, forget about everything — except friends and enemies.

Holmes started out to check on the FNGs and Duffy went into the jungle to check on an enemy.

Duffy knew that sneaking up on an FNG was easy. He also knew that lining him up for a clean shot would be easy. What he didn't know was that taking the shot was hard. Duffy was burrowed in beneath a bamboo stand. Lying prone, he had been sighting down his rifle for nearly two minutes. His brain kept screaming "Enemy!" but his eyes kept seeing a GI. The debate raged like a storm.

You got to take him out! He wants to fry Holmes, the best fucking soldier in the world. You can't let him do that.

You can't kill an American! He's a little fucked up but you can't kill him for that. You did nothing wrong. Take your chances with the captain.

He's the enemy! His uniform don't mean shit. He wants to take something away from you, just like the gooks. He's got to be dealt with.

Where does it stop, Duffy? When do you stop the killing? He's a GI, one of us. You can't kill him for being an asshole.

The arguments ran through his mind in rapid succession while he held his aim steady. The blade of his front sight underlined the FNG's chest. A gentle squeeze on the trigger and the debate, and the danger, would be over. Drop 'em, bag 'em and tag 'em. They'd probably even give the kid a medal and remember him in Tippy-Toe, Mississippi as a hero. The FNG would be just like a hundred other combat casualties. Or would he? How many others would have been shot by another GI? Duffy lowered his rifle. When he was an FNG he'd actually believed he'd make it through the war without having to kill anyone. Now, he was ready to kill an American. What was happening to him?

Survival, he answered himself. Survival had happened to him. The only thing that mattered was getting out of this shit-hole alive. Anything that threatened that was an enemy and enemies were fair game. It was simply a matter of survival. His choice was between bad and worse. Good couldn't get into Vietnam with a passport.

Up came the rifle.

Fuck this kid, Duffy told himself, he ain't playing by the rules.

His sight focused down the barrel and stuck under the kid's chin. One shot and it would be over.

The jungle was calm but inside Duffy's head, a voice was screaming.

Don't do it! You can't do it! He's a GI!

The snapping of the bullets through the still air ended the debate. Reflexively, Duffy's head dropped into the loam. He popped back up in time to see the FNG slump over the tree trunk, making soft gurgling noises as he did. Duffy bolted to his feet and charged toward the dying soldier. He never saw the body drop from the tree, not ten feet from his position. He bounded over the trunk and knew instantly he was too late. The blood spurted in red jets from a long rip in the boy's neck. Duffy threw a fist into the wound, groping for the severed vein, all the while lying to the boy.

"No sweat, GI! You're ass is mine now, cherry, and you're gonna make it, understand! You're gonna make it! You just hang the fuck on, cherry, just hang on!"

His hands fumbled as the boy watched with a surprised stare. Duffy was sinking deeper in the mud made by the bleeding. The boy's life was leaking into a million years of decay and there wasn't a fucking thing Duffy could do about it. A few seconds ago, he'd held the power of death over the FNG but that melted into the impotency of being a spectator as the boy coughed a last cloud of life into Duffy's face and went limp. Duffy cradled the corpse gently.

"Duffy! You OK?" Holmes screamed. "Let me hear you, buddy!"

"I'm Okay, but we got a friendly down and out! What the fuck is going on?"

"Sniper," Holmes answered. "He squeezed one off before I could zap his yellow ass. Who's down?"

"The big-mouthed FNG."

"Man, what a bummer! We got to find another way to grandma's. These woods is a motherfucker!"

Duffy laid the boy softly on the jungle floor. He stood, covered in blood.

"Wow, Duffy. You hit?"

"No, I'm OK."

"Shit, man, you look like you're about ready to croak your own bad self."

"Maybe just a little, Holmes," Duffy said softly as he slumped down against the tree. "I definitely died a little."

He put his face in his bloody hands.

"But there's worse things that can happen," he whispered. "There's worse things than dying."

Duffy had found something he hated more than the leeches.

—

Marilyn M. McMahon

Says author McMahon: "A Seattle native, I joined the Navy through its Navy Nurse Corps candidate program, thus making it financially possible for me to finish college. After graduation in 1967, I was assigned to the Philadelphia Naval Hospital, where I worked with Marine Corps combat casualties on the orthopedic service. I was stationed at the Navy's hospital in DaNang in 1969 and 1970, followed by stints in Oak Harbor, Washington and Oakland, California.

"A civilian since 1972, I am currently employed in a small business in Seattle. I started writing in 1985, and had my first poem published in an anthology, *Poetry and the Vietnam Experience* published by St. Lawrence University. Writing about being a Vietnam veteran has been a challenge, a healing experience, and the doorway to the establishing of deep connections all across the country and, to some extent, internationally."

In This Land

By Marilyn McMahon

In this land of lush jungle and squalid refugee camps, the beach and patio form a haven. A beach for play: smooth sand, gentle waves. The patio for sitting, talking, drinking: gray concrete, kept clean by mama-sans with hose and brooms; dotted with small tables, each with its brightly striped umbrella.

She sits in a lawn chair, aluminum with yellow webbing, exactly like those in Mom's backyard. He sits in another, green.

The tropical sun is warm, quiet, serene.

Last night's explosions are over, forgotten, as a bad dream is forgotten in the morning. The breeze from the north is cooling, salt laden as it moves from the Pacific across the harbor to where they sit.

The noises of war: helicopters, jets, boat engines; tanks, APCs, Jeeps, Hondas are ignored. Not heard. Only his deep voice, sharing items of interest to colonels, and her soft voice, responding to his rank and masculinity. Her dress is sleeveless, short, sunflower yellow, allowing her to bask in the sun. It is not important that her role is that of listener — admirer — the assigned role of her sex for hundreds of years. It is only important to feel warm, treasured, wanted; safe for the moment. She squints her eyes, idly scans the sun glittered waves, sips her gin and tonic, and listens with the part of her mind not otherwise engaged.

He speaks of his days: how it is to be a lawyer in a war zone, of a problem the Marines are having with the Army. He speaks of helicopter crashes, and botched rescues, and negligence. She listens, and nods, sunbathes and daydreams. She gazes at the water, today so similar to her own beloved Pacific, thousands of miles away.

She notes that something new has appeared on the waves. Idly she wonders that she had not seen it before. She considers where it might have come from, and what it might be. She watches, and sunbathes.

Her stomach begins to chill. She knows. She asks: look, what is it? She is afraid to say what she knows.

He cannot see it — continues to speak of what is important to him. She is silent. The sun glares, no longer warms. The ocean is foreign, alien, violent. The object — she cannot say its name yet — floats closer on the tide.

Finally others see it — but now there are two — they launch a boat, row out to retrieve the body. Another body. A third.

In flight suits, swollen with three days submersion. White. Blue. Black. Khaki.

She remains silent. Ice cold. Unable to see the white of the sun or the blue of the waves, only the black of shadows.

He becomes still.

The beach remains, sun drenched, wave washed. The patio is clean, flat. Empty.

—

The Kid

By Marilyn McMahon

His was the smooth, soft skin
of light blond hair and ruddy cheeks.
Easy to embarrass. Shaved once
a week or less, never
flunked inspections.
A boy who volunteered,
didn't wait for the draft.
Called "kid" by everyone
in the platoon.

A week of patrols,
then his squad went to China Beach.
"Three beers, I swear to God,
ma'am, he only had three beers."
The sergeant was crying.
The kid had fallen. A simple fall.
A head injury. Brain stem damage.
Inoperable.
No hope.

Three days, he lay there. A machine
breathing for him. Nurses
and corpsmen bathing him, turning
him, protecting him from nighttime
rockets. He didn't need a shave.
Test after test, no change.
No chance. A simple fall.
No bullets, no mortars, no chance.
The fourth day,
I removed the respirator
and waited.
Hours later, his heart stopped.

Confession

By Marilyn McMahon

Day before First Friday
we file from our classroom to the church
at our assigned time.
"Bless me, Father,
for I have sinned.
It has been one month
since my last confession;
I was angry with my little sister
I was jealous of her new doll.
I was selfish, and did not share
my roller skates.
I was proud, and I boasted."
In that dark, cozy place,
my eyes are tightly closed.
Father does not know
who I am.
A blessing, the Sign of the Cross.
I march to the altar rail,
gaze bent to the floor.
I kneel, hiding my eyes in my knuckles.
Three Hail Marys, and the Act of Contrition.
I am forgiven.
My soul is pure white.

Continued

Tomorrow, I may receive Holy Communion.
Sunday morning Mass
after ten-hour night shift
admissions, transfers, two deaths.
Armpits still chilled from warming
frozen plasma.
Fingernail stained orange —
Betadine prep for an emergency trach.
We sit wearily in metal folding chairs.
Bright, sun-filled quonset hut:
the Chapel of Saint Luke.
Slowly we stand as the priest
and his attendants file in.
We bow our heads,
one sign of the cross
sketched in the air.
My silent catalogue:
Bless me Father, for...
I was enraged, wanted to hurt another.
I committed adultery two, no three, times.
I was proud, would not pray.
Thirty others forgiven at the same time.
Our souls are purified
we may receive Communion.

Continued

Night
the black hour
when sleep has fled again.
Poison gas in Iraq and Iran.
In El Salvador, disemboweled priests
and two women.
Star Wars
and Minutemen.
Martinis and handshakes in Beijing
across one thousand bodies.
Blockades create starvation
and democracy.
Arms shipments.
I am enraged
and frightened of my rage.
I am appalled
and made helpless.
I am guilty of fear
helplessness
failure to believe or hope
having believed and having
asked no questions.
Where is forgiveness
and purification of soul?
Where is communion? and when?

The dark, private cubicle is empty
door closed tight.
The sun-filled chapel
was blown up by those
who believed in a different god.
Knuckles no longer provide
a safe dark.
I will not pray.

Bob Crunk

Bob Crunk served with Bravo Company, 4th Supply & Transport Battalion, 4th Infantry Division, in Pleiku, from April 1969 to April 1970.

Says author Crunk: "In the years after Vietnam, I got married and earned a Bachelor's Degree in Management, with the help of the GI Bill and my wife Nancy. Coming to terms with that year I spent in Vietnam, and the subsequent emotional odyssey, has further strengthened my belief that we still did the right thing."

Hell's Roller Coaster

By Bob Crunk

July 1969: the Central Highlands of South Vietnam.

A twenty truck convoy from the 4th Transport Battalion of the 4th Infantry Division has just left Camp Enari outside of Pleiku City on a resupply mission. This convoy is a wild roller coaster ride down the infamous An Khe Pass on Highway 1 to their ultimate destination, Firebase Charlie, an artillery stronghold perched atop a stark moutainside ten miles southeast of the tiny hamlet of An Khe.

The massive groans of diesel engines and stripping of gears echo sharply across the jagged mountains of Pleiku as the convoy meanders slowly down the shell-gutted highway in an uneven procession amid the smothering heat and nose-burning sting of diesel fumes that belched in chorus from the giant exhaust stacks of the iron behemoths called "deuce and a halfs."

Spec 4 Bob Crunk and his shot-gun mate Chuck Schultz are riding in battle scarred Number 204 near the back of the convoy as they begin their descent down "Hell's Roller Coaster," the An Khe Pass.

Schultz: "Firebase Charlie got hit pretty bad again last night, man. How many times does that make it this month?"

Crunk: "About the fifth time, man. Old Charlie must have definitely found out their hiding place by now."

Schultz: "Man, these damn convoys don't get any easier, do they?" he grumbles as he clicks his M-16 off safety and rests the barrel on the door ledge facing out into the green valley below.

Crunk: "They sure as hell don't anymore. It seems like we're always heading to An Khe or Qui Nhon."

Crunk rips through the gears as the two-and-a-half-ton truck lunges ahead through the blinding dust and jolting potholes.

Schultz: "Watch out! These damn bumps and craters the engineers call a road don't get any softer!"

Crunk: "What are you complaining about? You're getting real short now."

Schultz: "Damn straight, dude! September 18 can't come soon enough for me, and then your old shot-gun buddy will be on that beautiful freedom bird to home, sweet home!"

Crunk: "Your real lucky, man. But don't look back. I won't be too far behind you when you leave this hell hole."

The convoy begins its descent down An Khe Pass as the trucks' engines strain with the systematic down-shifting of gears.

Crunk: "Got a cigarette, man?"

Schultz: "Here, try a man's cigarette."

Crunk: "These damn Camels will kill you!" he says and coughs deeply.

Schultz: "Still hung over from last night, are you?"

Crunk: "Yeh, and this damn heat doesn't make it any easier. Whew! It must be at least a hundred degrees today," Crunk complains as he adjusts his stiff flak jacket over his shirtless shoulders and swipes away the sweat.

Schultz: "You got it! I could really dig an old Wisconsin winter about right now — skiing down some fast slope, chasing my old girlfriend to the bottom."

Crunk: "Man, I hope these damn brakes don't fail us today, especially with the load we're carrying," he said, yelling it over the engine drone.

Schultz shouts: "Those artillery dudes will definitely perk up when they see us pull in with all this beer! What kind we got rattling around back there, anyway?"

Crunk: "Good ol' Miller this time. Pabst last month and Bud

the month before. Leave it to the Army to dictate what beer we're going to drink."

Schultz: "Speaking of beer, you want one?"

Crunk: "You got the church key? Open it for me, man. This damn road isn't getting any easier to handle."

Schultz: "Look out, man! This stuff is really foamy today. I'm so used to warm beer for so long, I won't now how to act when I get a cold one!"

Crunk: "At least the stuff's wet."

Schultz: "Yeh, wet and messy, with all these bumps you're hitting."

Crunk: "I sure hope the mine sweepers did their job this morning. I don't feel like going home in a body bag today."

Schultz: "I'm with ya, man. Remember the Dak To convoy last month, when half the trucks hit those anti-tank mines?"

Crunk: "Sure do, man. I'm just glad I wasn't driving in it."

The pace of the convoy quickened as the trucks slid deeper into the valley.

Schultz: "How fast ya going? Feels like we're in a free fall!"

Crunk: "Got to stay up with the truck ahead of us or we'll lose it all. You know that, man!"

Schultz: "That's Willy's deuce ahead of us. He must be still on a hang over. He's weaving all over the place!"

Crunk: "That lifer is something else. It looks like one of his rear tires is ready to blow any second now!"

Schultz: "It's those heavy artillery shells banging the side of his truck bed that's giving him problems."

Scanning the mountainside, Schultz chambers a round in his M-16.

Crunk: "As long as he keeps moving ahead of us we'll all be okay!"

Distant cracks of sniper fire pierce throughout the valley.

Schultz: "Damn! Did you hear those shots? Sounds like they're coming off to our right."

Crunk: "Hand me a couple of magazines. I'm not taking any chances."

Schultz: "Just keep your eyes on the road ahead and I'll watch out for us, okay?"

Crunk: "We've been on a hundred or more convoys together, man, and I'm still scared as hell!"

Standing on the side of the road near his Jeep, the convoy commander waves his arm frantically in a circular motion overhead, signaling for the drivers to pick up speed.

Crunk: "Look! There's Captain Alvez. Must be trouble ahead."

Schultz: "Take it easy, man. I can still see the lead trucks. We'll be okay as long as you stand on it and keep moving! Remember back at Fort Dix—you never stop a convoy—always keep rolling no matter what. If you stop, you're a dead man!"

Suddenly a cloud of white smoke appears up ahead.

Crunk: "Did you see that?"

Schultz: "See what, man?"

Crunk: "Up ahead to the left, you idiot! The white smoke!"

Schultz: "Hey, man, that's CS gas! Where's our masks?"

Schultz searches frantically under the seat for the two masks as the deadly gas gets closer.

Crunk: "Find those masks, man! I smell the stuff already," he says, coughing.

Schultz: "Here, man! I found them! I'll hold the wheel. Put it on now!"

Fumbling with the rubber mask, Crunk hastily slips the mask on as the truck plows through the deadly white cloud.

Crunk: "Whew! Thanks, man. You really saved me!"

Schultz: "Say what? I can't hear you in this rubber bastard."

Crunk: "Damn! Those lousy dinks hit us with gas!"

Schultz: "Can you see the road?" he asked, coughing.

Crunk: "We're okay," he said, coughing. "I can still see Willy's tail lights. Are you okay? I can barely see you over there!"

Schultz: "Don't worry about me, damnit! Just keep going!"

The smoke cleared and the convoy races wildly down the An Khe Pass.

Crunk: "Wow! That was close, man! My face is burning up from that damn mask! Here, put the damn thing back under the seat."

Schultz: "Just keep this damn thing on the road. We've got to get through this pass or we're real gonners, man!"

Crunk: "Be ready, man. That sniper fire is sounding real close by."

Schultz: "God! I hope we make it through this!"

Crunk: "Calm down, Chuck! We've been in tougher convoys before. Just sit tight and stay alert!"

Schultz: "Man! Just get me through this pass one more time. I got to see my woman in one piece!"

Suddenly ear-splitting explosions erupt throughout the valley as mortar rounds and land mines detonate, bombarding the convoy.

Crunk: "Hey, man! We're really getting it now! The damn VC must have been waiting for us to come through!"

Schultz: "Look out, Crunk! They just hit Willy's truck! It's stopped. Look out!"

Slamming on the brakes, Crunk slides the truck sideways to a stop in the middle of the road.

Crunk: "Get the hell out of here, man! Now! MOVE IT!"

Schultz and Crunk leap from the stalled truck with '16s blazing, into the vast countryside, then jump into a nearby ditch for cover.

Crunk: "Goddamn, man! Get down quick!"

Schultz: "Man, this is suicide to stay here, out in the open. We've got to get out of here!"

Crunk: "Stay put and keep shooting, Schultz!"

Schultz: "All hell is breaking loose, Crunk! Who's that screaming up ahead of us?"

Crunk: "I don't know, man, but you got to stay down! Look out! Those rounds are getting closer!"

Schultz: "Look out! They just hit the damn truck! We can't stay here! We're sitting ducks, damnit!"

Chunks of earth shoot skyward as enemy mortar fire rains down on the stricken convoy. A group of frantic soldiers dash past Crunk and Schultz.

Crunk: "Where in the hell are they going? Those idiots are going to get killed!"

Schultz: "Oh, please, God! Where are those choppers? We're all going to get killed if they don't hurry up, man!"

A direct hit explodes on Number 204 in front of Crunk and Schultz, spraying the countryside with a foaming white shower of warm beer.

Schultz: "Damn! There goes the booze!"

Schultz panics, sprays the countryside with his remaining ammo.

Schultz: "I'm getting out of here, man! I'm not going to make it home if I don't! Are you with me, man?"

Crunk: "Stay put, Chuck, and save your damn ammo!"

Schultz: "I'm scared, man. Where's the captain? They'll kill us right now. We've got to go and get help!"

Crunk: "Schultz! Schultz! Listen to me. We've got to stay here together until help arrives. If you leave, you're a dead man, you crazy bastard!"

Cobra gunships dive into the valley, spraying suspected enemy positions with a barrage of rocket fire that swoosh over their heads.

Schultz: "Oh, man! I've been hit! I've been hit, damnit! Help me, man. I've been hit!"

Crunk: "Schultz! Schultz! Lie still, man. I'll crawl over to you. But God, please lie still!"

Schultz: "Hurry, man. Please hurry! I'm bleeding like a stuck hog!"

Crunk: "Where are you hit, man? I'll help you, but tell me where you are hit!"

Rolling over on his side, Schultz' hand uncovers a gaping stomach wound.

Schultz: "On my right side! It hurts, man! It really hurts! Get a medic, man. I don't want to die out here like this!"

Crunk: "The choppers are here, Chuck! The choppers are here! We're getting help. Can you hear them? There right overhead of us!"

Schultz: "Medic! Medic! I can't stand it, man!"

A burst of .50-caliber machine gun fire rips the air from a gun-truck near the front of the convoy.

Crunk: "Take it easy, Chuck. I'm putting this handkerchief over your wound to stop the bleeding. Just lie still and hold it. I'll take care of you!"

The explosions subside. The men are in chaos, trying to find their buddies.

Crunk: "Listen to me, Chuck! Just lie still. I'm going out to find help. Okay?"

Schultz: "Don't leave me alone, man! I don't want to be left here to die! You hear me!"

Crunk: "Stop crying and pull yourself together, man! Look! Halfway up the ridge, those tracers. Charlie's still out there! I'm going to find help."

Schultz: "Leave me a clip, man. I'm not going to die easy. And please hurry!"

Crunk crawls out towards the stricken convoy, unaware that a VC sniper is waiting in the ditch off to his right.

Crunk: "Medic! Over here! We need a medic quick!"

Schultz: "Look out! Crunk! Sniper! Sniper!"

Seeing the black-clad VC crawling up the ditch, Schultz squeezes a burst of 16 fire, hitting the VC point blank in the forehead.

Schultz: "Get down, Crunk! Get down!"

Crawling back to where Schultz lies, a look of horror creases Crunk's face. The VC slumps over in a puddle of beer.

Crunk: "God almighty! Where in the hell did that gook come from? Are you okay, Schultz?"

Schultz: "I'm still breathing, man. But please get me out of here, and hurry!"

Crunk: "I owe you one, big guy! Medic! Medic! Over here! Over here!"

The medics carefully load Schultz onto a stretcher for medevac chopper ride to the MASH hospital at An Khe as Crunk stoops down to his side.

Crunk: "Hey, big buy. I think you may have bought your ticket home early! The medics say you're going to be okay, and you probably will be going home. What do you have to say about that?"

Schultz: "I love it, man! I just love it! But hey, who's going to save your ass again if I'm back in the world?"

Crunk: "Save your breath, man. I'll be right behind you!"

A shaken PFC Williams rushes over to Crunk and Schultz,

ducking the chopper blades that swish wildly overhead.

Willy: "Hey, man, what the hell happened back there? You two really took a beating."

Schultz: "If you knew how to drive and dodge those damn mortars, I wouldn't be lying here, you idiot!"

Crunk: "What the hell happened, Willy?"

Willy: "Felt like a ton of bricks hit me when I ran over that damn land mine. Next thing I knew, I was lying in a ditch hugging the ground. Praying to God to save me!"

Schultz is loaded onto the med-evac chopper as Crunk leans over him.

Crunk: "Take it easy, big guy. I guess this means good-bye for now. I'll see you in the States."

Schultz: "Keep it on the road. And remember — don't stop for anything."

As the chopper flies off to the field hospital at An Khe, the convoy regroups.

Crunk: "Hey, Willy. How many guys did we lose this damn time around?"

Willy: "The captain says three dead and fourteen injured, including Schultz."

Crunk: "Man. It never stops. Let's get the hell out of this forsaken place."

The convoy commander waves his hand overhead, signaling for the drivers to get going.

Crunk: "Hey, Willy. Looks like I'll be needing a new shot-gun partner. You want to ride shot-gun next time around?"

Willy: "Forget it, man! I'll take my chances elsewhere. I damn sure don't want to end up like poor old Schultz!"

Crunk: "Hey, poor old Schultz is heading to the world, you fool! We all can't be so lucky!"

Under a scarlet sky the broken but resilient convoy resumes it course out of the An Khe Pass, towards their final objective, Firebase Charlie.

C. R. Hurst

C. R. Hurst served with Alpha Company, 3rd Tank Battalion, 3rd Marine Division, in I Corps, from December 1966 until December 1967.

Says author Hurst: "I was no great hero, no fierce warrior, sometimes a victim, sometimes mad and bitter, somedays a patriot, once in awhile happy, most often scared, always an American, and by the grace of the most high God, a survivor!

"I presently live in the small town of Ceredo, West Virginia with my wife and daughters. I work at a large plant and am a substitute school teacher. I have held down various jobs in my struggle to get past Vietnam, like so many other vets. Writing about Vietnam helps me share and let loose of my feelings. As a Vietnam veteran, I could never let them go!"

Never Was Blind, Only Shortsighted

By C. R. Hurst

I could see the two of them tenaciously working their way up the grassy slope to my left. I gave Sam a nudge and we quietly aimed our guns in their direction, and waited in anticipation.

"Rat-tat-tat, dow-dow-dow, we got you — you're dead!"

"No way — it wasn't fair!"

"Sam and I fired first and you both are dead. That's the rules we agreed to. We fired first!"

Playing war took a considerable amount of time while I was growing up, and as I grew older it only became more sophisticated and calculating. Many was the time I listened to an account of battle from veterans of wars past. I was intrigued by the stories and movies. This only reinforced the glamor of it. War was an obsession with me, like winning the first event in a track meet, making the football team, or kissing my first girl. I was mesmerized by it. War was the crowning of manhood, the catalyst by which I could attain the illusion without question.

West Virginia was thousands of miles away, along with Paris Island, South Carolina and Camp Pendleton, California. They were all just stepping stones toward the completion of my quest. All my younger life was geared to reaching that illustrious status, which I pursued, sometimes unknowingly, with fervent speculation.

I was awakened by the rattle of heavy anchor chains dropping into the sea. It was just two days before when the sound of those same chains, hauling in an anchor, echoed and pounded in my brain, making my first hang over a memorable occasion. The overcrowded troop ship only docked one day at Okinawa, after sixteen days at sea. There was only enough time to store seabags and get drunk before our tour of duty in Vietnam began, a tour which would start with a classic Marine amphibious assault on a hostile beachhead.

The smell of the Pacific Ocean was commonly familiar and I climbed onto the deck of the ship. A presence seemed to shroud me and a vague dark outline of something strange and menacing beckoned in the distance. It was December, 1966, and I knew the dark monster that was embracing all my being was not Vietnam, but the gotterdamn of war it promised.

The ship suddenly came to life, as if someone had kicked a giant anthill open. I scrambled to get my gear and prepare for the assault, in which I was to be a prime participant. I was surrounded by young Marines dressed for battle, waiting in the confusion for the order to climb down the ship's nets into the landing crafts.

Visions of John Wayne storming the beach in the movie, *Sands of Iwo Jima*, danced in and out of my brain as I climbed down the heavy wet rope of the dull gray troop ship. The air was warm with the salt of the ocean spray, awakening my nostrils, and all my senses were put on edge, waiting to explode. I was ready for the short ride to the beachhead and ready to act out the part I had played and seen hundreds of times in the movies.

The ocean was calm as the landing craft raced toward the hostile beach. I was perched in the front of the craft, ready to be the first to charge into the mouth of hell and taste, smell and embrace battle. I couldn't understand it. Bullets and explosions pounding the beachhead, and boats and comrades weren't exploding in pieces in the water. The sky was a faded blue as the sun made its morning appearance, looking like a red rubber ball sliding across a crystal plain. The signs of war were nowhere to be found. I could see the brown sand on the beach, the luscious green leaves on the curved rough palm trees, and exotic birds floating in the air. At any moment I expected to be swallowed in the noise of battle and to engage the oriental devils that were against everything I stood for and learned to believe in.

The sergeant yelled, "Get ready to disembark," and my stomach fell like a roller coaster.

The craft's landing ramp crashed down into the blue-green water and the beach looked at least fifty yards away. I charged out of the craft like a creature being pursued into oblivion. As I reached the end of the ramp it was as if a giant hand pulled the world out from under me and I was falling endlessly downward. I realized I was sinking fast, with more than eighty pounds of military gear hurrying my descent. In the murkiness my mind quickly erased John Wayne movies and I frantically stripped off gear as I plunged downward.

A barefooted, waterlogged, dark-green and exhausted young Marine crawled onto the warm brown sand of the Vietnam coastline. Other young Marines heard him thank God — the movies and his quest were only a reality of childhood, adolescence and the elusiveness of manhood.

The Cua Viet River Rat Races

By C. R. Hurst

The sluggish green C-130 cargo plane was banking eastward to begin its approach to Dong Ha Airstrip. I was looking out the window at the familiar terrain, which reminded me of my grandmother's half-finished patchwork quilts. I was on my way back from a week of R&R in Hong Kong. My CO had insisted I take a leave after our company suffered heavy casualties in fighting around Khe Sanh. After ten months of combat he decided even I needed a rest. I was among the few originals left in the company and was wondering what was next as the crew chief walked behind me.

"Hey, how bad do you need out at Dong Ha, Marine?"

"Pretty bad, Chief, why?"

"They're taking incoming down there and the skipper says he's only going to open the rear door, while I shove the skids out onto the runway. We're not going to stop and the only way for you to get out is to climb on top of a skid and hang on."

The airbase runway is metal and I've never seen a skid turn over, but the distance they sometimes slide makes for a wild ride.

"Chief, I'll go for it."

"Okay, groundpounder."

The huge plane lumbered in and the mechanical rear door whined as I climbed on top of a skid of beer. If I was going to die from being crushed to death, beer seemed a suitable way to go. The skid slid for what looked to be a hundred yards. I felt like a cowboy who just climbed down off a bronco as I limped toward Headquarters Company. It was late, so I sacked out for the night and woke up sore from head to toe. I was reaching for my M-79 and gear when the tent flap opened.

"Wilson, wake up!"

"I'm up, Gunney. What do you need?"

"You're shotgun and we're in the lead Jeep of a convoy going to Alpha Company near Cam Lo. Welcome back, Randy."

"Thanks a lot, Gunney."

The ride to Alpha Company was uneventful. We passed the same old rice paddies, water buffalos, and black clad people with conical hats in knee-high water. Traveling Highway One was like being in the present and all along both sides of the road was the past. Anyhow, uneventful means no snipers or ambushes. The gunney filled me in on his family as we rolled along.

I couldn't wait to see O'Reilly. We have been together since boot camp. The first time he told me his name I thought he was pulling my leg, because I was a country boy. "Alexander O'Reilly is my name," I remember him saying with a mile-wide grin. His skin was black and shiny like a new unmarked police car. He just sat there as he began his routine. "Hambone... Hambone, does I lie, or do this country boy thinks I jives!" His tale was that his mom married an Irish sailor who made his exit from O'Reilly's mom's world. He said he joined the Corps because he needed a job to support his now very ill mother. He sent the biggest part of his money home, and who was I to question. All I know is, I enjoyed his company. Where there was commotion and a poker game, you'd find Alex in the middle of it. I liked that because it helped me forget about our future, Vietnam. O'Reilly had this marvelous ability to fall into rosebeds, and when we got to Nam, somehow we ended up in Headquarters Company. It didn't last long. O'Reilly was playing poker and winning more than odds allowed according to the Major, although no one could catch him cheating. The Major shipped us both out to Alpha Company. We have only been separated twice, and both times one or the other was on R&R. The gunney thinks O'Reilly is a tad off, and says I'm becoming too much like him. But he instantly yells for both when the heat is on.

We pulled into the company perimeter near Cam Lo. I could see O'Reilly standing there like a mother hen, still flaunting that mile-wide grin. He was shouting at some boots, new Marines fresh from the States, unloading the back of a six-by, to follow him for orientation. It wasn't long before a boot went running, screaming, through the area, trying to brush off some harmless spiders. Three men wrestled him down and calmed him. O'Reilly was up to his old tricks, telling boots about poisonous snakes and spiders, then dumping some on one of the unsuspecting boots for entertainment. O'Reilly turned around and saw me.

"Hey, Randy. It's about time you came back."

"You know me, Alex. Chasing women and partying it up is time consuming."

O'Reilly got out some boned turkey and pound cake, while I began to heat some C-ration coffee. He filled me in on what had been happening. We began the ritual of eating with hot sauce in hand as he disclosed to me that we were being air-lifted to Cua Viet for an in-country R&R in the morning. The gods were certainly smiling on me. We pulled listening-post duty, just out from the perimeter, for the night. The morning sun brought the sound of chopper rotors in the distance.

O'Reilly began telling me about a plan to make some big money at Cua Viet, but decided to finish it on the chopper ride there.

"What's in the cans with all the air holes, Alex?"

"Two of the fastest river rats you've ever seen, country boy."

The noise of the choppers drowned out any chance to finish the conversation.

The South China Sea was warm, and its breeze felt good. I lay on the beach sipping beer and thinking about home. I noticed O'Reilly in the distance talking to some office pokes and SeaBees. It wasn't long before he came over and sat down beside me.

"Randy, everything is on for tonight. Everyone is going to be at the race. You be sure and bet on the black rat, double or nothing!"

"How do you know he'll win, Alex?"

"That's mine and the doc's secret, country boy. You just bet the way I told you and you'll make some bucks!"

As darkness fell, the beach area became crowded with spectators and speculators. Anticipation of the race was running high and a USO-show feeling prevailed. O'Reilly and the doc had soaked the black and gray rats in diesel fuel all day. Bamboo cages covered each one, and two boots stood ready to light them with torches on O'Reilly's countdown. The rat that ran the farthest before it exploded or keeled over would be the breadwinner. The count began, and the race was on. The rats were both fireballs in seconds. The gray one fell over and exploded, while the black one ran for about ten feet, to become the winner.

O'Reilly and I went to sleep that night $10,000 richer between us.

The morning stillness was broken by the sound of truck engines, and the gunney hollering orders for the company to saddle up. We drove about twenty miles, stopped and dismounted. Captain Jacobs gave the order to fan out on line. So began a three-company sweep through open country to the mountains, about thirty miles worth.

Our company was moving slowly because of the heat of the noonday Asian sun. Our squad was crossing another leech-filled rice paddy near a small village. A short burst of AK-47 fire cracked out. O'Reilly fell beside me. I pulled him over to the paddy dike for cover, at the same time trying to see how badly he was hit. I reached for a bandage and yelled for the doc. Alex grabbed my flak jacket with his right hand and pulled me close to his face.

"Country boy, make sure my money gets to the address on my next letter."

"Don't waste your breath, Alex. You can take it yourself."

Two seconds later he was dead.

I felt like part of me was gone as a squad from Second Platoon dragged two dead NVA from one of the village's huts.

During the next month a dull haze settled into my mind. The gunney joined my squad to keep me company when he could.

"Wilson, I got a letter here for Alex. Didn't you say you needed the return address from it?"

"Yes, sir, Captain."

"Wilson, you and the gunney grab your gear. We're all going back to HQ. The Major wants us, survivors, to get home in one piece, so we're going to hop the supply chopper back."

I stared blankly at the heading of the letter's return address, "Father O'Reilly's Orphanage," as the chopper flew over the land that reminded me of my grandmother's unfinished, patchwork quilt.

James L. Thomas

Says author Thomas: "I went to Vietnam at the age of nineteen, served with the 101st Airborne Division (Airmobile), the "Rakkasans" 3/187th Airborne Regimental Combat Team. My tour lasted one full year. I spent approximately ten and a half months with line companies as a combat medic. I carried an M-16 for myself and for the men I shared my tour of hell with!

"Seventeen years after I left Vietnam, I don't think a day went by that Vietnam didn't come up in my mind in some way or another. Anything could bring back a 'picture' that my mind had captured. One day I was reading the entertainment section of the newspaper, when one of those pictures flashed on the words "Hamburger Hill" — a battle I had survived and had helped give its nickname. The article told of some new movies in the making. I felt a need to find out more. I wrote to the Los Angeles Times in care of the article's author.

"A few weeks passed before I received an answer. When I did, I believe my course had been set. The author's name was Jay Sharbutt, with the Los Angeles Times, who worked the war for Associated Press as a correspondent. I called him on the phone and we began finding out about each other. We had crossed paths in Vietnam, on Hamburger Hill. (I found out later that Sharbutt's article about the battle was the one that got the people in America, especially Congress, aware of it, and its waste of human lives.)

"Sharbutt put me in touch with the film's production company in L.A. They paid my way to talk with director John Irvin. It was the first time in seventeen years that somebody wanted to talk to me about Vietnam and really listened. It was the beginning of a 'healing' therapy for me. At the end of our conversation Irvin made a comment that sparked a fire: 'It's too bad you hadn't written a book. It would have made my work much easier. You should still do it. People want to know about Vietnam.'

"One afternoon I received a phone call from Gary Sheperd, of Ted Koppel's "Nightline." They were doing a show about the wave of new Vietnam movies coming out of Hollywood. Sheperd and a camera crew came to my place of work, and to my home, to continue the interview, which included my family. My appearance on the show was brief, but to me and my family, it was our brief moment of fame.

"Twenty years after the battle for Hamburger Hill, I finished writing my story.

"I had always believed in my mind that I had someone watching over me while I was in Vietnam, a kind of Guardian Angel, if you can believe in them. One day while humping along a ridgeline not far from Hamburger Hill, RPGs exploded around us. One exploded a few feet in front of me. The explosion killed my comrade behind me and wounded the man in front of me. I was untouched. I had felt a firm push at my back. I turned my head just enough as I fell to see a soldier walk away from me. That push had saved my life. But the soldier was gone. That soldier was not of my war. His clothes were different, and I remember seeing "leggings" worn around his ankles. I believe that soldier was my uncle, who had been killed in WWII. Talking to my other uncle, I found out that his brother, my "angel," had been a newspaper reporter before he went to war, and when he left he told him that he would write a book about the war when he got home. He never did, but I did, and after all it was a newspaper man's article that got me started and kept me going. Call it fate, or a mystery of war. They're plentiful."

ONE MORE HILL

By James L. Thomas

It was our turn to go in! This wasn't like any LZ we ever went into. The choppers were exposed for a long time. They had to drop in through the dense jungle to a little tiny cleared spot to let us off. We would have to jump the last few feet. The jungle had screened out the sunlight and our eyes were still adjusting to the change in light when it was time to jump. The jump wouldn't have been anything except for the sixty-some-odd pounds of rucksack wanting to follow the law of gravity and taking you where it wanted to go. I scrambled to my feet hearing voices calling me.

"Over here, Doc!"

I recognized the voices of Sgt. Riley and Ron. I was beginning to see better, as the next chopper was getting ready to descend on the LZ. I heard automatic gun fire coming from what seemed to be the top of the hill. Sgt. Riley spoke:

"Nice LZ, huh, Doc?"

"Yeh," I answered. "What the hell's going on? This sure is a shitty place for an LZ, on the side of a hill!"

Sgt. Riley said, "It sure beats the hell out of the one we were supposed to come into. That one was really hot. The gooks must have been waiting for us. They hit the first six choppers going in. Now there's a handful who made it — stuck on the LZ and they're pinned down!"

"Where's the artillery support or air support?" I said.

"Can't help. Too many choppers in the air, and too many of us spread out along this ridgeline. They don't want to take a chance on hitting friendlies!"

"What are they going to do to help them?"

"Your looking at the help. We're supposed to try and link up with them as soon as the rest of the company lands."

Dreading the answer, I had to know which company was cut off.

"So who're the poor bastards on top?" I asked Sgt. Riley.

"Part of Charlie Company and some scared shitless door-gunners!"

Time was not on our side. It was getting dark, the climb was slow, the jungle was thick. We could not link up with the top LZ before night, and the LT felt it was too risky to try the linkup at night. They would have to hold out by themselves. Their firing was sporadic and there was no return fire. They might get lucky! The gooks might have been so proud, knocking out all those half-million-dollar choppers, that they might have split.

The night was filled with whisperings like "I think I saw something move over there." Gunfire followed the comments. A few flares were sent up, but no sign of any gooks.

We continued early next morning, trying to reach the top. As we reached the crest, we began to see the burned out skeletons of the choppers. It looked like a junkyard. The point man began to holler, "Coming IN!"

We saw friendly heads start popping up, then men walking toward us. The looks on their faces told us they couldn't have been happier to see us, even if we had been girls wearing bikinis. The LT gave the orders to spread out and secure the area. A detail was picked to get the bodies from the choppers. Most of the guys from Charlie Company had made it. It was the poor pilot and co-pilot that didn't have the time to get out. I avoided the body detail and asked myself if anybody in this world needed me. Looking around the hilltop, it was just so hard to believe the price we just paid to be standing there. For what?

The rest of the survivors were in good shape, with minor cuts and scrapes. Naturally, there wasn't a dead gook to be found. They'd built a small tunnel leading to a bunker, where they were hiding until the choppers came in. They just popped up once in a while to fire an RPG and some small arms, then back down, waiting for the next one to come in. And then they'd zap another. You can't help but give the gooks credit. It was amazing, how just a few could screw up so many and destroy so much equipment. No wonder the big brass was always so concerned about body count. We had to kill so much more of them to keep the books writing in the black!

The door-gunners and crew chiefs were pacing up and down, waiting for a chopper to come and take them back in. You could tell that they were feeling the pain of losing most of their crew members in such a short time. Their unit, the "Ghost Riders," was wiped out.

It had gotten hot that day. The chopper that would take out the dead came in none too soon. The heat was spoiling the flesh, filling the air with a sickening smell, and the insects were adding to the disfiguring condition. One of the door-gunners retrieved a fire extinguisher from one of the downed choppers, hoping the chemicals might help keep the bodies in better shape. It really bothered him, knowing the bodies were becoming almost unrecognizable. He had stayed close to them, lifting up their poncho coverings periodically and spraying them with the fire extinguisher, hoping to delay the inevitable. Man can destroy, but nature always takes over in the end.

Whoever was giving the orders wasn't wasting any time in getting this hill whipped into shape. Just as the choppers were leaving with the chopper crews and KIAs, two big Chinook choppers were circling overhead, each one dangling a bulldozer from its bellies. As each one landed, it loaded its net down, just long enough to let the dozer crew out with their gear. The dozer crews didn't waste any time beginning their task of leveling of the hilltop. The pace at which they worked was a dead give-away that they didn't like being out there. Maybe seeing our "chopper graveyard" was intimidating.

By late afternoon the dozers had changed the face of the hilltop. It was beginning to look like a firebase — Firebase Airborne! The bulldozers had turned the hilltop into an almost level red clay baseball field, and it didn't take long for someone to throw out the first ball. Before anyone realized it, work had almost stopped and the roar of a school playground seemed almost natural — in the middle of a dense jungle forest. The hill had really changed. Some guys still stood guard, and a few watched the sky for Blackjack's chopper. We knew he'd get the "ass" if he caught us.

One last chopper had made a stop with more supplies, and the all-important mail. There had been a screw-up somewhere and we hadn't gotten any mail, even while I'd been back in the rear area. Better late than never. Sgt. Riley passed out the mail and had a surprise for himself, a couple of packets of pictures that had been developed by the PX. Sgt. Riley had been taking pictures of us since he got to the platoon and this had been the first time he had gotten them returned. He broke out in laughter as he looked at them. We stopped reading our letters and crowded around him.

I pointed to one of the fatigued figures and asked, "Who's that?"

The sergeant looked closer and said, "It's you, Doc. Can't you tell. You and that nose. I'd recognize it anywhere!"

We all laughed, but I know we were amazed at the way we looked. The last six months had aged us greatly. We even looked different to ourselves.

The next few days were quiet. The gooks left us alone. We made some short recons around the hill, but nothing too far out. The firebase was coming along. A great deal of the loose dirt that we had played ball on had ended up in more damned sandbags. I accepted the fact that until I left Vietnam, sandbags would be a part of my life.

Blackjack had been to see the base a couple of times. He wasn't really concerned about the base as much as he was concerned about us, and not in a fatherly way. He didn't like his troops baby-sitting firebases. He wanted them out looking for gooks! I had the feeling we'd be leaving here soon, and my hunch was right. Third Platoon would head out tomorrow.

Our job would be to recon out a few days from the firebase. Since we'd had no activity around here, Blackjack wanted us farther out, to try and "shake some loose." We would leave at midday, so we would not be far out from the firebase the first night. I guess they figured that the gooks had been quiet too long and might try something, knowing that some troops had left.

We ate chow at noon, which we normally didn't, but LT figured we might be rushed and might not have time in the evening to set up a NDP where we could be comfortable enough to cook a hot meal. The LT said that the going would be easy, downhill for quite aways. We would be traveling down a "finger," coming off the hill to the north. The finger led down slowly off the top. It was fairly narrow, which gave us a good view to our flanks. The going was easy — a slight decline, just enough to make the weight of our rucksacks comfortable.

Our easy pace came to a halt. The point team stopped and had passed the word that they found a booby trap. We sat down and lit smokes while we waited for the trap to be clear. Word came quickly — it was a bomb, an unexploded bomb dropped from one of our planes, and the gooks had booby-trapped it. The captain had sent word to blow it in place. The Sarg would set the charge while the point gave him security. The rest of us were to pull back and get down. The bomb was laying off the left side of the finger, so we would pull back a good distance and cross to the other side and get down and use the top of the finger to block the blast from coming straight at us.

We were set for the blast. For a reason that puzzled me, the LT yelled out the universal signal before setting off an explosion — "Fire-in-the-hole" — three times. I would have loved to have had some gooks come sneaking up to see what was going on and boom! blow off the charge and watch them get a free trip back up north. The explosion went off, but sounded like it was only the sergeant's charge that went off. But before we could raise up our heads any farther, the bomb exploded. The ground shook like a great earthquake. You could hear the shrapnel whizzing through the trees, tearing hunks of bark off the ones that stood between us and the bomb. For a few seconds we paused and realized that if the point hadn't found the bomb, we all could have been dead center of the bomb's kill zone. I know I hated for Ron to be on point, but I was damn glad he was today.

Getting back in order didn't take long, and soon we were approaching the bomb's crater. I was curious to see the size of the hole it had made. The ground still felt like it was trembling from the blast, when a furious exchange of explosions and automatic gunfire broke out. The exchange lasted only the time it took for me to hit the ground. My helmet fell forward on my face as my rucksack slapped me in the back of the head. Then the yelling started.

"Get Doc up here quick!"

My stomach felt the full weight of my meal as I tried to get moving. I dropped my ruck and pulled my aid bag off it. My stomach cramped as I stumbled forward to the front. Our M-60 had started firing without any return fire. I reached my first causality. It was Jim, our Kit Carson Scout. I got to him just as he seemed to try and reach out for his last breath of air. He had caught a piece of shrapnel right in the side of his throat, severing his jugular vein. I reached down to press my hand against his neck, to try and stop the bleeding, but got to it just as the blood stopped it's pulsating flow.

I yelled out, "Jim's dead!"

I heard a voice yell to me, "Up here, Doc. The point team's hit."

My heart started to pound. My mind flashed — all kinds pictures of what I might find when I reached them. All the firing had stopped. I reached the LT and he told me that they were in the bomb crater. I crawled to the rim, pausing for just a second, then I hurled myself over, waiting for gunfire that never sounded. I continued to roll to the crater's center. I stopped just short of a twisted bloody figure. I reached forward to touch it when it rolled over toward me. I started to gag when I saw the half-missing head of Ron. I rolled away from the corpse, not wanting to see its pain-etched face, which was colored bright red. The sound of the M-60 firing behind me brought me back to the moment. I rolled flat on my back, feeling warm tears roll to the sides of my face. In my head I could hear the cry of someone in pain. I turned back toward the body that I had just finished eating lunch with a short while back. I really couldn't believe what I was seeing, or I didn't want to. The cries I heard seemed to fade. My sickness faded too, but I became angry, pulling my M-16 closer to me. I chambered a round, and still lying flat on my back, moved the selector switch to auto, and pulled the trigger. One round shot out. It had misfired. I chambered another round and pulled the trigger again. Still only one round. They had given my rifle a complete cleaning in the rear. Someone must have screwed something up!

I started to almost giggle out loud in a punch-drunk state.

I thought to myself, "How could all this stuff happen in just a matter of a few hours. My whole world has changed. Damn it, I want to go home. I can't put up with this shit anymore!"

I heard the sound of a AK-47 pop a few rounds in our direction. As I grabbed my M-16, I noticed it was resting on the side of my foot. The thought of a round, one of my rounds, entered my head.

"Yeh, that's a sure ticket home. One toe missing and I'd be home free! They always sent amputees home!"

The idea of doing it became real the longer I left the barrel of the gun rest on my foot. I even moved it in position, wondering which would be the one I needed the least. No one would suspect that I'd done it intentionally. It would be just an accident, especially the way I was lying in this crater. I wouldn't have to worry about the pain. I had the morphine with me. Or better still, I could give myself the shot before I pulled the trigger. I began to hear more of the guys moving up from behind me. If I was going to do it, I couldn't wait any longer. Someone might see me do it. I curled my finger around the trigger and took a deep breath. I paused and turned my head, straight into the eyes of Ron. The barrel of my rifle slipped from my foot. I couldn't do it. Looking at the pain-twisted face of my buddy brought the coward up from deep inside me. It told me it was wrong!

Ron looked different now. The corpse lying next to me wasn't him. I couldn't help but wonder if the expression on his face reflected the amount of pain he suffered just before death. Did Ron stop me from pulling the trigger?

The friendly voice of the LT brought me back to my senses.

He hollered, "Hey Doc. Let's go. No time for a nap now!"

I rolled over and got to my knees and in a quick start unassed the bomb crater.

"The gooks are gone. They accomplished what they wanted to do!" the LT said. "We're heading back to the firebase!"

The LT was right. The gooks had done their job. The score was 4 and 0. We lost 4 men and we didn't even get a blood trail! Blackjack won't be happy about this! We wrapped our dead in their ponchos and got them headed toward their way home.

It didn't seem like we had gotten that far from the firebase, but going back was uphill. Evening was closing in on us. We pushed ourselves to reach the firebase. Some of the guys from Second Platoon met us at the perimeter and gave us a hand with our dead. Not many words were exchanged, just looks of fear and the one everybody carried with them, the one that said "Gee, I'm sorry. But better you guys than us!"

Something was different about the firebase. It looked a little messed up. I asked one of the guys from Second Platoon what happened.

He said, "The gooks dropped in a couple mortars rounds about the same time they hit you guys!"

It wasn't hard to figure out that they didn't want us on this hill and it would take a lot to hold it.

I was trying not to think much about this afternoon as I got some chow ready to eat, but a can of meatballs and beans that Ron had given me, because he knew I liked them, was the first can pulled out of my rucksack. My appetite left me. I took out one of the packets of Kool-aid I had just gotten in the mail and made up a canteen full of "Goofy grape." It seemed to fit the occasion.

The gooks continued to harass us, dropping in a couple of mortar rounds at random, morning, noon, and night. Their aim hadn't been too good so far. We hadn't lost anybody. They had sent out our mortar crews from the rear and they had sent out rounds every time the gooks did the same to us. It had been almost two weeks since we got here and the firebase was almost complete. The concertina wire had been strung, the bunkers were just about finished, and the battery of 105mm's was operational. That was the whole purpose of this place — get the artillery in a place where it could provide fire support for us out in the field. We always bitched about the work, but once you needed them in the field, the bitching stopped.

Just when we thought life would get routine, the LT said we had just got word we were leaving. Not just to go out on a recon around here — we were leaving for someplace else that he couldn't tell us. We didn't like the sounds of that, not knowing where we were headed. It really didn't matter to me anymore. There was nothing I could do anyway. I had no control over my situation. I just had to go along with whatever happened.

The next day the choppers began to bring in our replacements. They were from one of the other battalions. A big shuffle was going on. The guys getting off the choppers looked in good spirits and healthy. We wondered what they had been doing to get that way. When they were all in, it was time for us to leave.

The choppers had continued to circle the base, waiting for us. The LT said they wanted us to leave as a group, which was unusual. The normal routine was, as a chopper came in and unloaded, we loaded right on. He figured we might be going a longer distance, to use the quick shuttle method. We all got airborne. I was glad to leave, even though we didn't know where we were headed. We did know we were heading east this time, and that was away from the Ashau Valley. The hills all started to disappear from below us. Our curiosity was getting stronger. We hadn't been in an area like this since we left the south.

The sergeant tapped my shoulder and told me to "Look over there, Doc. That's the ocean."

I strained my eyes and looked in the direction he had pointed to.

I finally turned back to him and said, "Yeh. I think it is. Where the hell are we going?"

Smiles started to appear on everyone's faces.

The sergeant tapped one of the door-gunners and yelled as loud as he could, "Do you know where we're going?"

The gunner yelled back, "China Beach!"

Why didn't we think of asking him before!

"China Beach!"

That was a place they used as an in-country R&R spot. Damn! Old Blackjack must be getting laid regular, to have the heart to send us here. As the choppers descended, the smell of the ocean filled our noses. It brought back the memories of my senior year in high school. We went to the beach all the time that year, listening to songs from the Beach Boys. We hurriedly jumped off the choppers, just to make sure they didn't change their minds about bringing us here.

The place was big. They even had some buildings that looked real — not just sandbags and screen. Some guy in Navy fatigues asked which company we were and directed us to a couple of buildings that were like ours back at battalion, but built much better. We hussled to get inside. There were nice bunks — enough for everyone. The LT told us to find a bunk, drop our gear, clear our weapons and store them in the racks that were next to the doors. After we had done that we were called for a formation. Out of practice, we looked like stumbling recruits trying to get in a proper formation.

The first sergeant yelled, "Let's go, troops, or I'll send you back in the bush where you belong!" With those words we snapped to. The first sergeant started listing the rules of conduct while we were here. He told us where the mess hall was, and we would have to be clean before we could go in. We would pull no details unless we fucked up! The beach was open daylight hours only. We would have three days, starting right now. And he dismissed us. A roar broke out as we all headed for the beach, stripping clothes off as we ran. Small cries and swearing started as the salt water hit our abused skin. The little cuts and half-healed sores seemed to get bigger as the salt burned out the poison. Some of the guys wanted to leave and I hollered for them to get back in the water. It would do them good. After awhile we got used to it. Even the cuts and scraps I had started to feel better. I hadn't lied!

The beach echoed the release of tension as we played like kids on an outing. It was soon chow time and we were being spoiled — all the cold milk you wanted, fresh vegetables, and meat and chicken, and not the canned kind, but like what we would have at home. We pigged out like it was the only meal we were getting.

Clowning around was a way of life to grunts, but sometimes it got a little rougher. The tension and hidden anger sometimes popped up at the wrong person. Two guys were at it, chasing each other around the area. It was starting to get serious as they ran through our hooch knocking each other down and then getting up again. As one entered, the other followed the last guy.

Showing a sign that the joking around had ended, one grabbed an M-16 and hollered, "If this was loaded I'd kill you."

As he squeezed the trigger our mouths dropped open as a shot rang out from the rifle.

It was loaded! The first player fell to the ground. The rifleman's aim was true.

It had been an accident, but someone had died. The man shouldn't have picked up the gun, even in the way he had intended it, and the guy who hadn't cleared his weapon contributed to the man's death.

The accident put a damper on our R&R. It was another "humbug," something that shouldn't have happened. Clowning around with a supposedly empty rifle got one man killed, one man going to stockade, facing a court-martial for a degree of murder, and another facing some kind of discipline for not having followed orders and cleared his weapon. A humbug!

All the weapons were checked again by us, and then in formation, like a regular Inspection Arms. No other weapon turned up with a round still in the chamber. At least no one would have said so, but still, the odds of that guy's picking up the rifle, out of all the ones we had, was tremendous.

Everyone was quiet the rest of the day. Most wrote letters or read old ones, and mostly just kept to themselves. They were showing a movie for us that night, complete with popcorn, and we all looked forward to it.

It was a clear night. The movie was on an outdoor screen. They showed a movie called "Barbarella," starring Jane Fonda. Life was certainly different in Vietnam, not what you would expect in a war zone, with all the twists and turns it makes, and the way we in turn reacted to them. Someone died, but it's still better them than us, him than me, and let's forget it!

Our three days were over. It was time to get back to business. Everyone seemed to be thinking, "What did Blackjack have in mind for us now?" Now that he had fattened us up! Word had it we were going back to the battalion area to get resupplied, and that was it so far.

This time we loaded into Chinooks for our ride to Camp Evans. When we arrived, trucks were waiting for us. Things were running smooth. Blackjack must have had something planned for us, to get us moving like this. My first stop was the aid station. I dropped my gear on the little porch we had in front and went in. My med platoon sergeant was changing names on our duty board roster — it listed which company we were assigned to. My mouth literally dropped open as I saw that my name was no longer listed under Alpha Company. My eyes quickly searched the board. I found it! It was listed under "Aid Station."

"Well, Jim, you made it!" the sergeant said. "No more going out in the field. Your replacement is waiting for you to show him around."

I could hardly believe what I was hearing. It would take time to sink in.

"Oh, by the way. Better get some Spec/5 stripes, before Top catches you without them. You know how he is."

I stood with my mouth hanging open, awed by all the good news.

"I finally have something good to write home about! It's time for some beer and bullshit tonight!"

It was hard to believe.

"The morning was here and the companies were getting ready to move out and I'm staying. Better start those letters and tell the folks the good news... Owe my brother one first!

'Hi Joe. Well, things are getting better. I'm no longer in a line company. I'll be working on firebases or here at the battalion aid station. It's a hell of a lot better than before. You probably read that the 101st was in the Ashau Valley. Well, just don't believe all you've read. It's a bad place, but they play it up more. I made one combat helicopter assault and made it, and that's enough for this tour for that place. Medals are not what I'm looking for. Medals won't buy any beer in the States or anywhere. Hope to go to the PX and get a camera. Want to take some pictures while I'm taking it easy. The guys say film is hard to get. Maybe you could send a few rolls. I'll need 35mm. Well, I'll close. I'll write soon. Be good!

Your brother, Jim'

"Well, that's one letter out of the way. Got plenty of time for letter writing. Now, as long as I can find things to write about!"

Al, my platoon sergeant, told me that the operation that the battalion was going on was a real big one — five battalions strong.

"God," I thought, "They must be expecting to run into a shitload of gooks! Hope everyone gets through it! I don't know why I should, but I'm starting to feel guilty about not going with them. Especially leaving my platoon with a cherry medic!"

Got to the PX and got my camera.

"Now, if I can figure out how to use it."

The sergeant had been listening to the radio on battalion frequency. The battalion had made the CA into a LZ nicknamed "Blue," and everything was going okay. It made me feel good and gave me my appetite back.

After chow I sat around the aid station, halfway listening to the battalion radio. Nothing was going on and no contact had been made.

"Sounds like this operation will be a piece of cake. Just a walk in the sun, ditty-bop down the trail."

I went to my hooch to write some more letters and suck up a few beers, and catch up on some more sleep.

"This might get boring, but I'll suffer through. It beats the field any day!"

I was halfway dozing off to sleep when one of the headquarters clerks came running to my hooch.

"Hey, Doc Thomas. They want you at the aid station right away!"

I jumped up, thinking someone was hurt and they needed me to help. I ran to the aid station, pulling open the back door, and was quickly told to be quiet and listen. I huddled around the radio with the sergeant and another medic.

The sergeant said between the garbled radio transmission, "Bravo Company just made contact, trying to get up this hill!"

"Anyone hurt?" I asked.

"Yeh, one of the cherry medics and three or four other guys. They're pulling back right now. It's getting too dark now, Jim," the sergeant said.

I stopped him cold.

"I know. Pack my gear!"

"Looks like this could turn out to be trouble."

I went back to my hooch and grabbed my aid bag, and

returned to the aid station. My bag was still well supplied, but I wanted to make sure. The sergeant had checked on a chopper for me. There was one leaving first thing in the morning with supplies. Nothing I told myself could help make me sleep. Taking advantage of my sleeplessness, I wrote the rest of the letters, and spent extra time cleaning and checking my M-16.

There was no time to get breakfast and I couldn't eat anyway. The sergeant drove me up to the chopper pad.

On the way, in as convincing a voice as he could, he said, "The first medic that we get in is all yours and, if your still near an LZ, I'll bring him out myself!"

On that chopper ride I knew exactly where we were headed. I had stopped in a headquarters and got one of the clerks to show me were the battalion was. The Ashau Valley was twenty-some-odd miles from Hue and we were going to the northern part of it, only a couple of miles from Laos. The hill the battalion was attempting to take was the biggest around the area, called Dong Ap Bia, or military style — Hill 937. The map showed it was steep, with only a few ridgelines that could make the climb to the top possible.

We made one stop at firebase Burges-garten, to pick up an officer I had never seen before. He looked like he hadn't been out in the field much. The dead giveaway was, he hadn't earned his CIB (Combat Infantry Badge) yet.

We approached the LZ and things looked quiet. I could see GIs moving around with their shirts off — a good sign not much was going on. When we landed, Dave Stryer was on the LZ. He had taken a message from the sergeant that he wanted me to go to Delta Company. I wanted to go back to Alpha Company, with my old buddies, especially if we got into some shit. At least I knew how the guys worked together and covered my ass, and each others. But it wouldn't have been fair to switch with a new medic.

Delta Company was in position close to Bravo, which was going to move up and get on top of the hill. Arty sent in a barrage of 175mm, to try and chase away any gooks remaining on the hill. 175mm sure can put a damper on someone's party. The blasts seemed to change the direction that the winds blew. They had really laid in some rounds. Nobody could be left after that. We waited, and listened for the signal for Bravo Company to move up. It seemed quiet so far. The captain of Bravo Company reported a negative sit-rep from the point for their last on contact. We went, helping on the LZ, unloading choppers that were bringing in more supplies. It took a lot to keep a whole battalion running in the field.

Just like the weather — things went bad in minutes.

An exchange of automatic gunfire echoed from the bottom of the hill.

The radio began to hum with questions being yelled at the tops of voices. Explosions began to join the firefight. Bravo Company was in the middle of some heavy shit. Dave and I headed out, with a platoon from Charlie Company that was ordered to move up, and helped with their wounded. The platoon moved along the ridgeline leading from the LZ to the base of the hill. Some of the wounded had already started making their way to a small clearing just before the ridgeline. Helicopters started buzzing around the area. Just as we were getting some of the wounded stabilized, one gunship began making the pattern they used in a gun-run — the swoosh of it rockets being fired were close. Before anyone could react, some of the rockets began to hit just forward of our position.

We scrambled to the ground yelling, "Tell them to stop! Can't they see! It's us!"

His pass was over, but not till he had sent in a volley of rockets, right on some of the wounded, who were trying to make their way off the hill. Screams and cries poured out.

I rushed forward with Dave, not wanting to find out how bad it was.

And bad it was.

Five of the wounded had went from WIA to KIA, thanks to the joker in the gunship.

Couldn't he see what he was firing at?

He surely couldn't have mistaken us for gooks.

Our workload had been cut short, thanks to the ultimate fucking humbug:

To be wounded by the enemy and get finished off by your own people.

I could see the telegram going home:

"Wounded in action by enemy gunfire — killed by 'friendly fire' same time!"

—

THE FOG

By James L. Thomas

In platoon-size strength, we were on a recon three to four good days out from the nearest firebase.

We were out of chow and were waiting for resupply.

The weather had been getting bad and it was harder and harder for the choppers to be airborne.

We were in a mountainous area, which added to their problems, and ours.

The choppers couldn't make it.

Would try tomorrow.

This went on for days.

We were humping toward the firebase, but it was dangerous and hard to be sure of our direction.

It was difficult to be sure of our position.

The LT had no land features he could check.

We were hungry and getting very low on water.

At night the LT strung a rope around our NDP from position to position, to give us a little feeling of security.

It had no real value other than it kind of "tied" us together.

With the fog, the night became very dark!

Hunger and thirst started to control our action.

We were quick to get angry and much worse, we were getting careless.

All we wanted to do was get to the firebase as quickly as we could.

On the sixth day, our luck started to change.

The fog started to lift, and the sun was breaking through.

Just as we began thinking it was over, a shot broke through our excitement.

A sniper had hit, and had pegged one of the men, right behind his left ear.

I moved forward a few steps to check him, when another round was fired.

Just as I heard the shot I felt something hit me hard in the back, which made me fall to the ground.

Then I heard a voice say, "They got Doc!"

I was confused and couldn't move.

My only thought at the time was, I wished the fog was still with us!

I heard somebody crawling toward me, quietly saying, "Doc! Doc, are you okay?"

I answered, "Yeh!"

The fog did move back in.

The sniper must have been dogging us for days, waiting for his chance to strike.

And strike he did.

But not as good as he might have seen.

My aid bag caught the bullet.

The saying goes:

"Never worry about the bullet you can hear.

It's the one you don't that will kill you!"

I heard that one Lima Charlie — LOUD AND CLEAR!

Kevin R. McPartland

Kevin R. McPartland is a native of Brooklyn, New York, and during his war years, 1966/67, served with Naval River Forces in the Mekong Delta. His short stories and poetry have appeared nationally in the small press, and he is currently engaged in work on his first novel.

Panjang Island

By Kevin R. McPartland

Six times in the last hour, he thought, he'd seen movement. First it was just in front, just where a large patch of elephant grass met thick shrubs, then to his right and left. Each time the American would lie perfectly still, his rifle tucked close to his body. Black ants would crawl over his hands and sometimes onto his face and neck, yet he would not move an eyelash in hope of seeing the Vietnamese through the brush. For the last hour the cat and mouse game of war was played between the two. Both were about the same height, the American a bit huskier in build. Both were eighteen years of age, one in his homeland... one far from home. It was the sixth day of the sixth month of the American's stay in-country. Things were changing. He'd been told they would. It was toward the middle of your tour that you would start to change, not care, not worry who lived or died, including yourself. The not caring had led him to this small grid of brush on the small island in the Mekong River... him and the other boy.

From the air the island was a speck, a narrow rough piece of jungle and rock separating two riverbanks. On one bank the 9th Infantry Division firebase at Dong Tam. On the other, a treeline and rice paddies that stretched for as far as the eye could see to a distant mountain range that was the Central Highlands. On this day as he lay silently in the brush his eyes would occasionally catch the sky. He looked at its vivid blue and deep white of the cumulus clouds that blew south to the mouth of the river, toward the South China Sea. He thought of the ships that sat safely offshore, their crews going about ordinary shipboard life. He thought of his situation, of its absurdity. He looked at the uniform he wore, at the jungle boots and green drab fatigues. He'd enlisted in the Navy to go to sea. He never believed he would end up on river-patrol boats. He never believed his luck would run this piss-poor. Behind him he could still hear sporadic gunfire from the river. They would be coming looking for him soon... his crew. He still couldn't believe he'd done it... jumping from the boat in the shallows and chasing the one Vietnamese up the riverbank. He thought of the look of fear on the boy's face. It reflected an image to the American that he disliked, almost feared. The fear was different, though. It wasn't of the possibilities of what could happen. But more a fear of himself. What he had become. What the war had made him. There was no one on the island but the two of them. At least he didn't think so, not unless a stray Vietcong mortar team lay in wait for darkness, to shell the firebase behind him. He doubted it, though. More than likely, just himself and his prey. At any time he could just end this thing, make his way out of the trees and back to the river. But no, he wanted the kill, he wanted this one close up. The Vietnamese had fired at the patrol boat. This was authorized from Washington. He had his license. The American crawled a few feet, hugging the ground so low he literally pushed the reddish brown soil with his body. He eventually straightened his body in a perfect line with the trunk of a tall palm, carefully looking around its side.

He wondered if he was being watched the way he was watching, if the Vietnamese had somehow made his way behind him. If that was the case he was in the open, hiding himself from nothing. He'd stand soon and begin to walk, draw fire maybe. He'd heard nothing or seen nothing move for the last few minutes. His crew would be coming for him soon. It was now or never, and he wanted this kill for himself. He touched the miraculous medal that hung from his dog tags. Before standing, the Vietnamese came clearly to his mind. He was somewhere near, maybe crouching like himself, the heat bothering him. Maybe sweat dripping in his eyes, burning, the underbrush touching his skin with a ticklish cutting sensation to its texture. In his mouth would be the Buddha medal he wore around his neck. His culture had taught him since childhood to bring Buddha close to his body when death was threatened or nearby.

The American stood and walked into a small clearing. Small brightly colored jungle birds startled by his sudden presence squawked and flew high into the jungle palms above. He turned in a wide circle, his weapon drawn up to his face. He squinted, looking for something in his sights, a sound, an odd movement in the treeline, something to fire at, but saw nothing. There was just the midday jungle heat and the droning chatter of the birds. He could smell his weapon, he held it so close to his cheek. It smelled of plastic, metal and lubricating oil. Through the trees the sun shone bright on the river. He took a few cautious steps and felt a flash of fear. He'd been afraid, but suddenly this was a different fear, a combination survival fear and the fear of himself... of dying and at the same time of killing. At that moment in the heat. In the lush green heat of the afternoon he lowered his weapon from his cheek. His face and cheek were covered with sweat. He wiped it with the back of his free hand. He looked about, fanning small insects from his face, and felt at peace. The others had told him about this also, how sometimes right in the middle of it all you just wouldn't feel like playing anymore. It was a strange feeling, such a sway of emotion. But it was true. He thought of the Vietnamese dead. He knew what he would look like. Red against black pajamas and a waxlike pallor to the skin tone. Why did orientals always look like wax figurines in death rather than what was once human? The sun beat hot on the American's head. Not only on his head, but in his boots, in the crotch of his pants. He probably stunk, he thought — what a stupid concern. He began to walk toward the treeline. Toward the thick trees where the shade would be coolest... where a breeze would be blowing from the river. As soon as he got to the riverbank he'd swim. He'd take off his hot dirty uniform and swim naked in the cool brown river.

The face appeared through the foliage as though an apparition: Hatless, eyes staring, weapon raised. The sun caught the face in a ray of stray light, it's expression reflecting generations of warrior. A face totally in sync with its environment and at ease with its present task. The American reacted slowly. There was one single shot from the Chinese Communist AK-47 rifle that struck with a stunning concussion. The American's eyes focused briefly on the hot jungle floor as it rose to meet him. He thought fleetingly of cold clear water and then thought no more.

—

William Robinson

William (Billy) Robinson was born in Charlotte, North Carolina on December 8, 1926. He dropped out of school in 1942 and entered military service, in the U.S. Navy, on July 14, 1943, at the age of sixteen. During World War II he served in New Guinea and Australia. He was reassigned to the USS Iowa after World War II and served in Yokosuka Harbor, Japan from January to March 1946. He was honorably discharged on April 25, 1946.

He then volunteered for active duty with the U.S. Army, because of the Korean conflict, on January 11, 1951, served with Company B, 27th Infantry Regiment, in combat, as Squad Leader, Platoon Sergeant, and First Sergeant. When he returned to the United States he served with Company C, 3rd Infantry (The Old Guard), Fort Myer, Virginia as Platoon Sergeant and First Sergeant in the Presidential Honor Guard. After serving with the Old Guard, he was assigned to Company K, 3rd Battalion, 10th Infantry in Germany, as First Sergeant and on August 21, 1955 became the Battalion Sergeant Major, the youngest and most junior Master Sergeant in the Battalion.

He returned to Fort Ord, California on December 18, 1955 and served with the U.S. Army Combat Development Experimentation Center as Sergeant Major and First Sergeant until 31 August 1959, when he was re-assigned to the 3rd Infantry (The Old Guard), Fort Myer, Virginia and performed duty as First Sergeant of Honor Guard Company. In December 1960 he was selected to accompany the American Battle Monuments Commission to the Philippines for the dedication of the Manila American Cemetery and Memorial. In January 1961 he was selected by the Chairman, Joint Chiefs of Staff to present to President Eisenhower, on 6 January 1961, serial number one, M-14 rifle. During September and October 1961, accompanied Senator Albert Gore, Chairman, Subcommittee on African Affairs and Senators Philip Hart and Maurine Neuburger on a 24,000-mile Congressional fact finding tour of Africa.

He was transferred to Korea in January 1962 and served as Platoon Leader, First Sergeant and enlisted Aide to the Commanding General, 1st Cavalry Division. He returned to the United States in March 1963 as Chief Operations Sergeant, Plans Branch in the office of the Deputy Chief of Staff, Operations and Training, 3rd U.S. Army. He was reassigned duty in Germany with the 2nd Battalion, 15th Infantry in December 1965, where he served as First Sergeant and Sergeant Major until volunteering for Vietnam.

Arriving in Vietnam on October 1, 1967, he served as Battalion Sergeant Major, 3rd Battalion, 60th Infantry and Brigade Sergeant Major of the 2nd Brigade (Mobile Riverine Force), 9th Division in the Mekong Delta until retiring from the U.S. Army on November 1, 1968.

His military awards and decorations include the Silver Star, Bronze Star with Oak Leaf Cluster, Air Medal with Oak Leaf Cluster, Combat Infantry Badge (Second award), Army Commendation Medal with Third Leaf Cluster.

If Robinson had remained on active duty, he might well have become Master Sergeant of the U.S. Army.

After retiring from the U.S. Army he became the Director of ROTC at Therrell High School in Atlanta, Georgia.

The Mobile Riverine Force

By William Robinson

As I walked down the hall I could see the man dressed in a white doctor's jacket standing in the hallway just adjacent to the waiting room. Almost automatically my hand came up in a salute when I reached him.

"Come with me," he said, without any emotion. My heart throbbed and quivered as I followed him. When we reached the door to his office he stood at the entrance.

"Go in and have a seat," he said.

As I took a seat beside his desk, I waited for Doctor Kenworthy to speak.

I could not imagine why it became necessary for me to seek help from a psychiatrist, but this was the beginning of treatment for my depression, which lasted nine months.

Doctor Kenworthy dug into every crevice of my life, and on one occasion, he said, "You have led an interesting life. Why don't you write a book?"

That was during March 1981.

You will find in these pages many things that you find hard to believe. Believe them because they are true. It would have been impossible for me to write this story if I had not lived through the events.

The author's baptism of fire came during the Korean conflict in 1951, near Kumhwa, where he became obsessed with killing the enemy. In his own words to his men, he said:

"I will allow no prisoners. You are to destroy your enemy; if you don't know how I will show you; if you run from your enemy I will destroy you."

The author loved the Army more than anything, even his own family. He was a professional soldier that got the job done regardless of the obstacles. He maintained high standards among his men and expected, without question, that they perform their duty in a commendable manner, and those that did not were dealt with by firm disciplinary action.

With hopes of being a thirty-year man, and possibly a nomination to the Sergeant Major of the Army position, the author's love for the Army vanished during his tour of duty in Vietnam. It was at this time that he witnessed the senseless killing of women, children, and old men.

"I will take my leave from the Army," he said, "because I do not want to be a part of this slaughter, about which I can do nothing."

Vietnam was a time when millions of people were divided — father against son, mother against daughter, brother against brother, and sister against sister.

With all of our problems, we live in the most wonderful country there is. We have an inherent right to do anything we please as long as we do not infringe on the rights of others, and it is within the purview of the law. Many men have given their lives to protect those inherent rights without resorting to such atrocities as committed at My Lai, Cairang, and many other places in Vietnam.

None of this is to suggest that all military men are barbarians. Our military training taught us how to defeat the enemy and protect those innocent civilians. But, somewhere along the line, some of our military men forgot their loyalty to humanity and became only savages that killed at their own pleasure, regardless of sex or age.

History will judge that the Vietnam war constituted one of our greatest military defeats.

THE MEKONG DELTA

It was late in the afternoon of August 25, 1967 when I arrived in New York, from Germany, with my family. I made a quick telephone call to the private vehicle holding area, in New Jersey, to check on my automobile, which I had shipped earlier. It had arrived and I was informed that I could pick it up, provided I got there before closing.

"What time do you close?" I asked.

"At 5:00 p.m.," the man said.

"I don't think I can make it by 5:00 p.m.," I said, "can you wait on me if I am not there by 5:00 p.m.?"

"I will wait a few minutes," he replied.

"Okay, I am on my way," I said.

We hurried and got a taxi to take us there, arriving about 4:50.

"That sure was a close call," I said, "we only had a few minutes to spare."

I had no problem getting out of New Jersey and around Washington. We made the trip to Jonesboro, Georgia without any delays, stopping only for gas, food, and using the restrooms.

Our furniture and the items we had shipped from Germany were in storage at Fort McPherson, so we rented a house in Forest Park.

After we moved into the rental house I had a thought, "Here we go again, renting houses when we should be buying."

After discussing it with my wife, Lou, I decided to go to the Veterans Administration to see if the mortgage on our previous house had been settled. When I was informed by the VA that the loan had been paid in full and that I was eligible for another loan, I was elated.

We began looking around for a new house to buy. Our search did not take us very far. The house we located was much bigger than the previous one and was located in a nice section of Forest Park. After contacting the builder, we started the paperwork. I hand-carried the necessary papers to the VA and requested that they expedite the loan because I was going to Vietnam soon, and they agreed to do so.

The builder allowed us to move into the house before the outside painting was complete. This made it very convenient for

us, because there were many things I had to accomplish before
I departed.

I said to myself, "Everything must be in order before I leave.
With the high casualty rate in Vietnam I might not make it this
time."

With this thought in mind I went to the Staff Judge Advocate's
office at Fort McPherson and made out my Last Will and
Testament.

On the afternoon of my departure to Oakland, California, Lou
and the children took me to the airport.

"Billy, you and Steve take care of things while I am gone," I
said.

"Okay, Daddy," they said.

As we said good-bye I could see tears in their eyes, and later,
as I looked out of the window of the airplane, I could see them
standing at the window of the waiting room.

"My family loves me and I am going to miss them," I said to
myself.

When I arrived at the Oakland Army Terminal I was issued my
flight orders and instructed to report to Travis Air Force Base for
my flight to Vietnam.

It was nightfall when we boarded a Braniff Airlines airplane.
The airplane was loaded to its maximum capacity. Most of the men
were wearing their winter uniforms and when we became
airborne they started taking off their coats and relaxing.

During the flight the stewardess would bring around some
soft drinks and coffee. On one occasion they showed a movie.
There was not much laughing and talking. The men seemed to be
in a state of repose, but I knew that was not the case. They were
in deep thought about Vietnam.

As we were landing in Vietnam the pilot announced over the
PA, "Men, we are now landing at Bien Hoa, Vietnam. The ground
temperature is ninety-six degrees. We hope you have had a
pleasant flight and the crew and myself wish you the best of luck
during your tour of duty in Vietnam."

When he completed his announcement I looked around at
some of the young soldiers and thought to myself, "How many of
these young men will not make it back?"

When the door of the aircraft opened and we started to unload, the sweltering heat and humidity felt like 120 degrees. It was then that we got our first smell of Vietnam. The smell, I learned later, was the burning of human excrement.

We were directed, by soldiers dressed in jungle fatigues and armed with M-16 rifles, to waiting buses with bars on the windows.

As we rode along the roads, in the air-conditioned bus, toward Long Binh, I could see many Vietnamese people who, except for a few young girls, ignored us.

I thought to myself, "It sure doesn't look as if a war is going on in this part of the country."

When the buses stopped at the 90th Replacement Battalion and we off-loaded I could hear an announcement being made over the PA system.

"All new replacements who already have assignment orders to a specific unit report to the In Processing building. All others will wait in the receiving area for your assignments."

Several officers, senior NCOs, and myself moved directly to the In Processing building.

It did not take long for me to process, after which I was informed that a truck from the 9th Division was waiting to transport all of the replacements to division headquarters at Bear Cat (Army base) near Saigon.

Upon our arrival at Bear Cat we were met by the division chief of staff and the sergeant major. By this time I was soaking wet with perspiration. After their welcome speech, the division sergeant major came over to me.

"Come along with me," he said.

"Okay, Sergeant Major," I replied.

He led me to his tent.

"After your processing," he said, "you can stay here until you leave for your battalion."

"Thank you, Sergeant Major," I said.

When I completed my processing, which included getting paid and drawing jungle fatigues, I went back to the sergeant major's tent. When I entered there were two other sergeants major sitting at the bar. I could tell that they had been in Vietnam for a long time. Their faces and arms were very tan and their jungle fatigues were faded. On their pistol belts were holstered .45-caliber pistols and trench knives. After they introduced themselves they asked if I wanted a drink.

"I would like a cold soft drink," I said.

One of them went behind the bar and opened a small refrigerator and handed me a can of Coca-Cola. A short time later they departed and the division sergeant major came in.

"Sergeant Major Robinson," he said, "the G-3 has looked over your service record and saw that you have experience in operations. He said that he would like for you to be his operations sergeant."

I was surprised at what he had said.

"Sergeant Major," I said, "my orders have assigned me to the 3rd Battalion, 60th Infantry, a maneuver battalion, and that is what I want. In all due respect to the G-3, I don't want to be his operation sergeant."

"Okay," he said, "I will inform him."

"Thank you, Sergeant Major," I said.

The next morning I went to the division post office and converted my money, two months pay, into money orders to send home. During the afternoon the division sergeant major informed me that I could ride with the commanding general, Major General O'Connor, and him, in their helicopter to my unit located in the Mekong Delta. That night I wrote Lou and informed her that I had arrived and enclosed the money orders, because I would be leaving for my unit the next morning.

●　●　●

Troops of the 9th Division, nicknamed "The Old Reliables," had scored major triumphs since launching combat operations in Vietnam in December 1966. Significant achievements include many overwhelming victories against Main Force Viet Cong units, initiation of sustained operations in the Mekong Delta, formation of a Mobile Riverine Force, and discovery of the largest enemy weapons cache of the Vietnam War. In addition, division units had reduced Viet Cong control in four populous provinces and helped foster a spirit of cooperation between the government and its citizens through civic action programs.

In 1966 the 9th Division became the first division to be organized, equipped and trained for deployment to an overseas combat theater since World War II, when the Department of the Army reactivated the division in February 1966. In early May, a warning order from the Department of the Army alerted the division for movement to Southeast Asia during December.

On 19 October, the 15th Engineer Battalion became the first echelon to arrive in Vietnam and immediately began developing a division-size base, Camp Bear Cat, near Long Thanh, about twenty miles northeast of Saigon.

Advance parties of the Division deployed to Vietnam by air, with the first group landing on 8 December. The rest traveled aboard naval transport ships arriving between 19 December and 2 February 1967.

The official entry of the 9th Division to Vietnam was recorded 19 December when Major General George S. Eckhardt led an increment of 5000 men onto the beaches of Vung Tau, where they were welcomed by General Westmoreland.

In mid-January 1967 the division became the first American infantry unit to establish a permanent camp in the Viet Cong infested Mekong Delta. The 2nd Brigade headquarters and the 3rd Battalion 60th Infantry, my battalion, occupied Camp Dong Tam, five miles west of My Tho on the My Tho River. Dong Tam base was built up by dredging mud from the My Tho River to form a hardstand above the water line surrounding silty rice paddies. Two companies of the 15th Engineer Battalion transformed the sand hardstand into a base camp by constructing roadways, laying foundations for buildings and establishing a defense perimeter.

In the division's first significant contact with the enemy on 20 January, 1st and 3rd Brigade units, along with the 3rd Squadron, 5th Cavalry, cut down 14 Viet Cong during operation Colby.

In March the 1st Brigade and the 3rd Squadron, 5th Cavalry joined Operation Junction City, the largest operation of the war. During this multi-division operation, the division encountered their first important battle. In the pre-dawn hours of 20 March, Troop A, 3rd Squadron, 5th Calvary was attacked by elements of the 273rd Viet Cong Regiment near Bau Bang, about thirty-four miles north of Saigon. A furious six-hour firefight left 230 Viet Cong dead, while friendly losses were four killed and sixty-seven wounded.

A few weeks later, another lopsided engagement near Rach Kien in Long An Province produced 207 Viet Cong killed against one American dead and fifteen wounded. A pre-planned air strike exposed underground Viet Cong positions and forced the Viet Cong to flee their damaged hideouts. Immediately the 3rd Battalion, 39th Infantry, together with the 2nd, 3rd, and 5th Battalions, 60th Infantry, boxed in the disorganized Viet Cong and slaughtered them.

Deeper in the Mekong Delta on 2 May, elements of the 2nd Brigade collided with a force from the 514th Viet Cong Battalion. Displaying exceptional resourcefulness, the 3rd Battalion, 60th Infantry and 3rd Battalion, 47th Infantry encircled the enemy as helicopter gunships and fighter bombers rained deadly streams of fire. A search of the Ap Bac battlefield, near Dong Tam, accounted for 195 Viet Cong bodies.

During mid-May, the Cam Son Secret Zone, twenty miles west of Dong Tam, became the target of a combined recon in-force operation. In this sweep, the 3rd and 4th Battalions, 47th Infantry, joined by elements of the 7th ARVN Division and several naval river assault teams, killed 113 Viet Cong.

Emphasized during the Delta fighting was the need for a mobile strike force capable of navigating the Mekong Delta waterways. In June the solution came with the formation of the Mobile Riverine Force, composed of two 2nd Brigade battalions and Naval Task Force 117. Operating from a fleet of 100 naval vessels, the MRF initiated extensive combat operations in the Mekong Delta marshlands.

In their first major contact 19 - 20 June, MRF units netted 256 Viet Cong kills at Rach Nui Canal, west of Rach Kien.

The focus of action shifted north to Phuoc Tuy Province on 10 July, as the 1st Brigade teamed with the 1st Australian Task Force, and two battalions of Vietnamese Marines to begin Operation Paddington. The six-day mission, designed to open

Viet Cong dominated jungles, resulted in ninety-three Viet Cong killed.

Another heated engagement came two weeks later as elements of the 11th Armored Cavalry conducted a major cleaning operation along Highway 20 in Long Khanh Province. Suddenly besieged by an estimated battalion of the 275th Viet Cong Regiment, the cavalryman mounted a savage counterattack which felled ninety Viet Cong.

Early in August, a joint American and Vietnamese force tightened the noose around a suspected enemy stronghold in the Cam Son Secret Zone during Operation Coronado II. After eight days, the Allies from the 2nd Brigade, Naval Task Force 117 and ARVN Rangers, Marines and Infantrymen counted 285 dead Viet Cong.

Encouraged by the success of Coronado II, soldiers of the 2nd Brigade, combined with two battalions of the 3rd Brigade and ARVN units, continued combat probes into the enemy haven of Can Son. Totals for the 27-day Operation Coronado II in September were 330 Viet Cong killed, and 11 individual weapons with 11,200 rounds of small arms ammunition seized from enemy supply caches.

On 21 September, after months of preparation by the 9th Division, the 2200-man Royal Thai Army Volunteer Regiment landed in Vietnam as the fifth free world force to join the South Vietnamese in their struggle. Operating out of Bear Cat, the Queen's Cobras began combat and civic action operations in the Nhon Trach jungles, twenty miles southeast of Saigon.

October was highlighted by the largest arms cache ever seized in the Vietnam war. During Operation Akron III, while clearing jungles thirteen miles southeast of Bear Cat, elements of the 1st Brigade and support units turned up a massive system of tunnels and bunkers. Nearly two weeks of extensive clearing and searching yielded 1140 weapons, almost 95,000 rounds of small arms ammunition, 3634 grenades, 2273 recoilless rifle shells and 452 mortar rounds. The cache included four 85mm howitzers, the first artillery pieces seized from the Viet Cong by U.S. Forces.

• • •

Next morning I was up early and anxious to get to my battalion. After chow I picked up my bags and went to the division commander's heli-pad to wait for my ride. I had learned a long time ago that generals never get in a hurry. But, when they were ready to go they did not wait on anyone. When the general, his aide, and the sergeant major arrived we loaded into the command and control helicopter, a UHlB, and were off to the Mekong Delta.

During the flight we landed at a company command post near Tan An. While the general was talking to the company commander I moved around and talked to some of the men. My questions were limited:

"How long have you been here? Where are you from? Have you killed any Viet Cong?" I asked some of the men.

Most of them I talked to seemed to have high morale.

As we became airborne again I asked the sergeant major, "How much longer will it be before we get to Dong Tam?"

"We are not going to land at Dong Tam," he said. "We are landing on the Benewah and you will have to catch a boat to Dong Tam."

"What is the Benewah?" I asked.

"The USS Benewah is a Navy ship. It is the command ship of the Mobile Riverine Force," he replied.

Of course I was not familiar with the Mobile Riverine Force either, but said, "Okay."

I was very disappointed that they would not drop me off at Dong Tam, because when we flew over the base the sergeant major pointed and said, "There is Dong Tam just below us."

When we landed on the USS Benewah I dropped my bags off to one side of the heli-pad and after asking several sailors how I could get a boat to Dong Tam I finally located the chief boatswain mate.

"Chief," I said, "I need a ride to Dong Tam. Can you help me?"

"Sure," he replied, "I will get you a ride."

He then led me to the chief petty officer's mess.

"Wait here until I can fine a boat going to Dong Tam," he said.

A short time later the chief returned.

"I have you a ride," he said.

"Chief," I said, "is there any way to radio the 3rd Battalion and tell them I am on the way, and have someone meet me at the dock?"

He answered in the affirmative. I went back to the heli-pad and picked up my bags and lugged them down the ladders, through compartments to a pontoon tied up along side of the ship where a boat was waiting for me.

The trip to Dong Tam took about forty minutes and when I arrived there was no one to meet me. I waited for about a half an hour and started looking for another ride when I saw a Jeep coming toward me. When it stopped a sergeant major got out.

"Are you Sergeant Major Robinson?" he asked.

I nodded yes.

"I was waiting at the other dock for you," he said, "sorry you had to wait."

When we arrived at the battalion area the sergeant major took me to his tent.

"This is your home," he said.

The tent was built up off of the ground about three feet. It was boarded up about halfway, with screen wire surrounding the top portion. There were sand bags stacked up, about five feet, around the outside. The tent looked reasonably comfortable.

"Sergeant Major Robinson," he said, "I will not be leaving for several days."

"Okay," I said, "I will not get in your way. That will give me the time to become familiar with the battalion operations and the Mobile Riverine Force concept."

"If you are ready," he said, "I will take you to meet the battalion commander."

"Okay," I replied.

The battalion commander would also be leaving in about a month. After meeting the battalion commander I decided to walk around the battalion area. None of the companies were on an operation and most of the men were in the battalion area. I was not accustomed to the heat and humidity and by this time I was soaking wet again.

My first stop was the mess hall, where I took some salt tablets and drank several cups of water. As I moved through the area there was a strong odor coming from the burning of human waste.

I noticed that some barracks were completed, with men living in them, and some still under construction. Outside of the barracks there were some men sitting around. As I approached them I saw that they had their jungle boots off. While I talked to several of them I noticed that their feet were red and raw looking.

I thought to myself, "These men have Immersion Foot."

I also noticed that their boots, drying in the sun, were covered with mud.

"How many pair of boots do you have?" I asked one of the soldiers.

"I only have one pair," he said, "but some men have two."

"How often do you have a chance to dry them out?" I asked. He laughed.

"Most of the time we wear them wet," he replied.

When I departed them I took out my notebook and made a note — "Boots."

As I continued through the area I saw a sign which read "First Sergeant."

"This must be the headquarters company first sergeant's tent. I think I'll go in and introduce myself."

When I opened the door and stuck my head in I saw three first sergeants.

"Come in," one of them said.

When I entered I saw that they had a fifth of whiskey setting on a foot locker.

After introducing ourselves one asked, "How about a drink?"

"No thanks," I replied.

We talked for a few minutes, and when I departed I took out my notebook again. This time I made the note — "Whiskey."

Many of the men were still living in tents and as I moved through the area I noticed ammunition and equipment scattered everywhere, and the area was cluttered up with trash, bottles, and cans . Of course I made more notes. When I entered one tent there were three soldiers lying on their bunks. As I talked to them I noticed several quart jars filled with some type of liquid and what appeared to be pieces of meat inside.

"What is that in the jars?" I asked.

They looked at me and laughed.

"Pickled ears," one said.

"Pickled ears?" I said, "what is that?"

"VC ears," one said, "we cut them off of dead VC."

Another laughed.

"Sometimes they are not dead," he said, "but we cut them off anyway."

After departing the tent I made another note — "Ears."

I thought to myself, "I have killed the enemy but I never, at anytime, mutilated their bodies."

•　•　•

The 60th Infantry was born 10 June 1917 at the historic Gettysburg National Park, Pennsylvania.

In World War I the allegedly impossible crossing of the Meuse River by the 60th was regarded by military experts as indicative of the skill possessed by the American fighting man. This crossing and the brilliant records accomplished at Alsace-Lorraine and St Mihiel were handed down to the 60th when it was reactivated at Fort Bragg, North Carolina on 1 August 1940.

The 60th battle honors during World War II date from the campaign fought to control the northern shores of the African coast and keep open the Allied lifeline in the Mediterranean Sea. Highlighting this campaign for the 60th was the seizure of the Kasba (Citadel) in early November, 1942. The 60th continued across North Africa with the Allies until the German-Italian Army Group Africa was totally destroyed.

Sicily was the 60th's next assignment and they landed near Enna, 24 July 1943 to support the 1st Division. After numerous actions the cities of Floresta and Basico became the last Sicilian strongholds to fall to the might of the 60th Regiment. On 14 August 1943 the 60th was ordered to halt and was put into service with the rest of the 9th Infantry Division to await its next assignment.

That next assignment called for the 9th Division to enter the battle of "Fortress Europe." The 60th's first taste of battle on European soil came 2 June 1944 when it joined the 39th and 47th Regiments for an offensive into France. The order was given to march toward St. Colombe. In this action the 2nd Battalion achieved outstanding results. Driving hard toward the objective, the 2nd Battalion completely outdistanced the rest of the division. They overran the German defenses, set up a bridgehead on the Douve River and held the position for seven hours until the rest of the Division could catch up with them. For this aggressiveness the 2nd Battalion was awarded the Distinguished Unit Citation.

During the next three months, the Allied pincers began closing on the Fatherland, but two major obstacles stood in the way - the Meuse River and the Siegfried Line.

After a lapse of twenty-six years, on 4 September 1944, the 60th again found itself on the west bank of the Meuse River.

By 17 September the Hofea position of the Siegfried Line was being patrolled by elements of the 60th. Later the Siegfried Line was breached and the Allied drive continued toward the Roer River. In a quick change of direction, the 1st Battalion of the 60th diverted to capture the vital Germeter-Huertgen road junction. In doing so, they captured more prisoners than they had men present for duty in the battalion.

The Ludendroff Bridge at the town of Remagen was used for a bridgehead over the Rhine River. German troops were preparing to destroy the bridge on 7 March when American troops captured it intact. The 9th Division quickly seized the advantage and prepared to cross the river. The 60th began crossing the bridge the night of the 8th under heavy machine gun and artillery fire. The crossing took twenty-nine hours.

Now the job of mopping up began. Thousands of disillusioned German troops surrendered. The last object of the war for the 60th and the 9th Division was Drohndorf, which fell 21 April . Then on 26 April a patrol of the 60th contacted elements of the Russian Army and the East and West fronts were now one. This link-up signaled the end of Hitler's Germany and of fighting in World War II for the 60th Infantry Regiment.

• • •

That evening, after chow, I could hardly wait to take a shower. "Where are the showers?" I asked the sergeant major.

"We don't have showers of our own," he replied. "We use the

Artillery showers," and he pointed toward them.

I wondered why our battalion did not have showers, so I made another note in my notebook — "Showers."

As I lay in my bunk that night many thoughts went through my mind:

"Even though this battalion is in a combat zone and has been in action many times against the Viet Cong, there is no justification for some of the things I saw today. A good battalion, if they expect to have any respect for themselves, must perform well in the base camp as well as in combat, and from what I have seen so far someone is not doing their job."

My thoughts were interrupted by a barrage of harassing artillery fire being fired about fifty yards from my tent.

"How often do they fire the artillery?" I asked.

"Oh," the sergeant major answered, "they fire all night long sometime. You will get immune to it."

As I began to doze I thought to myself, "If I expect to get anything done around here I will have to move slow and easy, because this battalion is not used to my type of soldering."

Dong Tam base, covering 600 acres, filled to a depth of six feet with more than eight million cubic meters of sand and sedimentary soil, was generally a secure area. The base was set up with emphasis on defense. Concertina and barbed wire, claymore mines, trip flares, and other devices were used around the base. Bunkers were constructed of sandbags, timber, and mud to complete fortifications. The bunkers were manned only at night. The jungle area around the base had been defoliated, I think with Agent Orange. Occasionally at night we would receive incoming rockets and mortar fire, and sometimes during the day we would receive sniper fire.

Viet Cong guerrillas were not the only enemies encountered by the soldiers. The treacherous terrain of the Mekong Delta region south of Saigon provided another formidable obstacle to the battalion.

As the muddy Mekong River flows from the Cambodian border, it begins to fan out into thousands of smaller streams, leaving very little dry land running through the Delta. During the dry season, Mekong waterways irrigate the fertile rice fields that checkerboard the region. When monsoon rains flood the streams and canals, the Delta is an immense sea of muddy water.

Under such conditions, every step turns into an individual battle. Paths follow the rice paddy dikes to ease movement, but these dikes often are booby-trapped by the Viet Cong, forcing troops to negotiate the mud.

More than a massive mudhole, the Delta wears many faces. About twenty miles southwest of Saigon begins one of the most barren areas in the Delta — the Plain of Reeds — a large sheet of stagnant water dotted by rotting vegetation. The Viet Cong regard the Plain of Reeds as an inaccessible sanctuary.

Only ten miles southeast of Saigon is the Rung Sat Special Zone, a water-shrouded expanse of mangrove swamp considered one of the most foreboding and desolate places in the Delta. Known as the Everglades of Vietnam, the Rung Sat cannot be penetrated except by water.

Many soldiers maintain that movement in Go Cong Province is harder than the Rung Sat. One exhausted trooper observed that he found at least an occasional root or stump to stand on in the Rung Sat, but in Go Cong there was only sucking, sticky mud.

For the next few days I only observed and made more notes of things I thought I might be able to improve.

War stories were very popular, especially when the old men wanted to impress new men arriving in the battalion. Telling of war stories was nothing new. Men have told them throughout military history. But some of the stories that reached me were very disturbing.

Stories of how they would use demolitions — C-4 — to blow up and to burn Vietnamese hooches, sometimes killing everyone inside; stories of how they would mistake the South Vietnamese for Viet Cong and kill them; stories of how one man put a .45-caliber pistol in the mouth of a Viet Cong and pulled the trigger; also stories about how they would rape young Vietnamese girls.

When these stories reached me I became furious.

"What kind of war is this?" I said to myself, "and what has happened to the American soldier to make him commit such atrocious acts?"

I thought back to 1951 when I was in Korea. I actually loved combat and felt like skinning the enemy of his 3500 square inches of skin on many occasion, but in my military mind I knew it was wrong.

Before the sergeant major departed I had an opportunity to become familiar with the Mobile Riverine Force.

• • •

Six months of combat operations by a powerful striking unit known as the Mobile Riverine Force accounted for over 1300 enemy deaths in the upper reaches of Vietnam's Mekong Delta. The Mobile Riverine Force, combining maneuver units of the 9th Division's Second Brigade and U.S. Naval vessels of Task Force 117, was based upon concepts and strategy during the Mississippi Delta Campaign of the Civil War. Modernized adaptations of land-water warfare carried the American unit, the second riverine warfare in the nation's history, to lopsided victories over Viet Cong battalions that once considered the Mekong marshlands and waterways their prized sanctuary.

In the fall of 1862, General Ulysses Grant packed 32,000 weary Union soldiers onto river boats and began the siege of the vital Confederate city of Vicksburg. Using the Mississippi Delta waterways to position Navy gunboats and to transport men and equipment, the superior Northern forces penetrated the river strongholds.

General Grant's forces, teaming with Rear Admiral David Poter's Mobile Riverine Force, carried the North's offensive deep into Dixie. Fleets of armor-protected boats provided fire support and ferried troops as the Union assaulted the series of fortifications along the Mississippi.

Thundering volleys from the Naval gunboats and mortar vessels played a decisive role in the North's successful winter and spring campaign of 1862 and 1863. After the defeat of the Confederates in the battle of Port Gibson on 30 April, the fortress of Vicksburg fell on 4 July. River assaults also played dominant roles as key Union victories claimed Belmont, Fort Henry, and Shiloh. Riverine warfare virtually split the Confederacy in two.

Today, 10,000 miles from the muddy banks of the Mississippi

and a century later, U.S. Army infantrymen of the 2nd Brigade, 9th Division and a companion force from the Navy's Task Force 117, employed river tactics based upon plans of Civil War strategists - the setting for the 20th century Mobile Riverine Force of the Mekong Delta with its hundreds of waterways twisting from the Tibetan Plateau through fertile Vietnam rice land to the South China Sea.

In Vietnam, General Westmoreland found himself faced with essentially the same geographic obstacles that confronted General Grant during the 1860s. The need to move combat elements into the 26,000 square miles of the Mekong — long an ideal sanctuary for the Viet Cong — prompted the forming of America's second Mobile Riverine Force.

Borrowing from the tactical successes of the Mississippi Campaign and French experience with a Naval Assault Division during the Indo-China War, General Westmoreland modernized the concept of riverine warfare and requested the formation of such a force. The Joint Chiefs of Staff earmarked the 9th Division, then training at Fort Riley, Kansas, for Delta mission.

The River Assault Flotilla One, later to accompany the 2nd Brigade into battle as part of the Mobile Riverine Force, was commissioned on 1 September 1966, bringing to an end the century of American isolation from riverine warfare. At Coronado, California, the Navy, guided by Captain Wade C. Wells, started to assemble 100 vessels to house, carry, and support the brigade's venture into the enemy's watery domain. Craft ranging from slow moving World War II landing craft to giant barracks ships and sleek gunboats were molded into the feet.

Two auxiliary barracks ships, the only two ships of their type in the U.S. Navy, were refurbished to provide housing for units of the 2nd Brigade. In addition to their berthing facilities, the USS Benewah and USS Colleton featured nautical design, which permitted them to operate in the shallow sedimentary rivers of the Delta. To provide facilities for two battalions of the Brigade plus supporting units, a non-self-propelled barracks ship was added to the fleet. For troop and crew comfort, the floating barracks were fully air-conditioned, equipped with snack bars, movie area, and recreation facilities.

Armored troop carriers, protected by armor plating and mounted with machine guns, cannons and grenade launchers, were obtained to provide transportation for the combat troops during missions from the floating bases to forward operational areas. Gunboats called Monitors and assault support patrol boats were attached to provide fire power and protection for anchored ships and for slower troop carriers during assaults. The gunboats also served as blocking and intercepting forces during riverine operations.

Other boats provided waterborne medical aid stations, complete with decks for landing helicopter-evacuated wounded soldiers. A landing craft, repair ship and various specialized supply repair ships rounded out the vessels of Naval Task Force 117.

Aside from top-level conferences between Brigadier General William B. Fulton (then Colonel) and Captain Wells, short briefing of top cadre at Fort Riley on boat handling, and a ten-day staff school at Corondo, members of the 2nd Brigade received no specialized training in riverine warfare. In fact, the vast majority of the brigade had no idea that the 2nd Brigade had been selected as the riverine element of the 9th Division.

At the outset, the two leaders met to develop operational concepts and plans for the American offensive into the network of rivers, paddies, and mangroves of the Delta. Merging of the two services into an effective fighting team required careful planning and organization.

The leaders agreed that combat in a riverine environment would be much like fighting a normal land encounter. Such warfare, they reasoned, was simply an extension of land fighting where the same ground tactics could be applied. The main difference would be in moving infantry units by boat instead of trucks or track vehicles. Living on barracks ships would permit the force to move during the night, thus ensuring that combat troops would be rested and fresh when they reached the operational objective. Life aboard the vessels would also enable infantrymen to dry out after being shriveled for days by wet boots and mud.

The waterways would serve as the transportation link — opening unsuspected routs of attack — for the infantrymen of the

2nd Brigade. The Delta's water lifelines would lead American units to enemy strongholds hidden in nipa palm, mangrove, and jungle thickets along the rivers.

Combat units of the 2nd Brigade arrived in Vietnam during early February. The land forces would begin operations and join their sister element four months later. With the sinking of a Navy mine-sweeper and an attack on two other ships in Long Tau shipping channel leading to Saigon, the brigade was immediately ordered into the half-land, half-swamp area along the channel known at the Rung Sat Special Zone. Though not yet an active part of the Mobile Riverine Force, General Fulton and his men quickly adapted to operating in the mud and slime of the Rung Sat, a way of life that would accompany future Delta operations.

During the same period artillerymen of the 9th Division were experimenting with mobile firing bases acceptable to the riverine environment. Barges became floating gun positions and the 3rd Battalion, 34th Artillery prepared to support Mobile Riverine operations with 105mm howitzers. The batteries would follow their infantry comrades along the rivers and provide fast and accurate support once their barges were secured snugly against the shore.

According to General Fulton, the single greatest innovation undertaken by the Mobile Riverine Force was mounting 105mm artillery and 4.2 inch mortars on the barges. The artillery section including battery, six firing barges and fifteen transportation boats is commanded and furnished by the U.S. Army. With the availability of artillery support, the 2nd Brigade was ready to go afloat and initiate Vietnam riverine operations.

The first large scale riverine assault was delayed until May when the brigade shifted to Dong Tam base camp. Dong Tam's location on the My Tho River, a major arm of the lengthy Mekong, classified it as the likely location to house river operations.

In mid-May, Naval assault boats picked up infantry units and carried them into a Viet Cong-dominated area ten miles west of Dong Tam known as the Cam Son Secret Zone. This marked the first Allied drive into the Cam Son in two years. The Cam Son, later to be the battlefield for numerous clashes with the Viet Cong, proved to be the site of the first riverine encounter. The Brigade troops tangled head on with the 514th Viet Cong Local Force Battalion and dealt them a stunning blow.

On a marshy battlefield the firepower of the 2nd Brigade, supporting Naval craft and Allied units killed 113 enemy soldiers. On 15 May, the 3rd and 4th Battalions, 47th Infantry loaded onto armored troop carriers and were taken to predetermined landing beaches along the Nam Than River. With naval assault boats blocking the waterways south of the land objective, the infantry units closed in from east and west.

The enemy was hemmed in on three sides with their only escape route, the north, blocked by the Army of the Republic of Vietnam forces. Air strikes and artillery fire, coupled with the air-mobile insertion of a reserve company into the area, forced the Viet Cong from their reinforced mud bunkers. Enemy defenses oriented toward land routes of attack and helicopter landing zones, had been foiled by the riverine assault. No longer could the enemy believe that the sanctuary of the Mekong Delta belonged to him.

The entire Army-Navy force was assembled on 1 June, at the Dong Tam base. The 2nd Brigade Headquarters and two battalions, the same units that took part in the Cam Son battle two weeks earlier, boarded the USS Benewah and Colleton anchored in the My Tho River on 2 June. With the entire Mobile Riverine Force together and functioning, the Coronado series of operations, named after the Navy's California training site, was underway. In the following months, battles erupting from riverine assaults during the Coronado operations would account for over 1300 enemy kills.

• • •

After my predecessor departed I felt that it was time that I began pointing out to the first sergeants some of the problem areas within the battalion that I expected to correct. Before I discussed them with the first sergeants I wanted to go over them with the battalion commander, so I went into his office.

"Sir," I said, "I know that you are a busy man and I do not want to bother you with a lot of problems. However, I feel that some of the things I propose will enhance the morale of the men."

"What do you have in mind?" he asked.

I then went into detail about boots, showers, and the condition of the battalion area.

"Okay, Sergeant Major," he said, "you take care of them."

"Thank you, Sir," I replied.

When I departed his office I had a feeling that he was not interested in what we had talked about. In all of my Army career, as first sergeant and sergeant major, I had always had good rapport with my commanders, but this time I felt distanced from the battalion commander .

During my first meeting with the first sergeants I wanted to be diplomatic but firm.

"This battalion has a good fighting reputation," I said, "and I am proud to be its sergeant major. Combat is not new to me and I know what you are going through. However, I feel that there is a laxity in standards when the battalion is in base camp. I see men with immersion foot because they have to wear the same wet jungle boots each day, and nothing is done about it. I see ammunition and equipment scattered throughout the battalion area and men ignore it. I see men not taking care of their personal hygiene and it is condoned. I could go on and on, but I think I have made the point. Does this result in a ready outfit? Is this the mark of a proud military organization with a great history and tradition behind it? Not for my money, it isn't."

One of the first sergeants interrupted.

"We are getting the job done," he said. "Just look at the body count."

"Yes," I replied, "the battalion has a high body count, but how long will that last if the men are not taken care of while in base camp."

I lit a cigarette and continued.

"The requirement of the battlefield is most important, and we prepare for it every moment that we are not actually fighting, which means that we must insure that there is no laxity in standards."

I then went into detail on what I expected from them. I instructed them to give me a report on how many men in their units had only one pair of jungle boots.

My last comment to them was, "It is okay to have a drink, but I will not tolerate drunkenness among my senior NCOs."

That afternoon, while on a Search and Destroy mission, one platoon, using Scout Dogs, ran into a Viet Cong ambush . During the firefight two men in the platoon were killed and four were wounded, and one of the Scout Dogs was killed.

These were the first casualties in the battalion since taking over as sergeant major and I was saddened, but I knew that this was only the beginning and there would be many more to come.

I called the first sergeant, whose responsibility it was to identify the dead soldiers.

"When you go to the GRO (Grave Registration Office) I want to go along."

"Okay," he said, "I will call you when they arrive."

It was policy and natural that the wounded be evacuated to the Army Field Hospital before the KIAs, so it was about an hour before the first sergeant arrived to pick me up instead of calling me .

When we entered the GRO the two dead soldiers were laid out on tables. I walked over and looked down at them. Both had been hit by automatic weapons fire, one in the stomach and the other in the chest. Both of them looked to be about eighteen years old. At this point I had a strong feeling of anger toward the Viet Cong.

My thoughts flashed back to Korea 1951: "These young men look like some of my buddies who were killed fighting communism in Korea. They had not begun to live their lives."

Late in the afternoon I went to the Field Hospital to visit the wounded men. This was my first trip to the hospital, but would not be my last. The four soldiers were in the same ward, which was filled to capacity with other wounded soldiers.

I asked them very simple questions: "Where are you from? Do you think you will be going back to the States now? Do you need anything?"

The next morning a memorial service, which was tradition, was conducted for the two KIAs. Their rifles were stuck in the ground by the bayonets, their helmets placed on the rifle butt, and their boots in front of the rifles. On this particular occasion the harness and leash of the Scout Dog was laid out. After a few words and prayer from the battalion chaplain, Present Arms was given in honor of the dead soldiers.

When I received the report on the jungle boots from the first sergeants I went to the battalion S-4 (Supply) sergeant and asked him to order enough boots to issue each man another pair.

"I will try," he said.

"Don't try," I said, "just do it."

In the meantime I started looking around the battalion for a "Handyman." A "Handyman," to me, was someone, possibly a short-timer, who could assist me in my projects. After talking to the first sergeants I came up with just the man I was looking for. He had been a carpenter in civilian life and had only three weeks remaining in Vietnam.

The morning he reported to me I told him that he would not be going on any more operations, that he would be working for me until he departed Vietnam. He was elated.

"Thank you, Sergeant Major," he said, "what do you want me to do?"

"Your first project is to get a battalion shower set up, and I will assist you in getting everything you need."

"Okay, Sergeant Major," he said, "just show me where you want it."

We then got in my jeep and found a suitable location.

After setting up two large squad tents he built walk boards for the floor. He them got several 55-gallon drums and built stands for them, after which he went to the Engineers, picked up some pipe and faucets and got the welder from the maintenance shop to weld them to the drums. He then came to me and requested that the water truck fill the drums each day and let the sun heat the water. The showers were in operation within a week.

I had not heard anything on my request for boots, so I went back to the S-4 office. When I entered the S-4 sergeant and S-4 officer were setting at their desks.

"What is the status of the jungles boots I requested?" I asked the sergeant.

As he was about to speak the S-4 officer interrupted.

"We cannot issue anymore boots," he said.

"Why not?" I asked.

"We are not authorized to," he replied.

"Listen," I said, "what is authorized and what has to be done are two different things. The men need another pair of boots and I intend to see that they get them. If it takes a special authorization to get them it should be done."

He looked at me and in a very harsh tone of voice said, "Sergeant Major, I am not going to authorize another pair of boots to anyone and that is final."

"Okay, Captain," I said, "we will see about that."

Later that day I went in and told the battalion commander about the conservation I had with the S-4. As soon as I departed his office I heard him pick up the telephone and call the S-4.

"You report to me immediately," he said.

When the S-4 arrived he went directly into the battalion commander's office. I could hear him making excuses about the boots.

I finally heard the battalion commander say, "You get the boots we need without delay."

As he departed the headquarters he gave me a very hard look. In a matter of days the men were receiving a second pair of boots.

I had never in my military career had to resort to such tactics to get anything done, but this time I felt good about it.

During the next few weeks I learned more about this very different type of war — all of the casualties were evacuated by helicopter called Dust-off, which was all new to me. Search and Destroy meant exactly that. Men would fight for several days to take a piece of ground and then leave it for the Viet Cong to take back. A body count had to be made after each operation and reported to the next higher headquarters. The only reason, I expect, was to tell the higher command that we were killing the enemy.

Up until this time I had not seen a Viet Cong, dead or alive. I knew they were out there, and some of the Vietnamese I saw during the day were Viet Cong at night.

With this in mind I decided to go on a reconnaissance patrol with one of the squads. The squad used an Armored Personnel

Carrier and patrolled along Route One leading out of My Tho.
We moved out at about 2200 hours. It was a long night and we never ran into any Viet Cong.

As we were returning to Dong Tam I mentioned to the squad leader, "I haven't seen a Viet Cong, dead or alive, since I arrived in Viet Nam."

He laughed.

"You will," he said.

A couple days later, when the Recon Platoon returned, early in the morning, they stopped their track in front of my tent. I thought this unusual.

"Sergeant Major," I heard someone say.

When I went outside I saw the same squad leader standing over a dead Viet Cong.

"Here is your dead VC," he said. "I knew you wanted to see one."

He and the other members of the squad laughed.

"OK," I said. "I get the point. Now you take him back and drop him where you killed him."

The expressions on their face changed as they picked up the Viet Cong and threw him into the track like a sack of potatoes and sped off.

It was during this time that I read an article that disturbed me. Civil rights leader Martin Luther King urged that all black and white Americans should declare themselves conscientious objectors.

"Negroes," he said, "are dying in disproportionate numbers in Vietnam. Twice as many Negroes as whites are in combat."

This was not the case in my battalion and I took exception to the statement King had made.

Early in December a new battalion commander, Lieutenant Colonel Hill, was arriving. Before he arrived, the battalion adjutant came to me.

"Sergeant Major," he said, "I have never arranged a change of command ceremony and I understand that you have experience in ceremonies, and I would like your help."

"Sure," I replied, "I will write up a plan."

My plan consisted of having two platoons from each company

— the Battalion Colors and the Division Band.

When I presented it the Adjutant he said, "Looks good, Sergeant Major. Can we do it?"

"Of course," I said.

After getting the first sergeants together I went over the ceremony with them.

"I want the men to look good," I said. "I want them to have clean jungle fatigues on and clean jungle boots, also new camouflage covers on their helmets. Headquarters Company will provide the color guard and I want them to report to me immediately to start practicing."

There was some grumbling, especially from the S-4 when he had to go to Division, at Bear Cat, to pick up new camouflage covers.

After getting the details started I went back to the adjutant.

"Sir," I said, "I think we should invite the brigade commander, division commander, and the Navy captain of the Mobile Riverine Force."

"Okay, Sergeant Major," he said, "I will take care of the invitations."

"Also," I said, "I will arrange for some refreshments with the mess sergeant."

The ceremony went well. General O'Connor, the division commander, Colonel David, the brigade commander, and Captain Salzer, U.S. Navy commander, attended.

The ceremony had been conducted in the morning and in the afternoon one company from the battalion had to move out on a search and destroy operation. The operation was into an area about ten miles east of Dong Tam and Colonel Hill wanted to go along with them to the landing zone.

When the company loaded the helicopters and started to move out, Colonel Hill and myself loaded into a UH-1 helicopter and flew directly behind them. When they hit the ground we hovered over them. All of the helicopters were in and out in a few minutes and the men on the ground deployed in a rice paddy. There was no Viet Cong resistance at this time.

"Let's go in, Sergeant Major," Colonel Hill said.

"Okay, Sir," I replied.

As soon as we jumped out of the helicopter it went back airborne, and we moved toward the troops, who were now receiving small arms fire from a wooded area to their front. When I heard bullets whistling past my head I hollered at Colonel Hill.

"Get down, Sir."

Both of us went face first into the muddy rice paddy. We then made our way behind a rice paddy dike and joined the troops in firing my M-16 rifle toward the woodline.

In the meantime the company commander called for artillery fire on the wooded area. As soon as the artillery fire ceased the company commander, at the request of Colonel Hill, called for our helicopter and he then ordered his men to move out, leaving Colonel Hill and myself in the landing zone alone. A few minutes later our helicopter came down and hovered over the rice paddy. In their haste to get out of the landing zone the company had left several cases of ammunition, so Colonel Hill and I loaded them into the helicopter. Before we could get all the ammunition loaded we started receiving small arms fire.

"Let's get out of here," the Colonel hollered.

Both of us were out of breath when we became airborne.

When we arrived back at Dong Tam both of us, and my M-16 rifle, were covered with mud. I followed Colonel Hill into the headquarters building.

"Sir," I said, "your first day in the battalion and you have already been in a firefight."

"Yes," he said, "we sure have."

Before getting myself cleaned up I went into my office to relax. As I was lighting a cigarette the Adjutant came in. He looked at me.

"You sure are a mess," he said.

"Yes, I know," I replied.

"Sergeant Major," he said, "those cigarettes will kill you."

I laughed.

"Yes," I said, "I am sure they will if the Viet Cong don't do it first."

He laughed and walked out of my office.

After taking a shower I felt exhausted and decided to lay on my bunk for a few minutes and relax. I was not exhausted so much from the activities as I was from the heat.

As I lay there I thought, "Today was my baptism of fire in Vietnam. It wasn't much but enough to earn me my star to my Combat Infantry badge. It would have been terrible if the battalion commander had been killed on his first day in the battalion." I also thought, "I know now what these soldiers are going through here in Vietnam."

In late December, before Christmas, the battalion had been ordered to conduct a search and destroy operation near Sa Dec, about twenty miles southeast of Dong Tam. Alpha Company was given the mission. The area was known to be infested with Viet Cong. The operations order called for insertion of the troops, by helicopter, to a predetermined landing zone.

As the helicopters began moving in with the troops, the Viet Cong were waiting. As the troops hit the rice paddy the Viet Cong opened fire with automatic weapons, mortars, rockets and small arms fire. The company was caught in an ambush and appeared to be surrounded with no way out. They were like rats in a trap. The gallant men of Alpha company, some wounded, formed a perimeter and tried to defend themselves. Several men had already been killed.

The company commander immediately called for artillery and an air strike on the Viet Cong positions. The battalion commander, in his helicopter, began to access the situation, but decided not to commit re-enforcements. I was walking through the battalion area when the action began and was not aware of it until I returned to the headquarters and the S-3 clerk ran into my office.

"Sergeant Major," he said, all excited, "Alpha Company has hit a hot LZ."

I immediately went into the operations center to monitor the radio. I felt helpless and wished that I were in the action. The fighting lasted about two hours, at which time the Viet Cong broke contact because of the heavy bombardment from the artillery and air strikes.

Later I heard on the radio, "We need Dust-offs immediately."

It was then that I got into my Jeep and drove to the Army Field Hospital to wait the arrival of the wounded men.

When the first Dust-off arrived it was almost dark. The medics wasted no time in moving the wounded into the pre-operations ward. Later another Dust-off arrived with more wounded. This went on into the night. There was not enough room in the pre-operations ward, so many of the wounded were left, on stretchers, outside the ward. In the meantime the battalion executive officer drove up.

"Sergeant Major," he said, "Colonel Hill wants to know how many men were wounded."

"Let me use your radio," I said, "I will call him."

"Okay, Sergeant Major," he said.

"Brandy Six, this is Brandy Six Alpha," I said.

"Go ahead, Brandy Six Alpha," he said.

"I have counted forty-two WIAs," I said, "but I understand that they are bringing in more."

"Damn," he said. "Thank you Six Alpha."

The evacuation continued. The doctors, nurses, and aid men were doing an outstanding job taking care of the wounded. My final count of WIAs, before I departed the hospital, was fifty-three, but had no idea how many had been killed, which would come the next morning when they were brought into GRO. Alpha Company's first sergeant was also at the hospital and he estimated that twenty men had been killed. When I returned to the headquarters we called division and gave them an estimated casualty report and requested replacements immediately.

I did not bother to go to bed that night. Instead I went to the mess hall and drank coffee. My thoughts were on the WIAs and KIAs.

I wondered, "Will our casualty report be given accurately to the press or will it be falsified like the body count report which I know is falsified."

About 0500 hours I went to my office. I knew that this would be a busy day for me. One of the first things I did was to look at the daily status reports from the companies because I knew that we would have to get replacements for Alpha Company. During my check I noticed that several men were on special duty with division at Bear Cat.

"These I will try to get back. Division should support them

selves and not take men from the battalions," I thought to myself. About 0700 hours the adjutant came into my office.

"Sergeant Major," he said. "Division is sending us replacements this morning. They should be arriving about 0900 hours at the landing strip."

"Okay, Sir," I said. "I will pick them up."

Shortly after I received a call from the first sergeant of Alpha Company.

"Sergeant Major," he said, "they will start bringing in the KIAs about 0800 hours."

"Okay," I said, "I will get a truck and meet them at the airstrip and have them taken to GRO."

"Okay," he said, "I will meet them at GRO."

I thought to myself, "There should be no problem. I have enough time to get the KIAs to GRO before the new men arrive."

I then called the motor officer and asked for two trucks. He said that he only had one available, which he sent me. I also got a four-man detail from Headquarters Company.

My policy was to always brief all new men coming into the battalion and I had instructed the first sergeants to have the men knock off the war stories to the new men. However, I knew that they would continue.

I was setting in my Jeep when the first helicopter landed carrying the KIAs. As the men started removing them from the helicopter one of them men on the detail became sick and I told him to walk back to his company. It was understandable why he became sick. Some of the KIAs were torn up very badly. There was one with a stomach wound, with his intestines hanging out, another with part of his face blown away, another with bone protruding out of the skin, some with legs and arms mangled from shrapnel. Most of them were less than twenty years old.

Shortly after another helicopter arrived with another load of KIAs, I went over to the pilot.

"How many more?" I hollered.

"I don't know," he replied, "they found one man still alive and I dropped him off at the hospital."

I thought to myself, "That poor wounded soldier laid in that rice paddy all night."

Before we got all of the KIAs off, another helicopter came in with more KIAs.

"This is all of them," one of the gunners yelled.

I had counted nineteen KIAs.

Before we completed unloading the last helicopter the men on my detail seemed to be getting in a hurry.

I hollered at them, "You don't throw them soldiers around, you treat them with respect," and they slowed down.

All of a sudden I looked up and saw a Caribou transport plane landing on the other side of the airstrip.

"Damn," I said, "that is our replacements. They are early."

I was very upset, because I did not want the new men to see the KIAs.

"Get a move on," I said to the detail, "and get them out of here."

I them approached the driver of the truck.

"You wash this truck out and come back here as soon as you can to pick up the new men."

In the meantime the new men had started walking across the airstrip with their bags. There was a young sergeant in charge of them.

When they reached me the sergeant said, "We are assigned to the 3rd Battalion, 60th Infantry."

"I am Sergeant Major Robinson," I said. "I am the battalion sergeant major. There will be a truck here shortly, so just drop your bags and relax."

One of the men spoke up.

"Sergeant Major," he said, "were those dead soldiers we saw when we got off of the airplane?"

I did not want to lie to them.

"Yes," I replied, "we ran into a little trouble yesterday and lost a couple of men."

While we were waiting for the truck I looked at the new men. Again most of them were less than twenty years old. They had a look of fear in their eyes and appeared to be disconcerted.

I thought to myself, "How many of these young men will die in Vietnam?"

In a few minutes I saw the truck coming toward us.

"Okay, men," I said, "pick up your bags. The truck will be here in a minute."

When the truck stopped I walked around to the rear of it. The driver got out and came around to open the tail gate. When he dropped the tailgate I saw that it had not been washed out. It still had blood, from the KIAs, all over the floor board. I turned to the driver.

"I told you to wash this truck out before you came back. Why didn't you?"

"Sergeant Major," he replied, "I could not find a water truck."

"Don't tell me that," I said. "Maybe a few trips to the rice paddies will help you to learn to obey instructions."

As the new men loaded the truck one of them turned to me.

"Is this blood on the floor?" he asked.

I just looked at him and did not reply.

After we arrived back at the battalion area I briefed the new men and Colonel Hill spoke to them a few minutes before we turned them over to the first sergeant of Alpha Company.

Later that day Colonel Hill and myself went to the hospital to visit the wounded soldiers and when I returned I wrote a note to the division sergeant major telling him that we needed all of our men, on special duty with division, back for duty in our battalion.

It had been a long day and I was exhausted when I arrived at my tent. My predecessor had left me with a small refrigerator and I had some beer and soft drinks in it. After taking out a can of beer I sat down at my field table. Laying on the table was a letter. I looked at the envelope. It was from Sandra, my first niece. I wasn't surprised at getting a letter from her because she had written me on many occasions.

I opened the letter and read it. She gave me all of the recent news of the family and in closing she said, "I am enclosing a poem that means a great deal to me, and I thought you might like to have a copy of it." I then read the poem titled, "HOME INSIDE."

I HAVE A HOME INSIDE OF ME,
A HOUSE THAT PEOPLE NEVER SEE.
IT HAS A DOOR THROUGH WHICH NONE PASS,
AND WINDOWS, BUT THEY'RE NOT MADE OF GLASS.

SOMETIMES I LIKE TO GO INSIDE
AND HIDE, AND HIDE, AND HIDE, AND HIDE,
AND DOCTOR UP MY WOUNDED PRIDE,
WHEN I'VE BEEN TREATED ROUGH OUTSIDE.

SOMETIME, WHEN I'VE BEEN TO BLAME,
I GO INSIDE AND BLUSH FOR SHAME,
AND GET MY MIND IN BETTER FRAME,
AND GET MY TONGUE AND TEMPER THE SAME.

I MEET MY HEAVENLY FATHER THERE
AND HE STOOPS DOWN TO HEAR MY PRAYER
TO HEAL MY WOUNDS AND CURE MY CARE
AND MAKE ME STRONG TO DO AND DARE.

THEN, AFTER I AM QUITE STRONG
AND THINGS ARE RIGHT THAT WERE ALL WRONG
I GO OUTSIDE WHERE I BELONG
AND SING A NEW AND HAPPY SONG.

AND THEN I HEAR PEOPLE SAY,
YOU'RE BLITHE AND BONNY, GOOD AND GAY.
IT'S JUST BECAUSE I FEEL THAT WAY,
BUT THEY DON'T KNOW THE PRICE I PAY.

YOU HAVE A HOME INSIDE OF YOU,
WHERE YOU CAN FIGHT YOUR BATTLE THROUGH,
AND GOD WILL TELL YOU WHAT TO DO,
AND MAKE YOUR HEART BOTH STRONG AND TRUE.

When I completed reading the poem I think tears came to my eyes.

"How true it is," I thought to myself.

The next morning I showed the poem to Chaplain Johnson, the battalion chaplain.

"I sure would like a copy of it," he said.

"You are welcome," I replied and shared it with him.

During 1967 more than 16,000 Americans had been killed in Vietnam. The inflated body count rose to 50,000. By the end of the year U.S. forces rose to 543,000 men.

In the early part of January I began having a problem with the new first sergeant of Headquarters Company. The first problem came when he came to me and said that he wanted to be recommended for the Combat Infantry Badge.

"Sergeant Major," he said, "I was walking the perimeter yesterday and was shot at by some Viet Cong and I feel that I have earned the CIB."

"Where were you?" I asked.

"Over near the river," he replied.

"Did you report it to the S-2 or S-3?" I asked.

"No," he replied, "I shot back at them and they ran off."

"That sounds absurd," I said, "Was there anyone with you?"

"I was by myself," he replied.

"Do you have a witness?" I asked.

"No," he replied.

"First Sergeant," I said, "I think you are lying to me. If you want to earn the Combat Infantry Badge, why don't you go out on an operation with one of the line companies."

At this point he puffed up his lips.

"That is not my job," he said.

"You will not be recommended for the CIB," I said, "and that is it."

He then stomped out of my office.

After he departed I thought to myself, "I better inform Colonel Hill about this just in case we get any static from him."

After telling Colonel about my conservation with the first sergeant he said, "I agree with you, Sergeant Major. That guy has never seen any combat."

My next problem arose with him a few days later when I called a first sergeants' meeting and he never showed up. Very few times in my Army career had a senior NCO ignored my instructions and I was very angry. After the other first sergeants departed I picked up the field telephone and called Headquarters Company. The company clerk answered.

"Let me speak to the first sergeant," I said.

"Sergeant Major," he replied, "the first sergeant is over in his tent."

"You tell him to report to me immediately," I said.

"Yes, Sergeant Major," he said.

I waited a half an hour and he had not shown up. I called the company again and the company clerk answered again.

"Did you tell the first sergeant to report to me?" I asked.

"Yes, Sergeant Major," he replied.

"You tell him that I want him now," I said.

"Okay, Sergeant Major," he said.

I waited again. Fifteen minutes went by and I was getting furious, so I walked out of the headquarters toward Headquarters Company .

When I was approximately fifty yards from his tent I saw him coming toward me. He was staggering.

"That sorry bastard is drunk," I said to myself.

When I reached him I felt like hitting him but restrained myself.

"Listen," I said, "you go back to your tent and sober up. I will see you later."

He turned around without saying anything, and staggered back toward his tent.

As I was walking back to the headquarters, very angry, I got an idea. When I reached my office I called the company clerk.

"Listen," I said, "your first sergeant is drunk and I want you to check on him and let me know if he passes out."

"Okay, Sergeant Major," he said.

I then called the battalion commander's driver into my office.

"I want you to get me a stretcher," I said.

He looked at me, very puzzled.

"Why do you need a stretcher, Sergeant Major?" he asked.

"I have a reason," I said. "Just get it."

Just about the time he returned with the stretcher the company clerk called me.

"Sergeant Major," he said, "the first sergeant has passed out."

"Good," I said.

I looked at the driver.

"Bring the stretcher and come with me," I said.

The driver still looked confused. We walked to the first sergeant's tent.

"Okay," I said, "help me put him on the stretcher."

"Okay, Sergeant Major," he said, "but I still don't understand."

"You will in a few minutes," I said.

As we moved him to the stretcher he mumbled some but did not wake up.

"Okay," I said, "let's pick him up easy and you just follow me."

The driver still did not know where we were headed. It was several hundred yards to the barbed wire and we almost dropped him several times. After locating a good area we carried him through the barbed wire to the rice paddy about fifty feet past the wire.

"Okay," I said, "set the stretcher down and help me lift him off."

He mumbled several times but still did not wake up. The driver began to laugh.

"Sergeant Major," he said, "you are something else."

As we passed the motor pool I asked one of the maintenance men to keep an eye on the first sergeant and call me when he came to.

When I reached my office I told the driver, "Don't tell anyone what we have done. When the first sergeant wakes up he will think that he wondered out there while he was drunk."

The driver laughed again.

I was still furious at him. After I settled down for a few minutes, I went into Colonel Hill's office.

"Sir," I said, "I have a drunk first sergeant and I think he should be reduced."

I then went into detail about the incident but did not tell him that I had carried the first sergeant outside of the perimeter and left him.

"Have him report to me when he is sober," he said.

"Okay, Sir," I replied.

It was getting late in the afternoon and since I had not heard from the man at the motor pool I was getting concerned about the first sergeant. I did not want to get him shot by some Viet Cong,

I only wanted to teach him a lesson. I got into my Jeep and drove to the motor pool. When I arrived I walked around the maintenance building and saw several men standing outside and laughing very hard. I looked out toward the perimeter and saw the first sergeant, still half drunk, covered with mud, tangled in the barbed wire. I stood there a few minutes and watched him. Finally he got clear of the wire and staggered toward his tent. I laughed as I drove back to the headquarters.

"Maybe he has learned a lesson," I said to myself.

Later that day I informed the first sergeant's company commander about the drunkenness of his first sergeant and what I had recommended. He said that he had also had problems with the first sergeant's drinking.

The next morning I called the first sergeant to my office. He was sober now and reported immediately. When he arrived I looked at him. His face and arms were scratched up. I went in and informed Colonel Hill that he was there.

"Send him in," he said.

I then walked back to my office and looked at the first sergeant.

"Report to the battalion commander," I said.

Colonel Hill reprimanded him severely and told him that he was transferring him out of the battalion. When the first sergeant departed the headquarters, Colonel Hill called me into his office.

"How did that first sergeant get so scratched up?" he asked.

I looked at him.

"Maybe he got tangled up in the barbed wire chasing those invisible Viet Cong," I replied.

Both of us laughed.

Colonel Hill was a brave infantry officer and sometimes I thought that he was putting himself into situations that he should not. He and I went on reconnaissance patrols with one of the companies. This suited me just fine, and I tried to keep an eye on him in case we got into trouble.

In the meantime the men that were on special duty, at division, were sent back to the battalion. I felt real bad when one of them, on his first operation, got killed. I learned later that he was performing duty as a clerk in division finance.

This was entirely a different type of war for me. Being a sergeant major of a maneuver battalion, in combat, was the highlight of my military career. However, I was not with the troops and missed the action. Even when one or two of our companies were on an operation I could not go along with the battalion commander in his command and control helicopter because it was only large enough for him and the pilot .

Colonel Hill always listened to my recommendations. When recommended to him that the short-timers, men with less than two weeks remaining in Vietnam, be allowed to remain in the battalion area and not go on any operations, he approved my recommendation. This went over well with the men and they looked forward to their last two weeks.

On 15 January the brigade sergeant major came to see me.

"Sergeant Major Robinson," he said, "I will be leaving the brigade in a few days and Colonel David has selected you as his sergeant major."

"Me!" I said.

"Yes, you," he replied. "Colonel David has looked over your 210 file and has already talked to Colonel Hill and asked me to come and tell you."

I was elated and almost lost for words.

"When does he want me to report?" I asked.

"Try to come on the 18th," he replied.

"As much as I hate to leave the battalion," I said, "I will be there."

"You know you will be living aboard ship," he said.

"I will have to get used to that," I said.

On 18 January, after saying good-bye to my friends, I caught a small boat and headed for the USS Benewah.

I thought to myself, "It is ironical that I started my military career in the Navy and now I will be aboard a ship, serving again with sailors."

When I arrived aboard the Benewah the brigade sergeant major showed me to my quarters, which was a four-man compartment directly across from the chief petty officer's mess. He then took me into the chief's mess and introduced me to several chief petty officers, one of which was Chief Boatswain

Mate Martin, whom I became very good friends with. He then took me to Colonel David's quarters and introduced me to him.

"Glad to have you as my sergeant major," Colonel David said.

"I appreciate you selecting me," I said.

"We will have a chance to talk more later," he said.

"Yes, Sir," I replied.

The present brigade sergeant major had a few days remaining before he had to depart for the States. This suited me just fine, because it gave me an opportunity to get acquainted with the brigade operations. When the brigade sergeant major informed me that I would be with the brigade commander in his command and control helicopter, during operations, I was elated.

"Now I can be where the action is," I said to myself.

Colonel Bert A. David — some called him BAD, taken from his initials — was an outstanding infantry colonel. He was a thorough tactician who expected the most out of his subordinate commanders and supported them in their decisions. He was very knowledgeable of Viet Cong tactics and was always one step ahead of them.

I tried to stay abreast of all intelligence matters within our area of operation as well as other heavy fighting in Vietnam. Sometimes reports were sketchy on other area of operations. We did receive a report on 21 January that their was heavy fighting around Khe Sanh.

My predecessor departed on 25 January and I was now the sole brigade sergeant major and ready for action. In the meantime I turned in my M-16 rifle and drew an AR-15, which would be easier to handle in the command and control helicopter.

A Tet cease fire had gone into effect at 1800 hours, 29 January but there were so many truce violations by the North that the truce was terminated.

Early in the morning hours of 31 January the American Embassy, in Saigon, came under attack by guerillas. Ton Son Nhut Airport also came under siege. This marked the beginning of the Tet Offensive.

Within twenty-four hours many towns across South Vietnam had fallen, among them Can Tho and My Tho, which were devastated by our own air strikes.

On 1 February Colonel David committed the 3rd Battalion, 60th Infantry and the 3rd Battalion, 47th Infantry into My Tho, now held by the Viet Cong. Against a World War II back-drop of burned-out houses and littered streets, the troops tangled with the Viet Cong for two days. The soldiers climbed walls, darted in and out of doorways, and drove their Jeeps up and down side streets in a meticulous house-to-house search. Aided by U.S. artillery and air strikes, the troops finally smashed the remnants of an estimated three Viet Cong battalions.

Colonel David was directing the action from our command and control helicopter above My Tho. As the battalions moved through the town and overran one position, the Viet Cong panicked and dashed through the open rice paddies. When they did, our command and control helicopter swooped down and the side-gunners and I opened fire and cut them down.

In the wake of the holocaust, countless civilians were killed, maimed or left homeless by the Viet Cong. Casualty figures from the My Tho battle showed more than 115 Viet Cong dead, against nine of our soldiers and eighty-six wounded.

In the meantime the 1st and 3rd Brigades of the division had swept through Ben Tea, which had also been leveled by air strikes. They accounted for 150 Viet Cong killed.

The brigade had encountered sporadic contact for several days in the vicinity of Vinh Long, twenty-five miles southwest of My Tho. The Viet Cong had rained heavy fire on the city and were mounting another onslaught.

On 6 February Colonel David committed the 3rd Battalion, 60th Infantry on a reconnaissance in force mission along the Rach Cui Cam River. Action flared as the battalion, mounted on Armored Troop Carriers, accompanied by three escort ships, was hit by rocket fire after destroying a bunker complex 100 meters north.

Immediately, the companies dismounted and maneuvered to outflank the estimated Viet Cong battalion. At dusk, one company from the 3rd Battalion broke the Viet Cong encampment. The stronghold was pin-pointed and pounded by artillery and air strikes.

The next morning when our command and control helicopter

sat down near the Rach Cui Cam River, the area where the fighting was the day before, I saw several men trying to get a body count. After getting out of the helicopter and walking toward them, I looked around. Bodies and pieces of bodies were scattered everywhere.

"How can you make an accurate body count out of this mess," I asked one of the men.

He looked at me and smiled.

"It's easy," he replied, "all you have to do is look for arms and legs. When you see two arms and two legs that equals one VC — just a matter of mathematics."

He laughed and continued, "We don't count ears because sometimes they don't have any."

"I get the point," I said.

More than 130 Viet Cong were killed, forty-five bunkers destroyed, twenty-four weapons, eleven grenades and large quantities of ammunition were seized during the operation at Vinh Long.

Colonel David was scheduled to go on R&R to meet his wife in Hawaii, but since the Tet Offensive had begun he had to call his wife and postpone his R&R.

On 13 February the Mobile Riverine Force opened a new chapter in 9th Division history when we dropped anchor in the Mekong Delta city of Can Tho. It was the deepest Delta penetration to date for a 9th Division unit.

During the first two days of operations, the brigade soldiers, working from U.S. Navy monitors and armored troop carriers, discovered a huge ammunition cache and killed at least twenty-five Viet Cong.

Responding to intelligence reports of a planned enemy attack on the city, Colonel David rushed the 3rd Battalion, 60th Infantry, 3rd Battalion, 47th Infantry from Dong Tam to the Phong Dinh Province capital city.

On 14 February the brigade units, sweeping on both sides of a small canal which empties into the Can Tho River, discovered a huge stockpile of ammunition, hastily covered with palm fronds.

By late evening, enough demolitions and ammunition had been uncovered by Company A, 3rd Battalion, 47th Infantry to equip three Viet Cong battalions.

A day later the brigade encountered their first enemy contact in the area. Sweeping southwest of the city, we collided with the Viet Cong on three separate occasions.

The 3rd Battalion, 47th Infantry killed fourteen Viet Cong, while suffering two soldiers killed and six wounded. The 3rd Battalion, 60th Infantry counted eleven Viet Cong bodies, without any casualties.

The Tet Offensive was smashed within ten days in the Mekong Delta. By the end of February 37,000 enemy had been killed, at a cost of 2500 American lives attributed to the Tet offense.

Shortly after the Tet Offensive I had a chance to go into My Tho. Such destruction I had never seen. Many houses and buildings were completely destroyed and the people were in a state of turmoil. The orphanage had suffered terrible damage.

When I returned to the Benewah I felt saddened by what I had seen. Chief Martin approached me.

"Sergeant Major," he said, "you look like you have lost your last friend."

"Chief," I said, "I have just returned from My Tho, where I saw a great deal of destruction that occurred during the Tet Offensive, even the Orphanage suffered much damage."

"I expect so," he said.

"Chief," I said, "why don't we do something for the Orphanage?"

"What do you have in mind?" he asked.

"We could take up a collection from the men in the Mobile Riverine Force for them," I said.

"That sounds like a good idea," he said, "let's do it."

"Okay, Chief," I said, "you get donations for the Navy and I will take care of the Army."

After contacting the sergeants major from the infantry battalions and the artillery we started our collection.

During the early part of March the officers and men of the Mobile Riverine Force and contributed over $400, approximately 48,000 piasters, to assist the Orphanage .

After completing our collection we contacted the Civil Affaires officer and informed him how much money we had collected and that we wanted to present it to them.

"Okay," he said, "when do you want to do it?"

"Tomorrow morning will be fine," I said.

When Chief Martin and I arrived at the Orphanage the Civil Affaires officer was already there. In a few minutes two Vietnamese men, one the director, came out with three Vietnamese girls. They were dressed in their best clothing. The men were wearing white shirts with ties, and the girls had on white dresses and looked very pretty.

The Civil Affaires officer had informed them earlier that we were coming and after I made the presentation, on behalf of the officers and men of the Mobile Riverine Force, they invited us to have refreshments.

Living aboard the USS Benewah was very comfortable. The Navy food was very good and seemed to be plentiful. The troops always looked forward to returning after an operation, getting themselves cleaned up and relaxing, as much as possible, before the next operation.

Normally, after an operation, Colonel David and I would reach the Benewah before the troops. After getting myself cleaned up I would go to the pontoon, tied up along side of the ship, and wait for the arrival of the troops. When they arrived there were men with water hoses to wash the rice paddy mud off of them. After they were washed they had to clean their weapons before going aboard ship. During this time they were given a couple cans of beer or soft drinks, whatever they preferred.

On one occasion, after returning from a four-day operation, the troops were covered with mud and some of them were removing they trousers. As I walked around talking to them I saw one man who had dropped his shorts. As I approached him I realized why he had dropped his shorts. He was trying to get leeches off from around his thighs. It was a pitiful sight. I then got one of the medics to help him.

We were always happy when an operation ended. It would give us time to catch up on our letter writing. In my case I had a small tape recorder and Lou and I would send tapes back and forth rather than writing.

In the meantime, on 16 March, an incident took place that would not be revealed to the American people until late in 1969.

Lieutenant W. L. Calley led a platoon of Charlie Company, 1st Battalion, 20th Infantry, Americal Division into My Lai, a village in the central Quang Ngai province and slaughtered between and estimated 200 to 500 women, children, and old men. It was learned later that he had led them, with their hands above their heads, into a large ditch and systematically shot them, and those who ran were also shot.

In the chief petty officers' mess we always listened to radio broadcast from the Armed Forces Network. On 1 April, while eating breakfast, I heard an announcement over the radio that the battle of Khe Sanh was over and then I heard President Johnson making a speech.

He started by saying, "Good evening fellow Americans. I want to talk to you about peace in Vietnam." He then announced that he was freezing troop levels, limiting the air strikes against North Vietnam and seekinging a negotiated peace. He then went on to say: "With America's sons in the field far away, and with America's future under challenge here at home, with our hopes and the world's hopes for peace in the balance every day, I do not believe that I should devote an hour or a day of my time to any personal partisan causes, or to any duties other than the awesome duties of this office, the Presidency of your country. Accordingly, I shall not seek, and I will not accept, the nomination of my party for another term as your President. But let men everywhere know, however, that a strong and confident and a vigilant America stands ready tonight to seek an honorable peace, and stands ready tonight to defend an honored cause, whatever the price, whatever the burden, whatever the sacrifice the duty may require."

Everyone in the chief's mess was silent. We looked at each other with surprise on our faces.

I thought to myself, "How can President Johnson abandon his responsibilities when our country is in war?"

By this time Robert Kennedy, campaigning against violence and the Vietnam war, appeared to be leading in the Democratic race for President.

On 5 April we were shocked when we heard the news that Martin Luther King had been assassinated while at the Lorrane Motel in Memphis, Tennessee by James Earl Ray, on 4 April.

Immediately following King's assassination riots erupted in 125 cities across the United States. Forty-six had been killed, 3500 injured, and 20,000 arrested. In Washington, D.C. 711 fires were set, causing $15 million in damages, seven were killed, 1166 injured and 7370 arrested.

Many soldiers, including myself, were saddened by the news. The morale of many of the men, especially the black soldiers, became very low.

I thought to myself, "What is happening to our country and our people? Why must they fight among themselves when we have enough killing here in Vietnam."

Our operations continued in force. On 17 April elements of the 3rd and 4th Battalion, 47th Infantry, were sweeping south toward Cai Lay in the Mekong Delta when they became embroiled in heavy contact with an unknown sized Viet Cong force at 1100 hours. The 3rd Battalion, 60th Infantry was air-mobiled south of the action as a blocking force. As they closed in, howitzers from the 3rd Battalion, 34th Artillery, pounded the area from floating artillery barges. When contact was broken about 2000 hours, U.S. soldiers counted seventy-eight Viet Cong dead and captured three. In addition, ninety-six bunkers were destroyed and three weapons, six tons of rice and enough clothing to outfit a Viet Cong battalion, were captured. Documents found on some of the dead Viet Cong revealed they were from the 514th Local Force Company and an element of the 261-B Main Force Battalion. Our casualties for the day were four killed and thirty-three wounded.

On 23 April the 3rd and 4th Battalions, 47th Infantry joined the 2nd Vietnamese Marine Battalion and moved into a day long operation twenty-four miles north of Can Tho. I could not go along with Colonel David because General Johnson, the Army Chief of Staff and Sergeant Major Wooldridge, the Sergeant Major of the Army, were scheduled to visit the Mobile Riverine Force.

When Sergeant Major Wooldridge, escorted by the division sergeant major, arrived at Dong Tam, Sergeant Major Messonia, the artillery sergeant major and I met them. Sergeant Major Wooldridge did not recognize me at first, but when I reminded him of his trip to the 3rd Division he then remembered me. We talked a few minutes and then Sergeant Major Messonia took him on a tour of the artillery barges. I then presented him a plaque from the Mobile Riverine Force.

Colonel David had finally taken an R&R to Hawaii and when he returned he informed me that he would be leaving the brigade for his new assignment in USAREUR, (US Army Europe) in late May.

On many occasions when we were not on an operation I would accompany Chief Martin on an inspection tour of the troop compartments. One morning he approached me.

"Sergeant Major," he said, "some of the men are smoking marijuana aboard ship and I intend to stop it."

I laughed.

"I have known that for a long time," I said, "just how do you expect to stop it?"

"I would like for you to accompany me on an inspection and see if we can find the place they are using for their pot parties."

I laughed again.

"Okay, Chief," I said, "I will be happy to."

During our inspection we went into every living compartment and into every possible place the men could use to hide their marijuana smoking. When we went into one compartment there was a strong odor of marijuana coming from a small compartment off the living compartment. As we entered the smell became stronger.

"This is the place," Chief Martin said.

"Yes," I said, "I think so."

We then began looking around. On the floor we saw marijuana butts and we continued our search. I looked behind some pipes and saw several plastic bags which were filled with marijuana.

"Chief," I said, "look what I found."

He smiled.

"Well, at least we found some but I am sure that there is more aboard this ship and I will find it."

"Chief," I said, "you are fighting a loosing battle. As soon as you find it, there will be more coming behind it."

Since we did not know who the marijuana belonged to, there was nothing we could do. I kept it locked in my desk for a while and then threw it overboard.

Early in May I decided to take R&R and meet Lou in Hawaii. Colonel David let me use the command and control helicopter to take me to Bien Hoa.

When our airplane arrived at Hickman Air Force Base, we were loaded on a bus and driven to Fort De Russy, in Honolulu. Many wives and girlfriends were there waiting. As I stepped down off the bus I saw Lou. She ran to me and we embraced and kissed.

"Sure am glad to see you," I said.

"Glad you are here safe," she said.

Lou had never been to Hawaii before and I knew that she would enjoy her trip.

After checking into the Lelikii Hotel we rented an automobile. I was trying desperately to get Vietnam and all the killing out of my mind but it was very difficult.

During the time we were together we drove around the coast, took pictures, laid on the beach, had dinner at a Chinese restaurant, and visited many places of interest. When my five days were up and it came time for me to return to Vietnam I was anxious to get back to my brigade.

When I arrived at Bien Hoa I had to scramble around and find transportation back to Bear Cat. I finally caught a ride on a truck and when I arrived at Bear Cat I went directly to the airstrip to catch a ride on a helicopter going to Dang Tam. I approached the operations clerk.

"I need a lift to Dong Tam," I said.

"I don't have anything going that way now," he said, "but if you can wait around maybe something will come up."

"I don't have a choice," I said, "I will have to wait."

In about an hour the clerk motioned for me to come to the counter.

"Sergeant Major," he said, "I have a helicopter going to Dong Tam but he has to drop off a MEDCAP (medical civil action program) team in a small village near Moc Hoa on the way."

"That will be okay," I said.

The helicopter was very crowded and I thought, at one time, that I would wait for another one, but I was anxious to get back to my brigade, so I got aboard.

When we landed near the village I could see Vietnamese people running about and wondered what was going on. When the MEDCAP team got out and started toward the village I talked to the pilot.

"Can I have a few minutes to see what is happening in the village?"

"Okay," he replied, "but don't be long."

"I will be back soon," I said.

As the MEDCAP team walked into the village I was directly behind them and was shocked at what I saw. There were several Vietnamese bodies laying on the ground with people gathered around them crying and talking in Vietnamese that I did not understand. One of the bodies was a young girl, about fifteen years old, who had been shot in the head. Another was that of an old man which was almost decapitated. Another old woman with her hand cut off. Several others had been shot.

In the meantime one of the MEDCAP team, who understood Vietnamese, was talking to one of the Vietnamese women. I walked over to him.

"What happened here?" I asked.

"This old woman said that Viet Cong soldiers came in last night and demanded food. She said they gave them all they had but the Viet Cong demanded more and they told them that they did not have anymore and the Viet Cong got mad and started killing the people," he replied.

"How long have they been gone?" I asked.

He turned to the old woman and asked her. He then turned back to me.

"About two hours," he said.

"Is your team going to stay here and help them?" I asked.

"Yes," he replied, "they need us and we have a helicopter coming to pick us up in about two hours."

"Okay," I said.

When I arrived back at the helicopter the pilot was anxious to leave, so I did not tell him what had happened in the village. We became airborne immediately. I took out a piece of paper from my wallet and made a note as to the approximate location of the village so I could report the incident to the S-2. As we approached

Dong Tam, all of a sudden I heard a loud cracking noise and the helicopter began shaking and started loosing altitude. I did not have a headset, so I could not talk to the pilot. We continued to loose altitude.

The pilot turned to me and hollered, "We are going to hit the ground hard, make sure your seat belt is tight."

"Okay," I hollered back.

The helicopter still had some power but we hit the ground very hard and bounced several times, coming to rest on the skids at the edge of Dong Tam airstrip. No one had been injured and when I started to unbuckle my seat belt I saw a large hole in the seat about six inches from me. The pilot came around and I pointed out the hole to him.

"I think it was a .50-caliber round," I said.

"Yes it was," he said, "it almost got you too."

As we walked toward the operations building I noticed another helicopter arriving. It was a Dust-off. When it landed there were two men waiting. I knew what they were waiting for, bodies of American soldiers. They lifted three bodies from the helicopter and placed them on a truck and drove off.

During this time the Mobile Riverine Force was on an operation and was not anchored near Dong Tam. I waited most of the day to catch a helicopter going to the Benewah and when I finally arrived, I thought to myself, "This has been an awesome day."

Later I went to the chief's mess and had a sandwich and then went on deck to the fantail.

As I stood there looking out over the water at the last flicker of sunlight I said to myself, "I am sick of this senseless killing. This is not war, it is slaughter. Professional soldiers don't kill women, children, and old men."

I knew more than most men that civilians get killed accidentally in war, but here in Vietnam they were being killed on purpose, which was very appalling to me.

My thoughts continued, "I love this Army. It is my life, and I volunteered to come here, but now I am dismayed and cannot do anything to stop this senseless killing."

It was at this time I said to myself, "I am taking my leave from the Army. I am going to retire when I get back to the States."

I then went back to my compartment and read the poem, "Home Inside," Sandra had sent me.

"Colonel David," I said the next morning as we were getting ready to move out on an operation, "I have decided to retire from the Army when my tour is up in Vietnam."

"What!" he said, "retire from the Army? I thought you were a thirty-year man."

"No, Sir," I replied, "I have given it a great deal of thought and have made up my mind."

"I thought you might end up as Sergeant Major of the Army someday," he said.

"I had those thoughts too awhile back," I said, "but now it doesn't make any difference."

"I hate to see you get out of the Army, Sergeant Major," he said, "but if that is what you want to do I can only wish you the best of luck in your future endeavors."

During the operation we caught some Viet Cong in the open. They were running toward a stream and we swooped down and opened fire on them as they hit the water. I could see the water turning red where they had gone in. Colonel David and I really liked catching Viet Cong in the open because that was about the only time we could kill them.

On 26 May the sergeants major and first sergeants of the brigade gave Colonel David a farewell dinner.

On 29 May Colonel David and I were invited by the commanding officer of the 3rd Battalion, 34th Artillery to fire the 400,000th and 400,001st 106mm howitzer rounds fired by them in Vietnam. Colonel David fired the 400,000th round and I fired the 400,001st round. Sergeant Major Messoni later presented me with the shell casing of the round I had fired. It was mounted on a wooden base with an engraved plaque from the 3rd Battalion, 34th Artillery.

On 30 May Colonel Robert E. Archer assumed command of the 2nd Brigade during a most impressive change of command ceremony aboard the USS Benewah. After the ceremony I rode in the command and control helicopter with Colonel David to Bien

Hoa, where we said good-bye. On my way back to the brigade I stopped off at division personnel and submitted my application for retirement.

Colonel Archer was a very soft-spoken man and seemed to lack the tactical experience that Colonel David had. I gathered the impression that he was unsure about some of his decisions. On one occasion I overheard one of the battalion commanders tell him that he had made a bad decision about an operation. I was not able to accompany him all the time in the command and control helicopter because he wanted the S-2 and S-3 with him.

Meanwhile, back in the States, the Democratic campaign was heating up between Humphrey, McCarthy, and Kennedy. Many people were demonstrating against the war. There was much anger and hate throughout America. The whole country seemed to be divided.

It was early in the morning on 7 June when we heard the news that Robert Kennedy had been assassinated at the Hotel Ambassador in Los Angeles, on 6 June, by Sirhan Bishara Sirhan. Everyone was shocked and I was saddened by the news. I thought that if Kennedy was elected president he would stop the war in Vietnam and create some peace and harmony in the United States.

While listening to one of my tapes from home, my son, Billy, who would be seventeen in October, said, "Dad, I have a good job this summer and I would like to buy an automobile and I would like your permission."

I thought about it for a couple of days and responded.

"Son," I said, "you have my permission to buy an automobile, but there are some things I want you to remember when you get the automobile. First and most important is that you must drive carefully. Next, you must keep up the payments and also have proper insurance."

After I mailed the tape I thought to myself, "My children have grown up. Where have I been? I love them dearly, but the Army always came first."

My first operation with Colonel Archer came on 17 June. It was our first operation near Can Tho since February. Company E, 3rd Battalion, 47th Infantry, beached nine miles south of Can Tho. The point element was moving out about 100 yards in front of the main force when it was hit by sniper fire from a woodline. The fire was so intense that they became pinned down. We were monitoring the situation and I wondered what Colonel Archer was going to do. When he ordered other elements of the 3rd Battalion, 47th Infantry to be inserted to keep the Viet Cong pinned downed in their bunker positions, I felt that he had made a good decision. With the Viet Cong unable to escape, fire support from the 34th Artillery was called in, followed by Air Force bombing runs and gunship strikes. A sweep the next morning produced thirty-three Viet Cong dead.

During June General Creighton Abrams replaced General Westmoreland as U.S. Commander in Vietnam.

One night, while in the chief's mess, I had a visit from one of the company first sergeants.

"Sergeant Major," he said, "I am having a problem with some of my men."

"What kind of problem?" I asked.

"Well," he replied, "some of the men are coming up with excuses for not going on operations."

"What kind of excuses?" I asked.

"Most of the time they say that they are sick and want to go on Sick Call and by the time they get back the company has already moved out, so they goof off the rest of the day."

"That will stop now," I said. "You let me know the next time any of your men pull that."

"Okay, Sergeant Major," he said.

The next morning I went to the dispensary and informed the medic that if men came in on sick call and nothing was wrong with them that he was to send them back to their first sergeant and mark them "Duty." I then went to the re-supply boat and asked the Boatswain Mate if he needed any help on the boat during re-supply.

"Sure," he said, "I can use all the help I can get."

The reason I selected the re-supply boat was because it was fired on by the Viet Cong about every day.

A couple days later the first sergeant came back to me.

"Sergeant Major," he said, "I have three men that went on Sick Call this morning and nothing is wrong with them. What do you want me to do with them?"

"Okay," I said, "I have a job for them. You take them and turn them over to the boatswain mate on the re-supply boat for detail."

I watched from the deck as the first sergeant led them to the re-supply boat. They seemed to be happy that they were not going on an operation, but they had no idea what they were getting into.

That day the re-supply boat came under attack and was hit by a Viet Cong rocket, wounding one of the men on the detail. After that the word got around that if you went on Sick Call to goof off, you would end up on the re-supply boat. We had very little problem with men goofing off after that.

Ninth Division organization day was 18 July and a ceremony, honoring the occasion, was scheduled for that day. The division sergeant major had scheduled a dinner and meeting on 16 July, at Bear Cat, with all of the division sergeants major.

The dinner and meeting went well and on 17 July we found ourselves with nothing to do.

"Why don't we go to Saigon?" Sergeant Major Rossetti, the Sergeant Major of the 3rd Battalion, 47th Infantry said.

"That sounds like a good idea," said Sergeant Major Miller, the brigade operations sergeant said.

I had never been to Saigon and thought, since we had nothing to do, I would go along.

Before we departed we went by the NCO club and picked-up a couple fifths of whiskey and had a couple drinks before we departed Bear Cat. We also made arrangements to have a bus pick us up the next morning in order for us to be back at Bear Cat for the ceremony. On our way to Saigon we had several more drinks. This was the first I had drank in a long time and it was affecting me.

When we arrived in Saigon we checked into a hotel, and when I arrived in my room I took off my boots and laid down on my bed and went to sleep. It was almost dark when I was awaken by a knock on my door. I opened it and Rossetti and Miller came in.

"There is a night spot with a dance floor and bar a couple floors up. Would you like to go along with us?" Miller said.

"Sure," I replied, "let me get my boots on."

As I started to strap on my .45-caliber pistol Rossetti said, "You better leave that here."

"Okay," I said.

When we entered the night club a loud Vietnamese band was playing and several soldiers were dancing with Vietnamese girls. There were several other young Vietnamese girls sitting around, some at tables and some at the bar. There were also several other soldiers sitting around, some with girls. I was sure that the girls were prostitutes .

After locating a table we sat down. I felt a little uncomfortable but after a couple of drinks I began to relax.

In the meantime several Vietnamese girls came to our table and in their broken English asked, "Do you want a Jo-san."

Each time we said "No."

I felt very relaxed by this time.

"I think I would like to dance," I said.

"Go ahead," Rossetti and Miller said.

I walked over to a table where three girls were sitting. After selecting the one I wanted I ask her to dance. She was very receptive and we danced several times.

When we finished dancing I went back to my table and sat down.

As I was about to have a drink I heard a loud voice say, "Stay away from my girl."

When I looked up I saw a soldier who appeared to be drunk.

"Are you talking to me?" I asked.

"Yes," he replied. "That is my girl and I don't allow anyone to dance with her. You stay away from her."

"Listen," I said, "I think you are drunk and if you don't want to get into trouble you better leave this table."

"I will leave when I get damn good and ready," he said.

When he said that, Miller reached over and pushed him away. The soldier reached under his shirt and pulled out a trench knife. As he did, Rossetti, Miller, and I jumped to our feet as the soldier charged at Miller with the knife. Miller grabbed a chair and backed up against the bar. The soldier lunged at him. As Miller came down with the chair to the soldier's head, he rammed the knife into

Miller's stomach. Miller struck him again with the chair and he fell to the floor, dropping the knife. I lunged forward and grabbed the handle of the knife about the same time the soldier grabbed the blade. I brought the knife up as hard as I could, cutting the palm of his hand to the bone.

Blood was squirting everywhere and the soldier was rolling around on the floor, holding his hand, and hollering.

I ran over to Miller.

"He got me," he said.

"How bad?" I asked.

"Bad enough," he replied.

In the meantime the MPs had been called and arrived about the time I started to take Miller to the hospital. Other soldiers had gathered around and were trying to get the bleeding stopped on the other soldier. The MPs called an ambulance and took Miller and the soldier to the hospital. I returned to my room with the knife. It was as sharp as a razor.

The next morning I went by the hospital to see Miller before returning to Bear Cat. He was hurting but would be okay.

When we arrived back at Bear Cat the division sergeant major had heard about the fight and was very angry at us. After explaining to him the circumstances surrounding the fight he seemed to understand our position.

On 1 July I received a Department of the Army message promoting me to Command Sergeant Major. I was elated, because the command sergeant major program had not been in affect for very long and I was on the third increment of promotions to command sergeant major.

On 26 July the headquarters of the 9th Division moved to Dong Tam, leaving the Reliable Academy at Bear Cat to give new men a basic Vietnam orientation.

The Mobile Riverine Force, with its unique team of 4500 Army and Navy fighting men, continued to forge its modern adaptations of historic riverine warfare into the Mekong Delta region. Despite fighting an evasive and native enemy, the kill ratio was more than eleven-to-one in favor of the American team.

On 8 August as the brigade was returning by boat, from an operation near Can Tho, they ran into a Viet Cong ambush. We were in the command and control helicopter flying over the convoy. Colonel Archer looked at me.

"Is that area a 'free fire' zone?" he asked.

I looked at the map and as best as I could determine it was. "Affirmative," I replied.

He then ordered the troop commanders to open fire on the Viet Cong.

During the ambush, in Viet Cong territory, the troops fought back with flame-throwers, and left many huts damaged or destroyed.

Colonel Archer was concerned about the artillery barges because they were loaded with 106mm howitzer rounds and one Viet Cong rocket could detonate the rounds and blow the barge out of the water.

After getting through the first ambush without any casualties, the convoy was ambushed again by the Viet Cong. The same treatment, as in the first ambush, was given to them and they broke contact.

As the convoy approached the village of Cai Rang they were ambushed again. During the ambush the troops opened fire with automatic weapons and M-16 rifles. During this time the South Vietnamese Marines, on the edge of the village, saw the gunfire, thought they were being attacked, and opened fire on the convoy. When they did, every boat in the convoy opened fire and racked the village with bullets. The artillery fired their bee-hive (106 shell loaded with pellets) point blank into the village.

When the firing stopped the huts were filled with wounded and dead Vietnamese civilians. A total of seventy-two dead and 204 wounded. We could not account for any dead Viet Cong.

The next morning I went back to Cai Rang with the brigade Civil Affaires officer. It was a pathetic sight. Many of the huts had been destroyed and many riddled with bullet holes. The bullets caught many women, children, and old men asleep, from which they would never awake. People were gathered around the dead bodies crying and talking in loud voices to each other.

I thought to myself, "What a tragic mistake we made, if it was a mistake. Maybe the map was marked incorrectly... No, that could not be. The map was correct." Later I thought, "Whatever caused the error, we killed and wounded many innocent people."

The division commander, knowing that many questions would be asked about the incident at Cai Rang, appointed an investigating officer to make a report on it.

Unknown to Colonel Archer, his last operation, northeast of Sa Dec, on 30-31 August, would be his last with the brigade. On 5 September General Abrams relieved him of command of the brigade because of the Cai Rang incident.

On 6 June Colonel George E. Bland assumed command of the brigade, without a formal ceremony.

The Mobile Riverine Force was not new to Colonel Bland. He had served, under Colonel David, as battalion commander, 3rd Battalion, 47th Infantry before being assigned to MACV. He was a superior tactician and a true warrior who gave nor expected any quarter. I spent many hours in the command and control helicopter with him. It was a pleasure to watch him in action.

His first question, after an operation was, "Did we lose any men?"

His second question was, "How many VC did we kill?

When my retirement orders arrived on 18 September I had mixed emotions.

"I love this Army," I said to myself, "maybe I am making a mistake by retiring. What am I going to do when I retire?" Many other thoughts went through my mind.

I began giving more thought to my future and remembered that while I was stationed at Fort McPherson, and was a Scoutmaster, Penney Jones the Scout district executive talked to me about getting into professional scouting. With this in mind I wrote a letter to Mr. Uffelman, the scout executive of the Atlanta Area Council, and asked about my chances of becoming a district executive.

In his reply he said that, with my military background and scouting experience, that my chances were very good. However, I would have to go through a training course in Virginia, and that I would not be guaranteed assignment in the Atlanta area. He went on to say that, if accepted, I would be subject to assignment anywhere in southeastern United States.

After thinking about his proposal I thought, "I have moved

around enough in the Army and certainly do not want to be moved around when I retire."

I then wrote Mr. Uffelman and told him, "Thanks, but no thanks."

My next consideration was the Junior ROTC program.

"This is really what I want. Maybe I can teach some of those young men how to survive in combat, if they end up in the Army."

I then wrote the director of ROTC of the Atlanta Public Schools. It wasn't long until I received a letter of acceptance from him.

On 5 October I received my port call orders directing me to report to the Division AG Section, at Dong Tam, on 19 October. They also advised me that I would be departing Bien Hoa at 0130 hours, 23 October.

A couple days later, elements of the brigade were scheduled to conduct an operation into an area forty miles southeast of Dong Tam.

"Sergeant Major," Colonel Bland said, "since you will be leaving soon why don't you stay back this time."

"Sir," I said, "I understand that we are going into an rough area and I would like to go along."

"Okay, Sergeant Major," he said, "but make it your last operation."

"I will, Sir," I replied.

After three days of fighting and chasing the Viet Cong, the 4th Battalion, 47th Infantry successfully penetrated the enemy's Thanh Phu Secret stronghold, killing twenty-nine Viet Cong. The thickly vegetated area had been in Viet Cong hands since the war began. Few forces ever ventured into the heavy mangrove swamps, rice paddies, thick strands of nipa palm and tangled vines and grasses.

The first two days produced little contact and just four Viet Cong were killed. But in the last day of the operation, twenty-four Viet Cong were killed after being dogged through heavy vegetation by the troops.

Later in the day, as Company C followed some fleeing Viet Cong, they were alerted to enemy holes in the area. Seconds after, the Viet Cong opened up with automatic weapons and grenades.

The troops countered, simultaneously maneuvering on the concealed enemy. In the exchange, fourteen more Viet Cong were killed. Two more were added later crossing a stream as they tried to evade infantrymen. Our loses amounted to four killed and seven wounded.

My replacement arrived on 12 October and I told Colonel Bland that I would like to go to Dong Tam early.

"Before I leave," I said, "I will give the new sergeant major a thorough briefing on the Mobile Riverine Force and maybe I could take him on a flight in the command and control helicopter and show him how to use the radio and a few other things about the helicopter."

"That will be fine," he said.

Before I departed the battalion sergeants major gave me a dinner in which Colonel Bland attended. They presented me with a plaque. Later, the chief petty officers on the USS Benewah also presented me with a plaque.

The morning I was to depart the Benewah I went into the chiefs' mess to have breakfast. As I sat there, eating, I listened to the chaplain's morning program on the Armed Forces network.

After the chaplain had spoken a few minutes he said, "I would like to read to you a poem that was given to me last December by the sergeant major of the 3rd Battalion, 60th Infantry."

At this point I realized that the chaplain speaking was Chaplain Johnson.

"The poem is titled 'Home Inside,'" he said.

He then read it.

After he completed reading I thought to myself, "I sure am going to tell Sandra about this. She has shared her poem with all the men in Vietnam. I know that she will be proud."

When I arrived at Dong Tam the division sergeant major invited me to stay in his quarters until I departed. While there he gave a party for me and another staff sergeant major who was also leaving.

After processing through the AG Section, on 19 December, I told the sergeant major that I was going to Bear Cat and stay until I departed for Long Binh.

"The division commander's helicopter is going to Bear Cat for some maintenance," he said, "maybe you can catch a ride on it."

After getting my bags packed I went to the airstrip and asked the pilot for a ride.

"Sure," he said, "but we will have to make a stop on the way."

"That will be okay," I said, "I am not in any hurry."

As we were about to leave, a truck stopped beside the helicopter. Two men got out and lifted a body bag off the truck and placed it on the helicopter.

"Our stop is at Grave Registration," the pilot said.

When we became airborne I looked down at the body bag and felt lonely and bewildered.

I thought to myself, "How old is this soldier? How was he killed? Where is he from in the States? How many children does he have? I will never know. He is just another statistic as far as the Army is concerned."

During my couple days at Bear Cat I stayed with the first sergeant of the Reliable Academy and got drunk.

HOME

As I was boarding my flight at Bien Hoa, young soldiers from an incoming flight were getting off. As they passed they looked at us.

One of them hollered, "Did you leave any Viet Cong for us?"

The men in my group only looked at them with pity in their eyes.

I knew that they were thinking the same thing I was, "There are many Viet Cong left and you will probably be meeting them soon."

When we became airborne I looked out the window into dark space and my thoughts flashed back over the past year.

"My hopes ran high when I came to Vietnam, but somewhere along the line I lost the desire to destroy the enemy. My temper was tested but I did not succumb to the pressures of battle. How many more men must die in Vietnam before Communist aggression is stopped."

It was later in the evening when we arrived at Oakland Army Terminal. I felt tired as we got off of the bus. We were led to the mess hall where the traditional Army steak was waiting for us. After eating we were led to the barracks and given a bunk for the night.

Most of the men, as well as I, were anxious to call home. So, after getting a bunk I dropped my bags and located a telephone and called home.

"When will you be home," Lou asked.

"Maybe tomorrow," I replied. "I will call you tomorrow and let you know what time."

The next morning, after processing, I called the airport and made a reservation on a flight to Atlanta and called Lou and informed her what time I would arrive.

I boarded the airplane and located my seat, which was next to a young girl about twenty years old. As I sat down she looked at me very hard but I did not pay any attention to her.

Shortly after we became airborne a stewardess came around taking orders for drinks.

When she asked me I said, "No thanks."

The girl setting next to me said to the stewardess, "I want to change my seat."

"Is something wrong with your seat?" the stewardess asked.

"The seat is okay," she replied, "I just don't want to sit next to a killer."

I was shocked to hear what she had said. I turned to her.

"Who are you talking about?" I asked.

The stewardess, who was as shocked as I was, said, "Come with me, I have an open seat."

The girl got up and turned to me.

"I am talking to you," she said and walked away.

I was very angry and if she was a man I would have hit her.

I thought to myself, "Men are giving their lives everyday in Vietnam for people like her."

In an effort to get the girl off my mind I ordered a double Scotch and began to relax.

During that quiet time my mind drifted back in time: "There has been many sad times in my military career, but there has also been some happy times."

My thoughts were interrupted by the stewardess.

"Would you like another drink," she asked.

I think she was feeling sorry for me.

"No thanks," I replied.

My thoughts continued, "I have been a professional soldier for many years. As General MacArthur said, 'Old Soldiers never die, they just fade away.' Maybe I will just fade away."

It was a happy occasion when I arrived in Atlanta. Lou and all of my children were there to meet me. After our brief reunion we began walking to the parking lot. My son Billy spoke up.

"I will drive, Dad," he said.

I smiled at him.

He looked as old as some of the soldiers I lost in Vietnam.

"Okay," I said.

When we reached Morrow Road in Forest Park, a short distance from our house, Billy slowed down, almost to a complete stop.

"What is the matter?" I asked.

"Look up, Dad," he said.

When I looked up I saw a banner spread across the street.

"WELCOME HOME DAD," it said.

I was lost for words.

I arrived home on 29 October and on 31 October my family and I were invited to a welcome home ceremony by the mayor of Forest Park.

When we arrived at the city hall a large group of people were already there. Many of them were our friends from the church. There were two other Vietnam veterans being honored also. During the ceremony the mayor presented each of us the key to the city. He then asked if we had anything that we would like to say. The other two veterans declined, but I felt that I must say something.

After expressing my appreciation to the mayor for honoring us and giving us the key to the city, I looked out at the people gathered there. I had no prepared speech and was a little nervous.

"I have served in three wars and have been in twenty-four different countries during my military career. I have seen men die in combat and have seen people starving to death in the streets."

I paused. Everyone was silent.

"I would like to say this to you. With all of our problems, we live in the most wonderful country there is. We have an inherent right to do anything we please, as long as we do not infringe on the rights of others, and it is within the purview of the law. I am here tonight, by the grace of God, to tell you that many men have given their lives and many, at this moment, are giving their lives to protect those inherent rights. Communist aggression must be stopped at any cost, or it will end up on our doorstep. I plead to you to not forget the more then 30,000 Americans who have died in combat in Vietnam, fighting the Communist aggressors since the beginning of the war. Thank you, and God bless you."

Ronnie J. Schmitt

Says author Schmitt: "I volunteered for Vietnam and I spent thirteen months there. Even though the years since the early 60s have dulled the memory, even though time has caused much of the pain to fade, even though there isn't nearly as much left of yesterday as once there was, I still remember Vietnam as well as I remember downtown Milwaukee.

"I served in the 611th Transportation Company at Vung Tau in the Mekong Delta. Although soldiers like myself, who were essentially ground crewman, were not required to fly, most of us did, simply because we were professional soldiers. Not to join the activity was unthinkable. The role played by the Army aviator and the importance of aircraft in Vietnam may never be properly told. In addition to our company providing direct support to the 5th Special Forces, it provided reconnaissance, recovery of downed aircraft, close air support, saturation bombing, strafing runs, medical evacuation, delivery of mail, and transportation. As sideliners, our rotor-wing and fixed-wing aircraft were used for sport parachuting skydiving that I took up in Vietnam, and I even jumped with Brig. Gen. Joseph Stilwell.

"The more involved a soldier got, back in those days, the higher esteem was he held by fellow comrades. I did not want to be second best. Most of us had close calls, some were wounded or killed. But we were in Vietnam because we volunteered to be there, and we flew in helicopters because we volunteered to. For most of us, the simple fact was that we were in war, and we believed we should put all our effort into winning it. We believed we would live to go home, probably with a few medals.

"I received many medals and citations while in Vietnam.

"In the early 60s, my strong conviction was this: That I could show no greater love than this — to lay down my life for my country. God. Duty. Country. Today, in 1990, it may mean this — wasted acts of heroism. Great patriotic crusade, fini."

Only Those Who Were There Will Know

By Ronnie Schmitt

I am an ordinary, run-of-the-town sort of guy that you wouldn't think a thing like this could have happened to, but it did. I thought I lived in an ordinary American environment. Maybe ordinary people think in ordinary ways and should not. Maybe they should begin to think beyond the ordinary, and then they would understand.

Maybe there were others who fell in love also, but I am sure that no one loved as deeply as I loved Tuyet Hoa. Little Hoa was only seventeen, doll-like and fragile as a flower, her black hair cut in bangs down her brow and from beneath this fragility, her almond eyes peeped out shyly. I saw her first behind a tiny bar in that little Vietnamese hamlet and the building looked about as sturdy as a cardboard box, and it leaned away from the wind. There was a piece of wood hanging over the door that displayed the word *BAR*. The rest of the village was almost as bad — photo shops, laundries, barber shops, bars, and a few massage parlours built to accommodate Americans. There was also a fish market to provide fish and rice to those refugees that had fled their burned-out village.

Ted and I had escaped the heat of the barracks on the base and, with our tongues hanging out with thirst, we pushed into the bar, because it was one that few GIs went to. Only one other guy sat at the bar, which wouldn't have seated more than nine anyway.

"Sit," said Ted, "we'll wet our tonsils and roll."

We could hear the high-pitched twang of oriental strings and smell the sweet odor of opium that tantalized the evening air. Leaning over the bar, I rapped.

"Hi', Ba-Muoi-Ba (two beer 33)," I announced.

"Yes, okay," we heard.

Up until then I had not seen Hoa. She barely showed above the bar top. Hoa served us our beer and I just watched her while I drank my beer.

Ted started talking about different aircraft, then he said, "I just don't want to go out on recovery. That's where you can get it. I just want to get back home to good old Milwaukee all in one piece, for that woman that I got waiting for me."

He pulled a letter out of his pocket, giving it a big smack.

"Sure," I said, not really listening, but watching that little doll behind the bar. The GI at the other end of the bar pushed his glass and asked for another.

"Yes, okay!"

Her voice tinkled. The guy was half bent over. He must have been drinking since he came off the compound. The drunk said something about running the bar all by herself, and Hoa said, with pride in her voice, that her brother had built it so that she could take care of herself and their mother while he went off to fight the Viet Cong. Her speech was a little hesitant as she groped for the English words. I turned halfway around on my stool and I saw the old woman sitting there. Her face didn't show expression and her arms were folded, and she rocked back and forth, back and forth, never stopping. The drunk started the old refrain about wasn't she lonely, and that he could really take care of that as he reached across the bar to get her. The little doll stepped back away from his reach. Ted dragged the back of his hand across his mouth and thumped down his empty glass.

"Let's amble," he said, "there must be more action than this somewhere."

And he got up to leave.

"You go ahead," I motioned with my head, "and take the drunk with you! Okay, Ted?"

He looked surprised, then he took in the little doll and his eyes went over to the reaching GI. Ted grinned and shrugged.

"If that's the way you want it," he said.

Ted had the drunk off his stool and on his feet before he knew what happened, and Ted pulled him through the door.

I didn't say much that night. I just sat there, filling my eyes with her. I found out her name and I liked the sound of Hoa on my tongue. I was careful, for she was a little shy. Funny thing. I was shy also. Hoa told me a little, in her mixed-up, hesitant English, about her village home that was in ashes — how her father was killed in a raid by the Viet Cong that left her mother speechless and empty, and how her brother had brought them here, then built the bar so they could live. And then he hurried off to the war to avenge his father's death. The way Hoa told it, in her sing-song voice, I really liked.

I didn't know until I got up to leave and reached the door. I turned.

"I will be back tomorrow," I told her.

"Nice," she said and smiled.

Right then and there I knew I was in love, and I galloped back to the base as excited as a kid, but a little sad also. A love like this — what could I do about it? I realized that the military officials disapproved of such fraternization. That night I went to sleep thinking of Hoa. And so it began.

Ted and I walked into the village each evening and he left me at the dilapidated bar and he moved on farther into the village towards the beach and other bars.

Each night I sat at the bar, up at the far end, filling my eyes with Hoa, and her mother rocked in the shadows, and the stragglers came in. Hoa would smile timidly at each customer.

"Yes, okay!" as she poured their beer and stepped out of their reach.

We talked between customers. Hoa told me about her home and the rice paddies. Hoa talked of the war and she told me about the raid on their hamlet. Then, with shinning eyes, Hoa listened to me as I told her of my country and my city, and she would hold up her little hand when I talked to fast or used words she couldn't understand. Then I searched for new ways to describe things to her. I sketched the house I lived in. I drew the rooms upstairs and down. Hoa stared at the drawings, shaking her head in wonder. She looked up, her brows climbing up behind her bangs, her almond eyes becoming big with bewilderment. I had never felt this before, wanting to give all of me and all that I had, wanting to possess and hold and protect her. Then I took out my wallet and I showed her pictures of my loved ones.

On my days off we often locked up the bar. Before leaving, Hoa would lean over that rocking old lady and comfort her with her sing-song voice, to which her mother made no response. Then we would go to the beach. There in the shade of the rocks I took Hoa in my arms and loved her.

"This is our place," I told her.

"Prace." Her tongue wouldn't fit around the unfamiliar PL sound.

I put our names together in the sand, and then she managed to understand.

I took pictures of us together. The top of her head just reached my neck. I set the timer on the camera, and she was fascinated.

"Will we be together in the picture?" she asked.

"Yes," I said, "we will always be together."

Time passed. Hoa's mother's rocking became slower, then at last it came to a stop.

Hoa bent over her mother.

"She is at peace now," she said softly.

I told Hoa to sell the bar. We bought a nice little house at Go Cong close to Hoa's home along the South China Sea. Go Cong was an off-limits area for Americans at Vung Tau. It was Viet Cong-dominated territory and the village was considered sympathetic to the Communist. Whenever I went to the hamlet at night, I would put on a pair of black pants and sedge-hat worn by Vietnamese peasants and by the Viet Cong. Because of this unauthorized activities, I had a number of close calls with the Viet Cong, and this created a serious disciplinary problem for me with my company commander, which resulted in the loss of rank on a couple of occasions.

In 1964 alone, intelligence reports estimated that over 10,000 NVA soldiers came down the Ho Chi Minh trail and infiltrated South Vietnam. There was a drastic increase of terrorism against the civilian population in South Vietnam. On August 4,1964, North Viet Nam torpedo boats fired on the U.S.S. Maddox, and the U.S.S. Turner Joy, in the Gulf of Tonkin. Because of this stepped-up aggression by the Viet Cong, my orders to leave Vietnam were cut and I was extended for an indefinite period of time. All American personnel were restricted to their compounds. All our war materiel was boxed up and loaded onto cargo planes, and we were on standby alert, to fly to a secret base in Laos.

In such a war without fronts, no one was safe, and no one was spared. Night had fallen over the four thousand villages of the Red River Delta, and the night belonged to the elusive Viet Cong. Despite the increased action in Vietnam I felt safe with the belief that nothing could go wrong in my life — never to me, but always to the other guy.

But something did go wrong: That tiny human error, even in the Atomic Age, can still shape human destiny.

My illusion of safety disappeared when all of a sudden a tremendous explosion shook the earth and a pillar of dense smoke rose in its center. It was 0435 hours, and this was the moment that the Viet Cong chose to make its presence known.

But the Viet Cong were not particularly interested in attacking Americans. Their emphasis was one of terror against the civilian population in the village where Hoa lived.

At first light I decided I would venture off the base and check on Hoa. I jumped on a truck that was leaving the base. There were two different ways I could get to Hoa's village. The easiest and quickest route was to take the road east just outside the main gate. But that wasn't advisable during daylight hours because you could be easily observed going to an unauthorized area by the MPs standing guard at that junction. I rode in the back of the truck due east for about a mile to Front Beach, and then slyly jumped off the truck. I took a Lambretta cab in a westerly direction around a mountain hillside over the gray-backed heights that rose abruptly from the flat plain on all sides. The road was approximately fourteen feet wide at times and soon became a ledge that winds its way along the steep fall of the mountainside. The dust stained clutch of vehicles grated forward, shuddering, dipping and bouncing at an average speed of thirty miles per hour. I continued out over the parched floor of the Mekong Delta valley that began to weave its way purposefully past a cluster of wooden bungalows on stilts, with thin threads of woodsmoke threading into the cold heavens and the soft, nasal lament of a solitary lull that had the nostalgic quality of distant bagpipes.

We headed down an asphalt road that had a surprising amount of civilian traffic, and small busses overloaded with people who looked at me as I passed by them. A long way off, diagonally distant from the road, was the jungle. The shelter of the V.C. The jungle had a deep dark green retreat, shrouded in silence, adding to the sense that it was a haven for someone else, namely the Viet Cong.

At the Ville, I walked down a mid-way between twin sets of bungalows, past a basket of hens and a pig tied to a fence, and squeals in a cross falsetto. Walking into the hamlet was ghostly. Something was amiss. My senses were working overtime, with the stench of blood in my nostrils, mingled with the smell of the field, the hay, the cattle, the manure and the elusive VC and their countryside, heavy in the damp morning air. Midway through the village I saw the first evidence of the foray of the VC terrorist as I passed by a demolished school house that was smoldering in ashes.

By the time I got to Hoa I knew that it was too late. God! was she in bad shape. With the blood loss that Hoa had, it was a miracle that she was still alive. She had numerous gashes on her face where she was beaten and mutilated, and the flies and other insects were eating at the exposed flesh. I had no morphine to give her to relieve her agony.

The things Hoa went through, in all that humidity, I would not want another human being to have to go through. The stench was unbearable. I became squeamish and couldn't breath. I was throwing up, until I had nothing more to throw up. Hoa was trying to get up and I was trying to hold her down and she kept asking for water — and with an open belly wound, you can't give a person water. Then Hoa saw that it was me.

"Wonnie," she said. "Wonnie. Why you not give Hoa drink?"

God! I never felt so helpless. You could actually see her intestines. I never prayed before for a person to die, but I prayed, "Dear God, please don't let her suffer anymore."

Tuyet Hoa finally passed away. Like her mother and father, Hoa was also at peace.

The villagers said that about twenty Viet Cong entered the village. Some of them were youths. They seized the village headman and his wife. They cut off his head then cut the throat of his wife to silence her screams so that the voice of their leader could be heard.

"They made us watch while they slit open the belly of Hoa and pulled out her intestines like a bloody rope," the leader said, and that they were being punished because the school built there wasn't really a school but an American fort. They blew up the school, and that was the 0435-hour explosion that was heard.

Hoa was buried at Ben-Dinh near Cap Saint-Jacques. Hoa always did love the atmosphere of Vung Tau. She was buried among the hundreds of unmarked graves, and she lay absolutely peaceful under the hot sun, looking as improbable a place to be disturbed as existed in all of Vietnam, and as peaceful as if war had never happened.

In only a few days I would be leaving the "LAND OF SIN AND SORROW."

Rest in peace my love. You will always remain a satisfying memory to me, Hoa.

I am back at the base, frozen stiff and steaming sweat. I thought of at least a thousand and one ways to convince myself that none of this was true, that it wasn't really happening. But I could not isolate myself from all of it. My haven of peace had been violated, and in this wacky world of Vietnam, there was no search for meaning... But none of that conventional wisdom relieved my conscience of the moral "right and wrong" of what happened. It's very difficult to adjust your thinking and accept morals that are completely contrary to what you've been taught. I became crazed because of the frustration I felt and the horror I had seen. And then, after Vietnam, the bitterness in the heart for having been in that terrible place that even my own countrymen back home could not understand and had refused to accept. I wasn't a tin soldier. I became emotionally torn apart.

So that is how my tour of duty ended. My conditioned remedy of consciousness-altering refreshment was alcohol. I stayed in an alcoholic stupor. I could analyze myself all I wanted, but the fact remained that I chose to fraternize with Hoa, and she died because of it. I felt a guilt that weighed heavily on my mind. All the analysts in the world wouldn't bring Hoa back. It couldn't answer the question that kept repeating itself in my mind since that day Hoa died, nor over years has the burden lightened. The question is, "Tai Sao? Tai Sao? — Why? Why?" I felt sick about it all. I was sick about the war and what it was doing to me. It was the dark, destructive emotions that I felt that disturbed me. I was shocked by what I had seen, yet I was powerless to stop it from happening. The total despair of HOPELESSNESS. Little did I realize that I suffered from PTSD, and that it would contribute to a lifetime of incarceration for me.

Editor's note: as *Adventures...* was being readied for press, Ronnie sent this last-minute message from prison, "David, still, in 1990, sometimes I stay up half the night because my mind bleeds from hell when it goes back to Vietnam."

Included with the note was a photocopy of photographs showing a Vietnamese woman and a baby. Atop the paper Ronnie wrote, "Anh raised my Amerasian child Nha after the VC brutally murdered Hoa. Anh and Nha were living at Qui Nhon in 1975, when I lost contact with them after the NVA takeover of South Vietnam."

D. A. Andersen

Andersen was a Navy Hospital Corpsman attached to the 2nd Battalion, 3rd Marines (Fox 2/3) in I Corps during 1968/69. Serving as a platoon medic in a company, he experienced much terror, pain and fear. While in the bush, Andersen contracted malaria, which almost killed him. He was sent to a Navy hospital ship, the SANCTUARY, to recover. Afterward, he was assigned to the northernmost medical outpost, which served as the Marine version of a MASH unit. There he worked with five surgeons, treating the scores of wounded Marines in need of immediate, "life-saving" surgical attention, until his tour of duty was completed.

During the last twenty years Andersen has been a professional writer and editor, with extensive experience in publishing, public relations and marketing communications.

About "Temescal Moon" author Andersen says, "It is fiction, with threads of my own experiences and vision sown together. My story is an attempt to capture the essence, or spirit, of my experience... I'm afraid that my use of profanity will shock some readers. I toned it down for my story. In reality, it was much stronger, and was included in every sentence and phrase uttered. The same goes for the gruesome action. It was toned down considerably.

"I was going to dedicate the book *Adventures...* to Bill Crider, a counselor at a Vietnam Vets Outreach Center, who had been in a Marine Recon unit. Until 1984, I had dissociated myself from anything that pertained to the Vietnam War, almost as if I hadn't even been there. I thought that post traumatic syndrome was for wimps.They say you can't die in your dreams, right? I did, every night, for months. I finally reached out. Bill Crider was there, like a Marine buddy in a jungle. And I'll leave off with just one interchange between Bill and me.

"'I have this heavy guilt, Bill. It's incredible I'm even here, alive, in one piece, and functioning at al!. Hundreds of the guys I treated were ruined, and many didn't make it at all... One afternoon, we were surrounded on a mountain-hill. I knew I was going to eat it, so I began writing a last letter to my mom. All of a sudden a short Willie Peter round landed ten feet behind me. Everything and everybody around me was sizzling. Not me. Miraculously. I lay curled up in a fetal position, whimpering like a scared dog.'

"Bill said to me, 'David, you're okay. You're okay now... I'm still visiting guys at VA hospitals who are still in fetal positions.'

"I don't know why, exactly, but it blew me away. It popped a bubble in my psyche.

"This story is dedicated to every guy who is still in a fetal position... we'll always be blood brothers.

"It is also dedicated to all those who were touched and troubled by a war that lingers on, like a recurring, weird dream in the subconscious and soul of America."

Temescal Moon

By D. A. Andersen

Prologue

Russ Heisler felt relieved after twenty-three hours of deliberation and debate as a juror. He looked down at the oak handrail of the juror's box with bloodshot eyes and rubbed his fingertips along the railing while listening to the court proceedings intently. Yet he seemed to be looking far away.

District Court Judge A. E. Wiggins hunched forward over his notes, clasping his hands and clearing his throat. Talk in the courtroom died.

Heisler rubbed the railing but stared ahead at the defendant, a medic recently home from combat duty in Vietnam. The defendant sat quietly staring at the judge.

"Mr. Abelman," Judge Wiggins said, turning to the jury box, "please read the jury's verdict."

Heisler had decided seconds after hearing the news on TV about the three grisly murders that Daniel Buck, the medic, was a crazed Vietnam vet. He was a disgrace to his country. When Heisler received notice to appear for jury duty he did so gladly, reminiscing about his WWII service in the Pacific.

"Yes, your honor," Bill Abelman said, glancing at the defendant. "We, the jury, find the defendant, Daniel Buck, guilty of first degree murder... on all four counts."

Several in the audience blew out audibly. Abelman sat down

and Heisler rubbed the railing, looking at Judge Wiggins. The impassive image on Daniel's face did not change with the verdict, but his upper lip twitched.

Heisler watched Daniel and the images of the newscast quickly flickered in his mind: the eight-months pregnant woman, ambulance cover pulled over her face, being jounced down the steps in the rain and slid into the van, flashing red lights in the misty air; two small children, both dead, covered and carried like carrion in bags atop stretchers; then the veteran, dressed in jungle fatigues, his hands cuffed behind him, looking at the camera with a one-sided grin as he was shoved into the patrol car. Heisler saw the TV report, saw those eyes, and heard him scream, "I said I'd get even, Brisling!"

Judge Wiggins deliberated, looking at his fingernails for a few moments, then unclasped his hands and read a prepared statement.

Daniel turned toward the jury and stared at Russ Heisler, as if sensing Heisler's WWII fighting service. Heisler stared at Daniel. The judge cleared his throat again and began his pronouncement matter-of-factly. Heisler looked at the judge.

"The jury has reached its decision and its verdict stands, that decision having been weighed with the fairness of law in this land... Just as Vietnam is part of our history, so too is this trial. We are setting precedent here, at this juncture in time."

Judge Wiggins cleared his throat again and looked up at the crowded room quickly, then continued in a monotone.

"The defendant is today found guilty of the most heinous crimes... While Dora Brisling, age 31 years old and eight months pregnant, her daughters Cora, age three, and Sissy, age six, peacefully reclined in their living room, said defendant did smash the plate glass window with a pistol. He then threw into the living room three North Vietnamese 'Chi-Com' hand grenades... That the defendant planned and executed these acts with a clear mind is now proven.

"I wish to add something here," he said then cleared his throat. "The Geneva Convention, established and agreed upon by all civilized nations, very clearly proscribes medics from carrying guns that are larger than small firearms, and that those weapons are intended for last resort self-defense only... As we have heard repeatedly during this trial's testimony, not only did the defendant carry a sawed-off shotgun, but also used it quite savagely. There is something unacceptable in all of this.

"To continue... Just as the combat veterans of World War II campaigns returned to their society and continued to mold themselves to its norms, so too must the veterans of the Vietnam Police Action be expected to adjust and grow back into the folds of society... Finally... the impact of that 'police action' on any individual cannot be accepted as reasonable excuse for crime."

Heisler's cheek twitched several times as he stared at the dark-haired medic.

The bailiff guided Daniel from the courtroom to a private cell, where Daniel stood motionless, looking at his bunk with a smirk on his face.

"Another fucking temescal," he said to an imaginary friend at his side.

Jungle Fever

Daniel lay on a cot in deep twilight with his long legs hanging over the side. He looked out through an upraised tent flap watching a group of Marines with a powerful pom-pom gun attached to a Jeep exploding rounds into a nearby tree trunk. In seconds the tree snapped at its base and crashed onto dense jungle foliage. The Marines laughed into the viny twilight, ramming the Jeep into thick elephant-eared growth alongside a bamboo grove, firing the mobile canon like a lethal toy.

The pastel shades of evening gave way to a darkness more awesome than Daniel had ever imagined. The moist jungle air of late twilight moved from entrancing purples to tar black. Life's only light was his glowing cigarette tip.

Staccato bursts of rifle fire crackled in the distant sky. Then the almost touchable quietness of the hostile jungle night set in.

"Jeez!" Daniel said in panic, looking into the raven-black night. "I need light!"

He snuffed the cigarette stub into clayey soil and swung nervously off the cot. Aggravation entwined with fear and foreboding in his head. When he arrived at Dong Ha days earlier, he had hitchhiked over ominous jungle roads from Saigon on everything from jungle-green cattle trucks to rattletrap Jeeps. Just as he arrived at Dong Ha the battalion headquarters was in motion, moving from Dong Ha to Phu Bai.

Added to the potential dangers of the jungle was Brisling, the "Top GI" to Daniel. Ever since Daniel's field medical training with the Marines, the top sergeant seemed intent on driving Daniel over the edge. And Daniel knew that Brisling would arrive in a day or two.

The sergeant in charge of the medical battalion headquarters, the sergeant Brisling would soon replace, instructed Daniel to go with two Marines who were taking a truckload of gear from the battalion medical center to the new location at Phu Bai. Daniel eyed the huge wooden crates of emergency medical supplies on the rear of the truck then hopped into the truck cab.

The truck bounced over a dusty road as it moved in and out of alternating patches of barren spaces and jungle. The truck crossed an old stone and mortar bridge then halted with a screech of brakes in a cloud of dust.

Daniel and the Marines arrived at the Phu Bai position at noon. They began putting up the tent as tent-dust filled their nostrils and sweat dripped from their chins. They cussed the foreign earth as they strained in the 100-plus heat. Their green dog tags slapped against their sweaty bare chests as they pulled at tent poles and ropes and drove long stakes into the soil and slapped at savage jungle flies. An hour later the big tent popped into full-blown life with Daniel standing inside, breathing in the dust and lighting a cigarette. He drew in a chest full of smoke and sighed.

The Marines waved farewell then took off in the empty truck, over the bridge and into the viny jungle toward the old compound at Dong Ha. Daniel stacked the medical supplies in haphazard piles. By late afternoon, still sweating in streams, he stood akimbo in the battalion medical center tent and awaited nightfall alone. As his sweat dried it turned into a salty layer on his skin.

The late afternoon air began to darken with night and he realized in a sudden flash that he would be spending his first night alone in Vietnam. He sat on a canvas cot and listened to its wooden tent poles chirp with tension from the canvas. He lit a cigarette and drew in on the smoke until it hurt his lungs.

He breathed out then drew in more smoke and shivered despite the warmth of the air. He bent over and fumbled in his backpack for a flashlight but didn't find one, then got up to look for a lamp and kerosene. His fingertips were his eyes in the darkness as he felt along rough pinewood crates. He pried up a flat board and jammed a splinter into his thumb next to his nail.

"Goddamnit to hell!"

He groped his way back to the cot without the sight of his eyes or his fingertips. The cot squeaked as he sat down and he drew in a last breath of smoke before dislodging the outsized splinter with shaky fingers. He felt the blood leak out and onto his boot.

Moments later he walked out the tent flap wiping thumb blood on his pants. He heard occasional tail ends of sentences from distances he couldn't determine. Three men in camouflage uniforms and faces painted with camouflage face paint hurried by in the harried shuffle of the all-night perimeter guards' first two-hour watch. "Looking for your temescal, guys?" Daniel said and snickered to himself in a whisper. He felt them look back through the darkness at him but couldn't see them. He shivered and said softly to the dark jungle, "A hothouse of pleasure and pain... It prickles the skin like hot dryness... Just like a Shoshone temescal." A month before his flight into Asia's hell began he and his friends had swallowed large doses of Purple Barrel LSD in the full moon light by the riverbed. They had built a replica of the Shoshone's strong grass hut by the river's purling edge.

HIS EYES WERE AS WIDE OPEN AS LIFE WOULD PERMIT. THEY HEATED BIG GRANITE STONES IN THE HUT'S FIRE, WAITED AND WATCHED THE STONES GLOW RED AND WHITE THEN POURED ON RIVER WATER. THEIR MOUTHS GAPED WITH SILENT LAUGHTER AS THEIR PORES OPENED AND BODY TOXINS PERCOLATED OUT LIKE SEAWATER. THEN THEY LEFT THE HUT ONE BY ONE AND FLOATED IN THE COOL RIVER LIT BY THE FULL MOON. THEIR BODIES STRETCHED OUT OVER THE RIVER'S SLOW MOVING SURFACE AS THEY GRASPED SHORELINE BOULDERS WITH

TINGLING FINGERS. DANIEL LAUGHED IN THE QUAVERING WATER THEN SAID, "LIFE'S LIKE A TEMESCAL, RIGHT?" HE WATCHED THE RIVER MOVE BY AND SAW THE UNIVERSE SPINNING.

He jerked his head forward and saw Vietnam. The smell made his nostrils flare in a quiver. The smell of the land was intrinsically foul to Daniel. He'd smelled it in Saigon, where he first landed, in DaNang, the big rural city in the north, then in Dong-ha, and now, Phu-bai. It was so strong and persistent it seemed like a disease seeping up into the air from the ochre mud.

He mashed his cigarette into spongy soil with a boot heel then turned to walk back inside the tent. He whispered "Some kind of circus tent" to himself then heard footsteps running toward him from the jungle. He stood by his cot and took in a deep breath as his spine tingled. He thought about reaching for the gun.

Footfalls became louder in the night air. The sound intruded into the tent and before he could pull the pistol from the shoulder holster the noise of the footsteps stopped.

"Don't go for the gun, Doc."

The tall figure came face-to-face with Daniel.

"Go for the medical kit, Doc... I'm a friendly."

Daniel's shooting arm moved in a reflexive jerk. He stood rigid, pointing the handgun.

The fighter grabbed him by the shoulder.

"I'm a friendly, Doc," said the camouflage-painted face.

"What..." Daniel began to say, following the man through the dark with a dazed stare as the fighter moved into the tent.

"Knee's bad, Doc. I need it fixed."

Daniel lit his lighter and looked at the man in front of him as if looking at an apparition. The vision before Daniel clutched an M-79 grenade launcher in his right hand like an abnormal outgrowth of flesh.

"Newby, right?" the fighter said, breaking into Daniel's trance.

"What? Newby what?"

"New, Doc... New inside the Nam," he said and grinned, studying Daniel's expression of bewilderment. "Fix the scratch on my knee, Doc." He lifted his right leg and the pants showed dark red in the flickering light. "A little stitchwork oughtta do, Doc. Gooks are waiting for me in the bush. I can feel the evil little fuckers."

Daniel flinched at the touch of the hot lighter and fumbled but caught it before it fell. He asked the jungle fighter to sit on a wooden crate while he found a flashlight. He found one in a box full of intravenous bottles and turned in the darkness, shining the light on the wounded knee. The knee cap shone through a razor-straight gash.

"Nice scratch," Daniel said.

The nocturnal fighter just grinned, sweating in the dark.

Daniel opened containers of medical supplies and felt for a suture kit then his face reappeared in the tunnel of light in front of the fighter.

"This definitely isn't the way to clean this sucker. And numbing it's going to be a bitch," Daniel said as he squinted to see the wound.

"Just sew it, Doc... People are waiting for me. Out there, know what I mean?"

Daniel pinched the torn skin together then stuck in a needle. He waited briefly for a flinch but got none. The Marine smiled and looked forward as if in a trance.

"Strange threshold of pain," Daniel muttered as he stitched. He tied a knot in the dark thread then stood up.

"Good work, Doc. You'll be okay... I can feel it."

"What?... Doesn't this hurt?"

"Bunch of mosquitoes... Don't sweat it... Got a smoke?"

Daniel offered a long filtered cigarette then lit it.

"I'll be godamned, Doc," he said and sighed with a grin. "First smoke in two days... What a rush."

"What do you... do? Face paint?"

"Hiding. To snuff gooks, Doc... But mostly hiding," he said then jumped from the crate onto the bad leg.

He walked in long strides through the darkness and out the tent flap.

"What's your name?" Daniel asked following the man out into the night air. "I've got to record your name in the log."

"One knee's the same as the next, Doc... You'll be okay."

"Just like a Shoshone leaving a temescal," Daniel whispered to himself as he lit a cigarette.

Daniel gulped a drag on the cigarette then stomped it into the ground. He sat on his cot just inside the tent flap rubbing his face. He lay down and closed tired eyes but couldn't sleep. Looking into the darkness of his eyelids or the tent was like seeing a shadow of death. He forced himself back in time to his hometown's riverside temescal, with friends.

THE HALLUCINOGENIC NIGHT WAS MOVING TOWARD DAWN. DANIEL CAME BACK INTO THE SIMMERING HEAT OF THE TEMESCAL FROM THE COOL ULULATING OF THE PURPLE RIVER WATER.

"WHAT IF YOU KILL?" ONE FRIEND ASKED THROUGH THE STEAM.

"I'M GOING TO SAVE LIFE, NOT TAKE IT," DANIEL SAID. "BUT I'LL HAVE TO DEAL WITH DEATH."

DAWN BROKE IN THE SKY, BREAKING THE SPELL THAT BOUND THEM AS FRIENDS.

"WE KNOW YOU," ONE SAID. "WHY THE SHOULDER HOLSTER? HIT MAN STUFF, HEY?"

"IT'LL KEEP THE GUN OUT OF MY WAY... I WON'T EVEN USE THE GUN."

SUNLIGHT BROKE INTO THE TEMESCAL AIR. A LAST HOT STONE SMOLDERED. ONE BY ONE THEY WENT OUT OF THE STEAM HUT TO LIE ON THE RIVER. DANIEL SHIVERED AS HE WALKED FROM THE HUT. HE WAS THE LAST FRIEND TO REACH THE RIVER'S COOLNESS.

Sunup. Daniel awoke with a start, shivering in the dank air of the tent. He raised himself up on an arm that was still asleep and prickly with rushing blood. He looked out the tent flap and saw an orange cotton-ball sun through foggy jungle air. The decaying smell was a taste in his mouth. He heard a Jeep squealing through mud in the distance and men digging, swearing with every impact of their metal tools biting the earth. He rolled off the cot and stood up rubbing his tingling arm.

He walked outside and watched large tents being raised in rows like hot air balloons at a fair. Small clusters of men dressed in sloppy camouflage fatigues sat on their haunches sipping coffee from C-ration cans while watching others pull at long tent ropes. One group gazed into the dense maze of jungle vegetation like aborigines. A story teller pointed beyond the horizon. Another small group finished raising a battalion tent and rested in a cluster, lighting small blue heating tablets under cans of cocoa or coffee.

Daniel squatted down, emptying a packet of coffee into a green C-ration can. He lit a heating tablet in another can that served as a stove. He lit a cigarette and stared at the blue flame of the tablet as he inhaled cigarette smoke, then stirred the heated water with a plastic spoon, watching the light colored foam swirl atop the brew. He looked up to see the fog rising like a steamy veil from the jungle foliage and tilted the drinking can by its lid to sip coffee. The sun became a distinct burning orb in daytime sky.

The Top GI was on his way to the new battalion medical headquarters where Daniel was sipping coffee. Daniel knew Brisling was determined to hurt him but the thought quickly faded as he watched a small plane whisk by above the jungle canopy, trailing a streaming cloud of defoliant.

Daniel took a final gulp of the muddy water as he heard a Jeep jerking along uneven road. Gears crunched as the driver slammed on the brakes and skidded through a puddle of mud twenty yards across. Daniel saw Brisling riding shotgun. Brisling stared at Daniel with a smirk. The "Top GI" was Daniel's head drill instructor during Daniel's Marine training. He was also the uncle of Daniel's best friend, a hometown temescal chum that flipped out then blew out his brains with a military-issue pistol. Brisling had said Daniel was to blame for the suicide and should die too.

The Jeep slid to a stop at the opposite end of the long tent from Daniel. Brisling's ruddy face twisted in a frown as he hopped out of the Jeep and walked into the tent.

"Getting closer to the front every day, eh, ass-lick?" Brisling said to Daniel, who stood at the far end of the tent.

Daniel stared at the approaching sergeant without comment.

"You're gonna get it right, Buck... Right?"

"Who knows, Sergeant Brisling."

"Getting a little cocky these days, maggot!... A maggot in the mud, creep."

Daniel stared at Brisling silently.

Brisling barked orders at his driver and Daniel to move crates, then he hurried out to inspect the new forward base.

Daniel and the driver pushed and shoved and finished remaking the tent innards in an hour, then Daniel grabbed his towel and was quickly gone from the tent. He laced his boots in the sun, then headed toward an old rock bridge with a stream running over mossy stones. He stumbled down the embankment and stopped at waters-edge, stripped off his sweaty fatigues and piled them on a jutting rock.

Cold water moved like crystalline air over the slippery moss-green stones. He gripped two slick stones from behind and lowered himself into the shallow water. Knees spread, his body floated in the billowing water as he splashed himself to bathe. In five seconds he was out again, the toes of one foot hugging a spongy rock. He gazed at the sparkling water and daydreamed of the riverbed, floating just outside the temescal with Brisling's nephew.

WHEN HE WAS FIFTEEN THE WATER IN THE RIVER RAN WIDE AND FAST. HUGE GRANITE BOULDERS SUBMERGED UNDER THE WATERLINE CREATED A TREACHEROUS SERIES OF RAPIDS IN THE 100-DEGREE SUNSHINE. HE LAUGHED IN IMAGINARY HYENA CALLS WHILE A FRIEND FLIPPED OVER FROM HIS INNER TUBE INTO THE CHURNING WATER.

The reflections of the Phu-bai stream created a moment's hypnotism in Daniel. He saw the group of them, several wild, incorrigible teenagers with truck tire tubes suspended over their heads.

THEY WALKED THROUGH DRY CHAPARRAL OVER NOON-HOT STONES BAREFOOTED. THEY HOPPED INTO THEIR INNER TUBES AT THE TOP OF THE RAPIDS AND BEGAN THE JOLTING RIDE DOWN THE RIVER.

AFTER THE TUMULTUOUS MILE-LONG JOURNEY THEY FLOATED INTO A HUGE POOL DAMMED WITH BOULDERS BY LOCAL TOWNSPEOPLE. THEY SWIRLED VICTORIOUS UPON THE COOL WATER. THEY LAUGHED AS THEY REGAINED THEIR BREATH, WATCHING FAMILIES RECLINING ON LOUNGE CHAIRS ALONG THE ROCKY SHORE.

He jerked his head up and refocused on the Phu-bai stream. He began humming, then whistling "Summertime" as he put on sun-dried fatigues. He clambered up the bank without using his hands and moved into the path of a Marine sergeant.

"What you doin' down in that stream, boy?" the sergeant said with a good-humored sneer on his leathery face.

"Just cleaning up, Sarg," Daniel said, his shoulders forward in the submissive but chesty posture he'd mastered at Pendleton.

"Fool thing to do," the sergeant said then looked forward toward his destination. "This place is still fresh... Stream's full of shit like leeches and snakes. Killed a gator upstream just two days ago."

"Oh, okay," Daniel said and shrugged.

"Fool thing to do, boy."

Daniel stopped and studied him from behind, then walked on with long slow strides. Yellowish brown mud slipped up over his boot ankles. He walked inside and saw Brisling's driver asleep on a cot with a drab green towel draped over his face. Brisling's voice screeched through the field radio by the driver's cot and the man grabbed the handset lethargically.

The brief message, decoded, said: "Tell that maggot Buck he's going out onto a hot LZ, probably tomorrow morning. End of line."

"End of life?" Daniel quipped, determined to keep his sense of humor.

He packed his gear.

Brisling was still away as sweaty afternoon turned to clammy night. Daniel finished checking and repacking. He took the .45 out of the shoulder holster and laid it on the cot by his rolled towel-pillow. The committed pacifist smiled at the pistol like a preacher at a whore. He'd proven that he could shoot the eyes out of a target. He put the .45 away like another hemostat and rechecked medications.

Brisling was still away at nightfall. Daniel swallowed a sleeping pill with chemically treated canteen water. Everything he possessed was stacked in a bundle. He was ready for his jungle reveille.

Without remembrance or warning it was sunup, and no birds sang. The Top GI sat behind a dark green desk in the dawn light and scowled at Daniel through blood shot eyes. He made no comment as Daniel left the tent with the driver. He stared with a snicker as the Jeep squealed in mud and left for the helicopter landing zone.

Daniel climbed up the metal ramp into the rear end of the chopper feeling like a fat gorilla crawling into the metal anus of an even bigger flying insect. The deafening sound of the engine and blades intensified his sense of unreality, of being in another temescal.

The chopper swung up into the air from the LZ like a preying mantis from a nap. Daniel watched a Marine in flight-gear gripping a machine gun that peered out a hatch with him. He studied the gunner studying the jungle below then looked out the wide opening of the helicopter at the second helicopter moving in tandem just behind and just above the thick jungle canopy. He vibrated with the revolution of the chopper blades' swack-flap swack-flap in the moist air.

He looked at his vibrating hands and remembered his last conversation with his grandfather John Buck, the pugilist. Thirteen-year-old Daniel had listened to the old man, who had puffed ears and watery gray eyes.

"LEARN TO USE YOUR FISTS, BOY. IT'S GOOD TO KNOW. BUT FIGHTIN' AIN'T THE WAY TO MAKE A LIVIN'... REMEMBER. YOU GOT TO GET UP AND KEEP FIGHTING... I USED TO GET KNOCKED DOWN IN THE RING. I'D GET UP, WOBBLING LIKE JELLY. I'D HEAR MY MANAGER SHOUTING, LIKE I WAS IN A DREAM, 'BUCK UP! BUCK UP!' HE USED TO

SHOUT... AND THAT'S THE IMPORTANT THING, BOY. TO GET UP AGAIN.
TO KEEP ON FIGHTING... IN OR OUT OF THE RING... YOU'LL BE OKAY,
BOY, IF YOU CAN GET KNOCKED DOWN THEN GET UP AGAIN, READY
TO FIGHT... IT'S THE SPIRIT, BOY, THE SPIRIT."

"YOU STOPPED BOXING, GRANDPA. WHY?"

"I KILLED A MAN, DANNY. SO I STOPPED BOXING."

THE WORDS STRUCK DANIEL'S NERVES LIKE A ROD ON THE SPINE.

DURING THE FOLLOWING MONTHS AND YEARS OF TEEN-AGEHOOD
HE KEPT REMEMBERING THE WORDS. THEY CREATED THEN REINFORCED
IN HIM THE BELIEF THAT HE HAD TO BE BOTH COMPASSIONATE AND
TOUGH. GRANDPA BUCK'S WORDS LIT A PATH INTO THE FUTURE THAT
DANIEL WALKED. HE BECAME A MEDIC.

Nineteen-year-old Daniel rode in the noisy flying machine just
above the invincible jungle's covering. He thought about his
grandfather's words, studying his dirty hands while swallowing on
a dry throat as he vibrated in the air.

"I'll jump out of this hothouse and take a swim sometimes,"
he said to himself and chuckled. "I'll get my swims in."

He instinctively jerked his head around to face the rear of the
chopper just in time to see the escort chopper explod in a rocket's
ball of fire. The NVA rocket exploded inside the chopper like a
huge firecracker. The exploded chopper seemed to float for a
moment then it sank in a burst of metallic flame. It hit the ground
and instantly sank in the jungle's humus bed and mud. He
clenched his fists and teeth as he waited for his chopper to
explode. But he heard only the nauseating whir of chopper
blades.

He unclenched his sweaty fists and blew out in relief,
swallowing hard on bilious saliva. He cringed and cried with no
tears.

"Let me out, fool. I want to swim," he said to the unhearing
gunner.

The gunner turned and looked at Daniel and nodded, then
quickly turned back to the jungle with his machine gun.

Liquid Life

The chopper landed on the metal grates of a staging area LZ. Tall stacks of supplies rimmed the LZ perimeter with sandbagged machine gun nests. Marines dressed in dusty fatigues and muddy knees moved slowly in the hot air of late morning.

Daniel squinted up into the spire of Vietnam sun-sky. He was part of a makeshift squad that walked warily through the tropical heat on a dusty road leading away from the staging area into the jungle. They were patrolling a mile long section of road for mines, booby traps and snipers. A convoy of cattle trucks would soon follow, bringing scores of men to their new haunts with Charlie Company.

Daniel felt as if he were wearing a gorilla suit, stuck as he was inside the heavy helmet, flak-jacket and backpack. As they walked along the road, little ochre-colored clouds of dust puffed up with each of their steps down on the winding road.

They walked slowly along both sides of the dusty road. It seemed to Daniel as though the jungle, 'the bush' as they called it, wanted to cover all roads and trails, suffocating everything on the human paths as a way of healing itself. He envisioned North Vietnamese soldiers popping out of slithery thick vines then opening up on the Marines with automatic weapons. He breathed deeply partly because of the steam-bath heat and partly because of fear. "Summertime" became his personal anthem. And the more ludicrous the tune seemed in the vicious land, the more he hummed it softly.

Daniel was the only 'gray,' as the blacks called whites, in the crew. The others, in all shades of 'black,' treated him coolly, mainly because he was a newby.

"Say, Doc," said a black with a machine gun balanced atop his shoulder, "Hummin' some kind of ol' black folks tune there, are ya?" he said and snickered.

Daniel grinned but kept walking.

"Don't look black to me," another black said.

Daniel nodded and tried to grin despite the sweat that ran into his eyes from under his heavy helmet.

"Don't mean a thing, Doc," Corns said while peering into the darkness of gnarled jungle vines but suddenly walking at Daniel's side. "They're just jiving you... Seems like most of us grew up in a jungle... And here we are again," he said and chuckled in a whisper, "still in the middle of hell." They all heard a vine snap and froze. After a few moments they heard nothing more and moved on, along the winding road. "Doc, do me a favor," Corns said and glanced at the machine gunner. "Be careful where you croon your tune around here, right?"

"I'm nervous," Daniel said then sighed.

They walked on together in silence. Daniel shifted his pack, helmet and flak-jacket, trying to work out knots in his neck and back muscles. They reached their destination, where an almost indecipherable trail crossed the dirt road. Corns raised a hand in signal and the makeshift squad spread out into a defensive perimeter, lying in the dust facing out into impenetrable green darkness. Sweat ran down Corns' dusty forehead and off his broad nose.

"You aren't nervous because you're a newby, Doc," Corns said. "You're nervous because you're in this deadly place called Nam... New babies grow up fast here... You either grow up... or down, into the ground," he said then looked at Daniel and smiled. "And the only thing you've got to shit in over here is your pants. Got to wear the same ones for a long time, so you learn to hide your nervousness."

"You trying to encourage me?" Daniel said and chortled with a grin.

Daniel offered Corns a cigarette and Corns signaled that everyone could smoke.

"What should a newby know," Daniel said.

Corns smiled at the prodding.

"Who knows, Doc," Corns said and drew in smoke. "Don't get caught on Charlie Blood Ridge more than once, I guess... Not at all. Cornell Hovington," he said and tapped himself on the chest, "did it once. Don't you try it... If you can avoid it, by all means do," Corns said and chuckled.

"Why're you called Corns?" Daniel said.

"My feet always hurt over here," he said then checked on the men's positioning.

"What's this Charlie Blood Ridge?"

Broad-faced Corns grinned.

"Total fucking insanity, Doc... A month ago, we were on a big hill with a rocky ridge. No big deal... The entire battalion was supposed to be there... in strength, right? But Echo and Fox companies got stuck on another hill at nightfall. They weren't very far from us. Far enough," Corns said and drew in cigarette smoke. "Everything seemed okay, at first. But when it got dark we felt something bad in the air. And you can bet your ass we were scurrying, hacking out foxholes..." Corns drew in smoke and simply stared into the bush for long moments. Then he continued, smoke drifting out of his mouth as he spoke. "We set up perimeters with claymores... Shit hit the fan all at once. The whole world exploded in on us. Must've been an entire NVA company charged up the hill and across the ridge. Motherfuckers were jammin'... We poured everything we had into them. Lucky we'd just gotten ammo with our C-rats. Gooks just would not stop coming at us. Crazylike. Zombielike... I don't know. Seemed like they were on drugs to me. Hyped up on their cause... We got one thing to be hyped about... Being alive."

Daniel wiped sweat from his face with a sweaty wrist, slowly drawing in cigarette smoke while studying Corns.

"They weren't scared," Corns said slowly as he stared into the jungle. "It sent fright up my spine, Doc. Guys' '16s were jamming because of the mud and stuff. And they got mangled by the gooks. You hardly knew where somebody was going to come at you from. They just kept coming, running up the hill, through the bush and over the ridge... Feisty fucking gooks. More than once I'd empty a '16 clip into a gook and he'd keep running at us. Spitting up blood. Still running. I'm telling you, Doc. It was very strange... Good thing my main man, Willard Henry, had one of the few M-14s."

"You mean the heavy old infantry rifle. John Wayne stuff?"

"Right. More powerful than a '16... I'd put a whole clip through some slope and he'd keep running at me. I tell you I was abso-fucking-lutely freaked. Like my rounds just made him madder... I'd whisper, 'Willard!' and he'd roll over to me and pow! One round. The gook would splatter... It went on till dawn, Doc. Wave after wave across the ridge and in among us. The only ammo left was a round or two for the grenade launcher. Scatter shot... 'Save it till the end'... And Willard had four rounds."

Corns lit a fresh cigarette from the butt of the one he was smoking.

"Didn't come again... Soon as the air started getting light, they just vanished... It'll never leave my brain... Still makes me shiver sometimes." Corns looked around to check men's positions then looked at Daniel without smiling. "You stay close to me, Doc. I'll help you get through this nightmare. And you'll be close enough to help me... if we have another Ridge."

The dense vegetation seemed to bulge and grow in the near-noon sun as if some plant amphetamine or steroid were infused into the ground and sucked up by thirsty roots. The air was clear but felt like light steam. The cattle trucks pulled up to a stop in a cloud of dust. They hopped in and faced out into the jungle as the huge truck bumped along the twisting road with ten more trucks making a convoy headed toward Charlie Company's new haunts. They crossed a new bridge made of U.S. steel and passed through a village made of bamboo, cardboard and corrugated metal roofing.

Small Vietnamese children in tattered clothes reached up from the sides of the road with grasping hands, hoping for C-rations or cigarettes. The Marines in the truck with Daniel ignored the children until a group of ten-year-olds yelled, "Doo mau mee! Fuck your mother!" The ultimate Vietnamese insult roused instant vengeance in a chunky Chicano. He stood and spun around on the wooden truck bed, pulled out a C-ration can from a jungle pants pocket. In the same fluid motion he chucked like a second baseman. The can struck the youngster just above the nose, crushing his forehead. The Chicano sat down nonchalantly as Daniel looked out through guardrail slats at the dead body as the truck moved on in the convoy.

Bouncing on the wooden benches to the beat of the road, their attention shifted to the dusty staging area they entered as the truck passed through mounds of barbed wire.

Daniel followed Corns as the black fighter weaved around two-man tents and found an empty patch of dust above dozens of small tents on a hill and threw down his gear. The gear made a giant dust cloud around Corns.

"You might just as well make your tent here, Doc, with me," Corns said.

"What'll these guys think?" Daniel asked quietly, indicating the mass of Marines.

"Not a thing, Doc. My name's Corns... People know it... and don't mess with me."

Corns unstrapped his plasticized poncho from his backpack and signalled for Daniel to do the same. Corns pulled out two extension rods from his pack and began showing Daniel how to erect a jungle pup tent.

"You've got lots to learn, Doc," he said. "Learn how to stay cool in the heat, warm in the cold... Keep the scorpions and foot-long centipedes out, the land-leeches off your ass... Learn how to make a tent that'll keep you dry in the monsoon rains, and hope no poisonous snakes shack up in it. You'd die for sure if one bit you... And learn to sleep in your clothes, smelly old muddy things, so they'll dry from body heat."

Corns kept up the phrases in rhythm with the tent construction.

"Lot's you've got to learn, Doc," he said as he drove in a stake at the base of the tent. "Luck is one of the most important... Firefights might kill you... Might kill you, but won't wear you down... like the motherfucking jungle... Bad motherfucker if I ever did see one... Wild... Wild like nothing you've ever seen... Anyway," he said, raising up on his knees and looking around, "tent's taut. We're set for the night."

"New Doc's staying here for now," Corns said in a full voice, then pulled his pack inside the low tent. He stuck his head out of the tent and said with a grin, "Hey, Doc, gimme one of those cigarettes you're so proud of."

Daniel handed him a nearly full pack.

"All I need's one, Doc."

"No problem," Daniel said as he crawled on hands and knees to enter the tent. "I've got a shitload in my pack."

"Okay. Listen. Go on ahead and get settled in... I got a feeling we'll be here tonight, but gone in the morning. Company looks about full again... I'll be back in a while. I'm going to look for Willard. And see if I can't find something to smooth the evening out a little," then winked as he crawled out of the three-foot-high tent.

Daniel unrolled a nylon camouflage spread to sit on. He unstrapped his pack tie then looked out into the dusty light of day as if falling into a sudden daydream. After minutes passed he lay back on the nylon spread and sighed as he stretched. Afterimages of aging but beautiful Francine shot into his mind like prism reflections. He pressed on tired eyelids and colorful phosphene patterns only covered images of sex. Her summer dress was unbuttoned and drawn to the waist from the shoulders and knees. Events took him by surprise:

IN AUTUMN 1968 DANIEL TRIED TO STUDY WESTERN CIV BY THE FIREPLACE WHILE LOW RAIN CLOUDS MOVED SLOWLY OVER THE HOUSE AND INTO STEEP FOOTHILLS. CAROL KNOCKED ON THE FRONT DOOR, DRESSED IN HER FATHER'S BLACK OVERCOAT. SHE DROPPED MERCEDES KEYS ON THE COFFEE TABLE THEN LEANED OVER DANIEL. THE COAT OPENED AND DANIEL REACHED IN FOR BARE SKIN.

THEY WERE LYING STOMACH TO STOMACH, WATCHING THE FIRE FLICKER AND SNAP.

"WHAT DID YOU DECIDE ABOUT THE DRAFT?" SHE ASKED IN A WHISPER.

"I'M GOING TO JOIN THE LOCAL NAVY RESERVE UNIT AND MAYBE AVOID THE WHOLE MESS... AND WE'LL HAVE ANOTHER YEAR BEFORE I GO ON ACTIVE DUTY."

SHE STOOD UP SUDDENLY AND STOOD WITH BACKSIDES TO THE FIRE, LOOKING AT DANIEL.

"LET'S GO TO MY PLACE," SHE SAID AND PUT ON THE COAT WITHOUT A PAUSE. "MOTHER SAID YOU HAVEN'T COME BY FOR A WHILE. 'DON'T ACT LIKE A STRANGER,' STRANGER."

THEY SPED AWAY IN THE BEIGE SEDAN AS SWOLLEN GRAY SKIES RUSHED PAST THEM. CAROL PULLED INTO THE LONG CURVING DRIVEWAY. THEY WALKED UP THE STEPS AND THROUGH WHITE

COLONNADES TO THE SCULPTED FRONT DOOR. FUMBLING COLD KEYS, CAROL WINKED AT DANIEL AS SHE OPENED THE DOOR AND WALKED INTO THE DARKENING HALLWAY.

"MOTHER!"

THEY WALKED OVER AN ORIENTAL RUG TOWARD THE REAR OF THE HOUSE AND TOWARD THE BRUNCH ROOM. FRANCINE ENTERED THE HALL AT THE OPPOSITE END WITHOUT SPEAKING AND SAUNTERED TOWARD THEM WITH HIGHBALL GLASS IN HAND.

"THERE YOU ARE. HI, MOM," CAROL SAID. "I BROUGHT YOU A PRESENT," THEN SHE HURRIED UP THE STAIRCASE TO DRESS.

TIPSY FRANCINE GREETED DANIEL WITH A SMILE AND A MOIST HANDSHAKE.

"YOU'RE LOOKING WELL," FRANCINE SAID THEN SIPPED FROM THE GLASS.

"LIKE A DRINK? STILL SIPPING ON WILD TURKEY, DANNY BOY?"

"THANKS. IT'S GOOD TO SEE YOU."

DANIEL STUDIED HER FROM BEHIND AS SHE LED THE WAY IN HER LIGHT, FLOWERY DRESS.

"IT'S AMAZING HOW MUCH YOU AND CAROL LOOK ALIKE," HE SAID AND BLUSHED.

"WHY THANK YOU, DANIEL. I DO MY BEST TO KEEP UP... YOU'RE NOT GETTING TOO SERIOUS ABOUT HER, ARE YOU? SHE'S NOT READY TO MAKE A NEST YET."

CAROL BOUNDED IN ON THE WOOD FLOOR IN TIGHT JEANS AND A SWEATER.

"WHAT ARE YOU TWO UP TO," SHE SAID WITH MISCHIEVOUS SUSPICION.

AFTER A DRINK AND SMALL TALK DANIEL AND CAROL DROVE THROUGH ORANGE GROVES TO THE HIGHWAY. STREET LAMPS SHED WAVES OF IRIDESCENT LIGHT IN THE MIST. DANIEL LOOKED OUT THE SIDE WINDOW, QUIETLY WATCHING REFLECTIONS OF HIS HALF-LIT FACE EACH TIME ANOTHER LIGHT POLE PASSED.

THEY KISSED AND DANIEL WALKED INTO HIS HOUSE.

WITHIN AN HOUR, THOUGH, UNABLE TO STUDY, HE GOT ON HIS
MOTORCYCLE AND FLAILED AGAINST THE WIND AND RAIN.

FRANCINE GREETED HIM AT THE DOOR, DRESSED IN THE SUMMER
DRESS. THEY TOUCHED HANDS AND FRANCINE LED HIM UP THE STAIRS.

"CAROL AND HER FATHER LEFT TO DO SOME CHRISTMAS SHOP-
PING."

Corns kicked up small dust clouds as he walked and chuckled,
talking in a jesting whisper with Willard. Daniel stuck his head out
of the low tent to see the tall black. Willard smiled and bent over,
trying to get Daniel to hit fists in the intricate black greeting.
Willard settled for a regular handshake then stood up and looked
at Corns quizzically.

"He's definitely white," Willard said then grinned. "Better be
cool if you want to stay cool," he said and looked at Daniel.

"Move on over," Corns said to Daniel as he bent to crawl into
the tent. "Me and my main man are ready to do a little partying."

The trio sat hunched over and forward, filling the small space.

Corns handed Daniel a letter.

"Nice you got mail from The World so fast, Doc," Willard said.
"Smell's like a chick wrote it."

Willard pulled a pint of stateside whiskey from his deep jungle
fatigue pocket. A look of surprise came over Daniel's face.

"What's with him?" Willard said to Corns, then took a swig.
"You a teetotaler?"

Corns chuckled and studied Daniel.

"You're going to have to learn to party when you've got the
chance, Doc," Willard said and handed the bottle to Daniel. "And
you better goddamn well enjoy it," he said and grinned. "Cost me
a lot of piasters."

"Thanks," Daniel said as he gagged on the warm liquor.

Corns lit a tightly rolled joint, drew in smoke from it, then
passed it to Willard.

"I bet you're a regular tripper, aren't you, Doc?" Willard said
before drawing in a chest full of smoke."

"I try," Daniel said and took the joint from Willard.

Corns burst the smoke out in a laugh.

"Hey," he said and sighed. "I'm the only jokester around here. You want to be a comedian," he said and smiled at Willard, "you better find another squad, in another platoon."

"Oh shit be careful Doc this jokers jealous and his ego's as big as a bucking waterbo and he ain't even rich or white," Willard said then hit Corns mid-thigh with a fist.

"Doc!" Corns said in maudlin seriousness. "This nigger. I mean, this very dark Negro type asshole... Well, I think you should kick his ass for picking on me. What say? Let's do it together."

"Here," Daniel said and sipped on the bottle, then handed it to Willard. "You guys always carry on like this?"

"Go on, Doc," Corns said and coughed. "Take care of this nigger for me."

"Doc's got to be smarter than that," Willard said, then pushed Corns over.

"This is some fine, fine smoke," Daniel said. "Thanks."

"Thank that little mama-san down the hill," Willard said. "Sold ten of them to me for ten bucks. Bitch would sell her daughter for a buck."

"There's an idea," Corns said. "I'll go first!" he said and chuckled.

"Aren't we being a little too open about this?" Daniel asked Corns.

"We've been here a long time, Doc... We do what we've got to do when we've got to do it. When we're in the rear like this, people leave us to recuperate."

"Survival, Doc," Corns said as he lit a cigarette. "We survive however we can," he said then took a freshly lit joint from Willard. "You'll see soon enough. We're going back in tomorrow, just watch."

"Enough of that shit, man," Willard said and took a gulp from the bottle. "Let's party."

"I thought I was," Corns said and burned the hair on Willard's arm with the tip of his cigarette.

"Ouch!" Willard said as he jerked away. "See what kind of shit I've got to put up with in this squad," he said to Daniel. "But I'm stuck. Can't do anything about it... one, because he's the squad leader... and two, even though he's the squad leader, we're the baddest ass squad in this piece of stinking shit country. I mean, for Chris'sake, even Uncle Ho knows who I am."

Corns laughed and slapped Daniel on the knee.

Daniel chuckled, relaxed, with eyes bloodshot but gleaming.

"That's why ol' Uncle Ho keeps coming around, Doc," Corns said to Daniel. "Knows there's nothing but a skinny ol' nigger humpin' around in the bush like an ol' skinny assed bear."

Willard grabbed Corns and they wrestled in the small tent. Daniel lay against the other side of the tent and laughed without sound in a stoned glee. After a minute Willard managed to pin back the shoulders of burly Corns.

"Okay, nigger," Corns said between gasps for breath, "you win... Now give me some of that whiskey."

Willard took a final slug from the bottle and handed the empty to Corns.

They finished another joint then Corns and Willard crawled out of the tent to find more booze.

Corns stood up outside the tent and stretched, then bent over to peer in at Daniel.

"Be careful of those crazy white Southern boys while we're gone, Doc. I need a good Doc close by when shit hits. Don't let those crazy red-necks get at you before we get in the bush."

"Why?" Daniel said, looking up into the broad black face.

Willard leaned forward and said, "Because they don't like niggers, Doc." He said it seriously. "You're part of our killing team now. But they'll mess with you, just as sure as shit, for being with us."

"I have football buddies at home who're black," Daniel said.

"Just watch yourself," Corns said, then the two blacks walked away.

Willard stopped abruptly and Corns stopped with him. Willard walked the several steps back to the tent and bent over.

"You any good with that pea-shooter?" he asked, referring to the .45 in the shoulder holster.

"Why?" Daniel asked. "I'm a medic. The Geneva Convention says..."

"Forget the Geneva fucking Convention, Doc," Willard said. "Are you any good with that thing or not?"

Daniel paused, looking into Willard's eyes.

"Top three percent," Daniel said, then glanced at Corns. "But I'm a corpsman..."

Willard and Corns backed up then looked at each other with ironic smiles of understanding.

"Doc, gimme one of those cigarettes you're so proud of," Corns said slowly and took one from the pack extended by Daniel, then walked away quietly with Willard.

Daniel looked out of the tent at the sun setting behind distant green mountains. He lay back and opened the letter from Francine. A brief note wished him well, said to come home soon, but that Carol was already seeing other guys. Daniel burned the envelope and letter. He thought about Francine and Carol and wished for home.

As deep dusk set in Daniel crawled from the tent and stretched tall, looking at the river at the bottom of the large hill and down, across a wide grassy area. The dusty road led through grassy flatland, over a series of knolls, then into the hundred-foot wide river. Beyond the river the road turned into a muddy path leading into and between two jagged mountains that formed a horseshoe with the river at its mouth. He lit a cigarette and gazed at the purplish blue river as if in a trance.

"How are ya," a voice said from behind Daniel, startling him.

Daniel turned to face four whites who formed a semicircle facing in on Daniel.

"Hello," Daniel said, "how's it going?"

The Southerner spoke as the others were silent:

"Okay, Doc," he said in a Southern drawl, "but we'd like to talk to you."

"Shoot," Daniel said.

"We aim to," the southerner said and looked at a cohort. "We're pretty new over here ourselves, Doc. And we think we ought to stay separate as much as possible."

"Separate?" Daniel said, checking out the three companions.

"You know what I mean, Doc... You can stay with us... and away from them... Sure, you got to treat 'em if they get hit, but you can stay with us, down the hill."

"Corns is the squad leader of the squad I'll be moving with. And his buddy Willard knows what's going on. I figure I should stay close to them."

"I said you can stay with us," the curly-haired southerner said.

"I'm already set up here, thanks. And it's getting dark."

"You can say that again," Willard said as he weaved his way around the tent and up next to Daniel. "We plan to keep the evening friendly."

"You boys got a problem?" Corns said, coming up behind Daniel.

"No. I reckon not," the curly-haired white said. "We'll be seeing you guys tomorrow, hear?"

"Yeh, I hear," Corns said.

The whites moved down the hill in a group.

Corns smacked Daniel on the shoulder with an open hand in jest.

"But I don't like what I hear," Corns said.

Corns and Willard gave each other a knowing glance.

"Best not get that shit in your head, Doc... We're you're buddies... You'll see," Corns said.

"Those jerks are about as much like me," Daniel said seriously, "as my skin is black."

Willard chuckled quietly then crawled in the tent.

"I'm sleeping here, Doc," Willard said as Daniel and Corns crawled in.

Willard uncapped a bottle of South Vietnamese whiskey and handed it to Corns.

"Here, Doc," he said, handing Daniel the bottle, "forget it. It ain't all that bad... Come on," he said, lighting a match to a joint that drooped from Corns' mouth.

Corns took a drag, handed the joint to Daniel, then lit a candle.

"You sure you want to spot us with that light?" Willard said. "I don't need a frag for dinner."

Daniel studied Corns.

"What the hell," Corns said, then took a swig. "I got luck."

Willard chuckled.

"Here, bro'," Willard said, "give me some of that whiskey... My middle name's 'luck,' like yours."

"Well, shit," Daniel said, reaching for the bottle. "I can use some of that myself."

Willard and Corns laughed.

When the candle stub burned out, the trio lay tucked up into fetal positions inside the tent and slept until dawn.

●   ●   ●

While the trio slept, John R. Murwood, Captain, USMC, also slept. He was a man who never wavered once he made a decision. An order was the ultimate decision. He followed orders and he made sure his men did too.

Across camp, Clay Brown wasn't dreaming. He was thinking about his buddy, Jimmy.

Clay was as black as the sky. He made no shadows or noise as he inched his way through the low tents. He held a buddy's razor-sharp bowie knife.

"Murwood sent Jimmy in, Murwood sent Jimmy in," he repeated in a murmur only he could hear.

He stopped at Murwood's tent and looked around, then lifted the tent flap. Within seconds he was outside again, looking around, crouching down and wiping the bloody blade clean in the dust. Ever so quietly he slipped away and through the night. He crawled back into his tent without waking his buddy. He slid the huge knife in his buddy's pack.

●   ●   ●

Sunup. Daniel felt coolness on his face as he awoke. He rolled over, lifted the tent's edge and looked down the hill. He pictured himself floating down the Vietnamese river in an inner tube, wearing cutoffs as a fifteen-years-old.

Outside the small tents men were stretching off the hardness of the ground and soundness of their foreign sleep. Some were hunched over C-ration cans of food and coffee and hot cocoa.

Daniel felt a tension in the air, like a thick enveloping cloud of crisscrossing mental energy that reached up from the ground to just above their heads. There was a sense in the strangely slow morning air that a long operation was beginning. The weathered vets of the bush looked coolly, moved coolly. The newbies looked about suspiciously, like young women walking down dark city streets. No orders had yet been given. But intuition filled the air like a mist. Daniel felt it and looked about suspiciously, trying to act coolly, trying to look about coolly, like Willard and Corns.

Corns kept stirring his coffee, constantly moving a C-ration can atop a blue-based flame.

Willard polished his M-14 rifle barrel with a cloth he kept in a dry and clean nook of his pack.

Daniel sat on his haunches and learned the fine art of imagination while preparing and eating the monotonous canned food. He still liked beans 'n' franks.

The expected orders came.

Gradually, one by one, the tents came down and men began gathering in squads and platoons. Loaded down like mules ready for a long trip, the men walked down the dusty hill toward its base. It seemed to Daniel that they were all moving instinctively, without orders, toward the knolls at river's edge that marked the beginning of a long hump. They stared grimly at the river that glistened light purplish blue in the morning light. They squinted to see beyond, into the dense foliage of the bush in the huge mountainous horseshoe.

· · ·

Daniel waited to cross the river in a line. He was absorbed in afterimages of the light purplish water sparkling like a string of gems in front of him. He shifted and reshifted his hundred-pound pack on knotted shoulder and back muscles. He looked up into the mountains, then farther up, into the sky, and saw the reflections of the river water in the sky, like a surrealistic vision, with men crossing through the river, waist-high on some, chest-high on others.

The first squad was nearly out of the river and into light brush on the opposite bank. Corns' squad started into the water from the muddy bank with Corns leading the way. Halfway across the river, most of the squad stretched out to the water's glassy edge. Corns' eye reflected the sun as he turned to check on his troops. Daniel moved through the glittering water as if in a glowing yet bad dream.

In a burst like unnatural lightning the air cracked open around Daniel. He choked on the breath of air he was taking in as North Vietnamese soldiers poured in machine gun fire from sandbagged nests in the deep green mountains of the horseshoe. Within seconds the tense but dreamlike morning became a perverse nightmare.

Groans and shouts of pain came from the brush across the river. The first squad was chopped up and trapped. The Marine in front of Daniel, one of the Southern whites from the evening before, sank in the water like a sandbag, as if he were trying to hide. The head of the man quickly bobbed back to the surface, attached only by throat skin and sending off inky red clouds into the water.

"Get out! Go Back!" Corns shouted, his voice quavering. "Get out! Go back!"

They turned and hurried back to the riverbank.

"Fucking nightmare! Fucking nightmare!" Daniel said over and over as he tried to change adrenaline panic to calmness.

"Like running through molasses! Like molasses!" he whispered to himself as he dragged himself onto the muddy bank with all his water-heavy gear. He looked back and saw another of the southerners ripped open from behind. The body sank then bobbed to the waterline. It floated downriver beyond the mouth of the horseshoe and into the jungle.

The battalion dug into the dozens of serrated knolls leading to the muddy riverbank. A thick qualm permeated the moist air around the Marines. Corns, Willard, Daniel and the rest of the squad made it back to the knolls closest to the river. The entire first squad was chopped into the muddy soil on the opposite bank except for two. Their bodies floated down the river.

Adrenaline created keen vision and a muffled hysteria.

No one yet saw the wounded Marine lying under a bush with legs in the river and upper body on the muddy bank. Everyone was behind a knoll.

The machine gun fire ceased all at once and an almost breathless quiet filled the air.

Suddenly a miraculous survivor on the other side of the river sprang up through the bush. He jumped into the river and began trying to run through waist-high water. He began a frantic dive forward, but a single shot from a North Vietnamese AK-47 rifle struck him in the spine. He landed in the water in a grotesque swirl, his back mashed through his stomach and into the water. As if on cue, the Marines opened up from behind the muddy knolls. Unable to see the source of the incoming fire, they sprayed lucky bullets into imaginary machine gun nests.

The firing ceased on both sides of the river at once. The lone survivor, the Marine mashed from behind as he dove, floated downstream after untangling from a clump of soggy branches at river's edge. Those that saw him from behind the knolls paid a silent homage to him with wide open eyes. Daniel shuddered as he watched the body float away. He was beyond the fright of the riverbed now. The surrealism of it all puzzled him. He tried to shake the sensation that it was the beginning of a long, drawn out dream.

That morning Daniel had met the Marine who'd just floated downstream. He was a farm boy from Nebraska named Chris. He remembered the blond farmer because of his nickname, Corn. It was so much like Corns. He remembered Corn talking.

"The whole thing is bullshit, this Vietnam, Doc. But, by God, we're the Green fucking Machine and we're gonna kick the slants outta them slopeheads." Then Corn said he was going down the hill to "rendezvous" with the rest of the scared but tough machine.

The string of words uttered earlier by Corn now slipped up against Daniel's mind like slivers of ice and he began shaking. Afterimages ran in his mind like water reflections. He saw the farm boy's blond arms and fingers clutching at the air. He saw the inner scream fade before it reached his face. He saw life float away in the glittering water. Daniel stopped shivering as a wave of numbness overtook him.

"Corpsman up! Corpsman up!"

The call to immediate emergency action cleared the numbness and replaced it with another jolt of adrenaline. Daniel snapped out of a seeming daydream. He dumped his pack and jumped up with his medical bag. He ran through the choppy mud toward the wounded Marine whose lower body lay submerged in the water. Daniel lifted branches of the bush and ripped open the man's flak jacket and shirt. The raspy sound of a sucking chest wound became a reality to his ears. Then all of a sudden mud around them started popping up in little chunks that splattered all over their fatigues and faces.

In one very small moment there was a blur for Daniel, a blink of his eyes. He felt as if he were an all-seeing being dressed in the shades of camouflage. His perception took on imprints from some eerie primordial world. He stopped unwrapping a large gauze bandage, suddenly seeing himself in slow motion. The unearthly crystalline images of his vision seemed to be a branding of his mind. The images before him were vision cast in the forces of passion and will, in the colors of an otherworldly rainbow. He forced the vision away, the will to "Buck up! Buck up and fight!" pulsing through his mind.

He unwrapped the battlefield bandage with clawlike fingers suddenly strong enough to grasp and crush arms or necks.

Milliseconds upon nanoseconds filled to bulging with the realization that the mud was flying up in violent chunks. The distant sounding thud-thud-thuds of machine gun fire came to Daniel through his vision. Machine gun rounds were ripping at the muddy bank all around them. He saw blood gushing from a new wound, spraying onto him from the man's thigh with the force of an artery. Was it the other man's wound or his own?

He couldn't feel his own body.

"Machine gun fire!" he yelled in a hysterical whisper.

In his altered vision he saw far off into the branches and trunks of bushes and trees thousands of yards away. His eyes were like out-of-control machines, looking through a light green tint at everything in magnified detail. He watched as men crouched near the top of the horseshoe mountain. They were firing their weapons at him.

A jungle green tank jerked up and over the closest knoll and lunged to a stop in the mud near Daniel and the wounded grunt.

Daniel looked at it as if he were staring at a huge metal dinosaur. He hooked the grunt's arm around his neck and dragged him toward the back end of the tank. Daniel and the grunt were one long step from the tank's protection when another machine gun round ripped into the grunt's back. His body jolted, then sagged. Daniel's crazed eyes searched the immediate environment like a vicious machine. The tank fired a round from its barrel that shook the ground and sent off a percussion like thunder. The tank barked another round and Daniel focused on its graffiti-scrawled name, "Bucephalus."

He could feel death reaching out for him. He drew in a last breath and stretched his face upward, into the late morning sky. He gazed into a spire of sunlight and his whole life craned upward, as if in prayer.

Two Marines ran from the nearest knoll. They picked up the dead Marine by the arms and legs and carried him away. Daniel envisioned a temescal.

"There it is," he said and sighed. "The temescal."

Minutes later he found himself lying behind the same knoll from which he'd run to help the wounded grunt. He was laughing but there was no sound. He looked at himself from afar and made his jaw stop moving. He lit a cigarette with trembling hands and surveyed himself with medic's fingers, then laughed out loud. Then he bent his face into an elbow joint and sobbed.

"Put that cigarette out you dumb motherfucker!" someone yelled. "They'll spot you."

The command was like an elixir shot directly into his veins. He took a drag on the cigarette, then looked up.

"Screw it," he said, and took another drag. "Like Uncle Ho said, 'Fuck 'em. Let's fight.'"

Platoons and their squads were moving up, closer and closer to the river, as the violent commotion continued. Another corpsman, a newby, ran up then dropped next to Daniel. He looked anxiously at Daniel as he pulled his medical bag close to him.

"Corpsman up! Corpsman up goddamnit!"

The other corpsman jumped up and ran out into new volleys of machine gun fire.

Corns came near Daniel in leaps and slides. He gave instructions to his men with hand signals.

"Get ready to go downstream," Corns told Daniel in a whisper. "Haul your ass through that patch of mud then jump your ass into the clump of trees."

Corns jumped up to run first but plopped back down on his back when he heard a thunderous shriek above them. Two Phantom jets shot by at tremendous speed. The jets circled, then came back for the kill. Daniel watched with a deep sense of pleasure as burning napalm jelly spread through the horseshoe mountains. Corns and Daniel hid their faces away from the heat of the fireclouds across the river.

Corns ordered his men to run to the clump of trees. The waves of deadly machine gun fire had been silenced by the napalm, but a lone sniper remained. Corns took off through the mud like a fullback. A sniper's round missed his head by inches just before he jumped into the clump of trees. An entire company opened up on the invisible sniper. Next to run was Willard, a sprinter made into a sluggard by his gear and the mud. The sniper fired again but missed. A company of grunts opened up again.

"Buck!... Buck!... Buck up!" Daniel heard Corns shout.

Daniel ran through the choppy mud feeling suspended from time and space, his eyes wild with resolve. He ran with the spirit of a tight end tailing in the game and ready to catch the long pass down the middle of an artificially lighted field.

"What a joke! What a fucking joke!" he shouted halfway through the muddy run.

He heard Corns and Willard laughing in guffaws.

"Give 'em hell, Doc! Give 'em hell!" Corns shouted.

He broad-jumped through the last ten feet of mud, landing in the thicket on his pack.

"The sniper must've got it just before you took off, Doc," Corns said and sighed.

The long distance firefight was over. The troubled tension in the air eased into wariness, weariness, then fatigue. Daniel sat on a rock in a stupor that came over him as the firefight broke. The squad moved back to the knolls but he didn't notice.

"You goddamn coward!"

The curly-haired Southerner shouted from another dimension into Daniel's woozy face. The words brought Daniel out of an inner haze. He looked around and saw that the two of them were separated from the others.

"Get up and fight!" the Southerner hissed, spitting into Daniel's face. "You coward! Get up and fight!... That was my friend died in front of you. In the river, asshole... Should of been you!... Should of been you!"

Daniel imagined his grandfather telling him how to punch. He grabbed mud in his left hand and threw it into the ruddy face. As the Southerner brought up both hands to wipe away the muck, Daniel slammed his right fist into a jutting jaw. He heard the chin snap and felt it shatter. The man crumpled to his knees, bent over and passed out with his forehead sunk into the mud.

"I'll kill you next time," Daniel said, then picked up his gear and walked along the riverbank toward the knolls, shaking his head.

Corns got back to the clump of trees to check on Daniel just as Daniel hit the bellicose Southerner. He let Daniel walk away.

"Corpsman up!" Corns yelled.

Daniel turned to watch another medic run along the bank. He sat down on a rounded knoll and stared at the sparkling river water.

"Shut up, Doc"

Daniel stood in a line stretching into the same jungly mountains that blistered with gunfire and napalm the day before. His platoon was one of the last to cross through the purplish water of the river. The advance teams of the line were already passing by the scorched North Vietnamese machine gun nests. The sickly thick air pushed them past the charred enemy bodies. Daniel again entered the waterway. Halfway across he turned and caught a glimpse of Willard, who was just entering the water from the choppy bank. Willard's face was cast down near the sparkling water as he strained to pull himself and his gear through the flowing water. He noticed Daniel's glance and looked up, then smiled.

Daniel was out of the river safely except for two leeches that clung to his buttocks. He trudged through beaten back foliage, his boots heavy with mud and moisture. He approached the first burned out nest of dead enemy soldiers. He watched, aghast, as veteran grunts hunched over in the sandbagged pit and cut off charred ears.

The battalion humped on and on, up, down and around hills and mountains, and Daniel hummed "Summertime." They marched on in the wet heat of the shade then out into clearings where the sun created an oven within their helmets and flak-jackets, in and out of entangled vines and leaves that grew up from the yellowish earth like writhing snakes. The men drank their two canteens of water and humped on, cotton mouthed. The snakelike line of men moved through the jungle, in and out of the sunshine, in and out of sniper's range. But no one seemed to feel like fighting and the line moved on.

By late afternoon the air was oven hot. Water was long since gone for most of the grunts. They walked on, through tall clumps of elephant grass that slashed at fingers and forearms like rusty dull razors. Then came the order for a reversal, for them to march back to the river they had crossed that morning. The combinations of cussing and groaning were mighty, despite spreading cotton mouth. They waited on the sides of trails to begin retracing their steps. Daniel discovered the two leeches swollen to the size of thumbs on his butt. Another grunt lit a Marlboro and touched the lit tip to the leeches, making them plop to the ground, where Daniel stomped on them with his boot heel and watched his blood spurt out onto the mud. The reverse march began and Daniel walked along in an irritable daze that was like a case of minor delirium. Images of his Marine training flashed in his hot head:

"WE'RE GOING TO STRIP YOU DOWN!" THE TOP GI SHOUTED INTO DANIEL'S FACE.

DANIEL LOOKED OUT OVER THE BLACKTOP PARADE GROUND WITH DOZENS OF OTHER HOSPITAL CORPSMEN STANDING AT ATTENTION. THE FLUSHED DI GLANCED DOWN AT DANIEL'S NAME TAG THEN QUICKLY REFOCUSED HIS EYES ON DANIEL'S.

"THIS HERE'S THE MARINES, BUCK," BRISLING SAID IN A MENACING

WHISPER. "THIS AIN'T THE NAVY, BOY. WE DON'T WANT TO FLOAT AROUND THE WORLD AT UNCLE SAM'S EXPENSE. HELL NO! WE'RE HERE TO KILL PEOPLE. YOU OUGHT TO ENJOY THAT, BOY... YOU'RE A KILLER, AREN'T YOU, BOY?"

"THOSE SQUINTY WEIRD EYES. THOSE SQUINTY WEIRD EYES," DANIEL SAID TO HIMSELF, WITHOUT SOUND.

THE LAST DRESS INSPECTION AT CAMP PENDLETON WAS ALREADY INTO ITS THIRD HOUR. DANIEL WAS IN AGONY AFTER STANDING ERECT ON THE HOT BLACK PAVEMENT IN SUMMER SUN. AFTER BRISLING MOVED DOWN THE LINE, DANIEL IMAGINED HIMSELF A TOTEM POLE, A SPIRITUAL COLUMN OF PAST CARVED BY EXPERIENCE, GLARING INTO THE FUTURE. HE SAW THE OTHER CORPSMEN IN THE SAME VISION, EACH STANDING MOTIONLESS AND IN PAIN, WAITING TO BE FED LIKE WOOD INTO SOUTHEAST ASIAN BONFIRE. HE STOOD THERE AFTER MONTHS OF RIGOROUS MENTAL AND PHYSICAL TRAINING, AFTER MAKING THE DECISION TO BE A MEDIC. EVERY NIGHT SLEEP CAME ONLY AFTER LONG DOUBTING MINUTES AND HOURS. HE THOUGHT ABOUT GETTING OUT SOMEHOW, BUT ALWAYS ENDED UP WITH AN INNER DETERMINATION TO STICK IT OUT. SLEEP THEN CAME.

THE NEXT DAY AT DAWN BRISLING STOOD BY HIS SECOND TIER BUNK, SHOUTING.

"BUCK, YOU'RE NOT GOING TO MAKE IT. THEY'RE GOING TO CHEW YOUR ASS UP AND SPIT IT OUT IN THE MUD, BOY... I WANT YOU TO KNOW, ASS-LICK, THAT I JUST GOT YOUR ORDERS. YOU'RE GOING RIGHT UP INTO THE DMZ. ME TOO, BUCK. I'LL BE RUNNING YOU, BOY."

The men received new orders to halt the hump and dig in on steep hillsides. The grunts soon gained a second wind and began digging foxholes and setting up defensive perimeters with claymore mines. Daniel discovered a way to make a lean-to tent with his single poncho, then watched the men hacking away at the hillside below him. Shouts of joy rang out from the swollen-tongued grunts as a first chopper hovered above them. The first net to touch ground contained a crate of hot beer.

Corns trudged up the hillside to Daniel's tent with four cans of beer, his face still streaming with sweat. He set the cans down and snapped one open, watching it as it foamed over. They exchanged only glances. Corns pulled out a flask and filled the beer can to the top with gin.

"Hell of a day, Doc," he said, stuffing the flask into a deep pants pocket. "Know when we get beer, Doc?"

"Oh, shit, I can feel this one coming. When?" asked Daniel.

"The day before we're expected to make major contact. Happens every time... Only time it didn't happen was on the Ridge."

Corns and Daniel looked down at clusters of men digging and sipping their one- or two-can ration of beer.

"That was a nightmare today, Corns. I feel like shit."

"I know, Doc... You'll get used to it... The monsoon rains will be setting in soon. Got to kick some ass before the gooks lay low... You did okay yesterday, Doc. And now you haven't got those crazy whites to worry about. That curly haired bastard is out of here for a long time, thanks to you... I heard talk you might get a citation for yesterday."

"What, for messing up that guy's face?... Citation for what?"

"Being brave, Doc. You get medals for that kind of shit, man."

"Kind of like Brownie Points? They should give me a Silver Star just for getting rid of that Southern red neck."

Corns sighed and finished the gin-beer in a long gulp.

"You're not digging a foxhole, Doc?"

"When shit hits I'll be up running around anyway, right?"

"It's your ass."

"I know."

Corns walked up the steep hill sideways ten yards.

Daniel watched more choppers hover then lower the huge rope nets full of water, food, and ammo. He grabbed his canteens, ready to descend the hill for some precious liquid, when Willard came up the hill walking sideways for footing. He handed Daniel a full canteen, from which Daniel took a long soothing drink.

Platoon Sergeant Lockwood, nicknamed The Cutter, came up

the hill from the grassy LZ at a straightforward lope. His whole being exuded fierceness and tenacity as he bent over into Daniel's face.

"So you're Doc Buck," he said and glanced at Willard. Willard nodded then moved obliquely up the hill to Corns. "You did good yesterday, Doc. But don't go hitting on my men no more, no matter what you think. Got it?"

Daniel just stared into the tanned and creased face in front of him.

"I said, don't mess with my people, no matter how fucked up they are. You got it?"

"Yeh, I guess so."

"Okay. We can use a good Doc. Now why in the hell ain't you digging a foxhole?"

"When shit hits the fan, I'll be up working anyway."

The Cutter studied Daniel, then turned to check on business at the bottom of the steep hill.

"Why do they call you 'The Cutter,' Sergeant Lockwood?"

Lockwood smiled a smile of dark humor, laughed in snort, then stood up straight.

"Because I cut things off... I cut things off that ain't needed... Are you dumb or what. They're sending over newbies who think and ask questions first now, right?"

"I just want to do my job, Sergeant."

"The first thing to learn in your job you learned yesterday. Stay scared. The next thing is to get mad... You don't look mad, Doc, just scared... And another thing. My name ain't 'Sergeant.' It's 'The Cutter' to you." Lockwood started to walk away then stopped and looked at Daniel. "That means you're a friend. Let's stay friends, Doc. You wouldn't do so good trying to break my face."

The Cutter loped sideways down the hill, using a low voice to bark out greetings and advice to men digging in. He tossed one of his beers to someone who was trying to dig through roots in the clayey soil.

Soon the hillside camp was silhouetted in a sweltering jungle dusk. Daniel warmed a can of pork slices, dusk-dreaming, staring out at the bush. He finished the pork slices and ended his meal by drinking the syrup from a can of peaches. When darkness came he was fast asleep, wearing his boots.

• • •

Leech-sized raindrops smacked onto Daniel's poncho, then onto his poncho liner and his face just before dawn. He awoke quickly and passed from jungle dreams to reality. Light slowly filled the air and he looked out into the barrage of monsoon rain. His gear was covered in mud washed down from the freshly dug foxhole of Willard and Corns.

"They'll wait until this shit stops for sure," he said in a sigh to himself then took off his dog tags to use his C-ration can opener on a grand breakfast of round crackers and jam. He swallowed chemically treated water and almost gagged. But the liquid felt so good he drank a third of a canteen, followed by five cigarettes.

When there was enough daylight for Marines to see their boots the long march began. Daniel saw grunts working their way up another steep, slippery hillside through a grove of rotting trees. A man moved up on all fours ten to fifteen feet, then slid back on his belly. Then up again.

Hours that seemed like eons later, it was late afternoon and they were told to dig in atop the mountain they were climbing. Foxholes being dug filled with foul water nearly as fast as entrenching tools pulled mud out. Daniel spread out a poncho atop runny mud and tried desperately to light a last wet cigarette with wet matches. Meanwhile veteran grunts scurried near Daniel, moving about in the rain as if it were the perfect opportunity to shower and have a smoke at the same time.

Daniel rolled up inside his nylon poncho liner and ate ham slices. He licked ham juice and mud from his lips then flipped the liner back. He looked out into the dusk and saw a tired fire team setting up a perimeter down the hill in the mud above a giant felled tree. Over the crest of the mountain, a gunship hovered in the air and fired a last volley of rockets into the viny jungle canopy before hurrying to a forward base for the night.

Sergeant Nicholas Reese, a lifetime member of the Green Machine, just back from R&R in Sydney, spread out his gear on a poncho near Daniel. Daniel looked up and realized that he must be near the company command post, but he barely noticed Reese because he craved sleep. He flipped up half of his muddy poncho over himself and wiggled himself into the mud. Reese muttered to himself about his wife. "The bitch runs away with a nigger," Daniel heard him say. "Damn it," Reese mumbled to himself.

Daniel had just fallen asleep when he felt a nudge on his boot. It startled him but he quickly calmed down. It could have been a rat. It could be an NVA, ready to charge into camp. He worked his hand slowly under the muddy poncho without a sound and put his fingers on the .45, pulling it slowly form the shoulder holster. He waited but heard nothing, and relaxed. A tap on his boot brought him to awakened life, but he couldn't see anything because of the jungle darkness, not even his feet. He pointed the pistol and started to pull the trigger then suddenly remembered Reese. He let up on the trigger in horror. He decided as a final caution in his crazy quick analysis of the situation to shout out the sergeant's name, then fire one second later if there were no response.

"Reese!" he whispered.

"Yeh?" Reese said, half a second later.

"Oh... nothing," Daniel whispered, then slid the gun away. Within a minute he was again asleep, dreaming of blond women with painted red lips wearing fur coats. They smiled in their arrogant sashay down bright big city streets in The World. Monster drops of rain pounded on him throughout the night.

Daylight struggled to fill the soggy air as Daniel awoke, the poncho still flipped over him. The ground on the mountain was so slippery, and the hillside so steep, a grunt on perimeter slept on his back with feet propped up on a tree trunk. Daniel flipped open the poncho and a thin lime-green snake crawled out and wriggled away through the mud to a clump of bamboo.

He watched a tired grunt walk down a section of the hill to retrieve a claymore, the hand-operated mine that cut like the giant Scottish sword of legend at waist level. An NVA had turned it around and inserted his own firing cord during the night. Just as the grunt bent over to pick up the mine he was cut in half by the explosion.

Everyone awoke at once.

Daniel jerked up into a sitting position then slowly spread open the poncho while staring at the halved body as another platoon's medic ran up to help. Stealing glimpses at the coffee he prepared, he stared at the commotion down the hill. The fresh smell of smoke and burned flesh mingled with the mist and rain in the new morning air.

The grunts pulled themselves up into readiness and began slip-walking down the hill past the halved Marine that was covered by a muddy poncho. The grunts started humping toward a next mountain, where the gunship had fired rockets the evening before. Daniel waited by his sleeping spot for the point platoon to pass. Willard came up over the top of the mountain and smiled at Daniel. Willard's clothes were dry and it seemed unreal to Daniel.

"How you doing, Doc?" Willard asked as he set the butt of his rifle on top of his boot next to Daniel. "Still got your sense of humor?"

"Yeh, but I never thought about living like a jungle animal before... Night before last the mud seemed dirty. All I noticed last night was that it seems warm under my poncho."

Their platoon began filing by and the two fell in.

"Your doing okay for a white boy," Willard said as he began humping in the line. "Keep thinking about the rear, Doc. And some woman."

The hill became unworkable with steepness. Willard followed by Daniel slid down a slippery mud path. At the bottom of the long slide they were coated in mud except for Willard's M-14, which he twisted in the air like a talisman. They stopped in a crouch at the rapid bursts of a machine gun and several AK-47s just over the next rise. The first platoon entered onto a hair-pin curve as it descended into a tree-splintered gulch. The intense gun fire represented immediate fighting. All Daniel and Willard and the others could do was listen to the deafening staccato of the firefight from a short distance away.

"Seems like they're miles away, Willard," Daniel whispered. "But it's going on just over that hill. Can't be more than twenty to thirty yards from us."

"Be glad gook bullets can't go through the hill, that's all... We'll be up there soon enough," Willard said then forced a slight smile for Daniel's sake.

"I'm so scared I can't think right," Daniel said.

"I'm scared too, Doc... Don't sweat it. Death ain't so bad, especially when it's over there... and we're here... Fuck it, Doc. I'll protect you... you scuzzy low-life poor white trash."

Daniel snorted a laugh and looked up at Willard just as Corns and The Cutter crawled up to them.

"First platoon's down and bruised," The Cutter said. "Corns is taking you in... Doc, First Platoon's doc is frozen. You're going in first, with me. Corns, cut Willard loose. He's coming in with Doc Buck and me." The Cutter looked at Daniel for seeming long moments, then quickly at Corns. "We're gone," The Cutter said as he jumped up and lurched forward, loping into the gulch followed by Daniel then Willard.

Mortar rounds thudded amidst NVA positions and pandemonium pulsed in the heavy damp air. Twenty more mortar rounds tore up the ground like huge firecrackers exploding from under the mud. The air was so choked with smoke and misty rain that it was difficult to see. The Cutter moved slowly in a crouched walk, twisting his body from side to side as he stepped over felled bodies. AK-47 rounds crackled in a bush to the left of Daniel. The rounds whizzed by Daniel and ripped a dead grunt. The Cutter and Willard fired in the same split second on the barrel flash of the AK-47. Daniel saw the frozen corpsman and moved slowly toward him. He tried to pull the man's head out from his hands but the man's frightened strength made it impossible. Daniel stuck a needle through pants cloth into the man's thigh, squirting in a quarter-grain of morphine, then he wrote out a med-evac card and tied it to the man's blood-caked wrist.

An NVA with a bayonet attached to his Russian assault rifle sprang out of a bush at Daniel. As the NVA reared back to thrust, The Cutter began a banana clip at crotch level and zipped up the spine to the eyes. The creature wiggled in the mud irritably. Willard pointed the big rifle and blew off the creature's head into the mud. The Cutter signalled to Willard to save on ammo, and to stay with the frozen medic. He signalled Daniel to go forward with him. Just as they began to move, another NVA rushed at them from The Cutter's blind side. As The Cutter turned 180 degrees, Daniel pulled the .45 from the shoulder holster and fired one round.

The Cutter blew out.

"Now there's a crew cut, Doc," The Cutter whispered, looking at the face without a skull.

Daniel trembled as he slid the smoking pistol back into its leather case in his armpit.

The Cutter studied Daniel then motioned for them both to wait at the edge of the trail.

The firing stopped abruptly and they sensed that the NVA who survived moved quietly away like silent spirits through the jungle. Daniel saw a foot-long centipede with giant pincers climb atop the helmet of a dead grunt. It stretched and wiggled its yellow head in the air.

They were up and moving again, along the trail and through very intense quiet mist. The enormous crack-boom! of a grenade made them stop in mid-step along the undergrowth next to a slippery narrow trail. First Platoon's point man tripped a booby trap. He lost his face to the machete-chop of the NVA grenade that hung like man-made fruit. The man's life fluids leaked out onto the mud, filling his footprints in little pools.

• • •

Later, the three battalion companies surrounded a rugged mountain from three directions. Corns and his squad led Charlie Company into what looked like an open jungle graveyard. Only hours earlier several hundred Marines and at least as many NVA perished on the mountain outcroppings and in the mountain crevices and blind gulches. The mountain had been abandoned by both sides, until now. A once tree-covered mountain rose up in the mist denuded of its trees. Exploded trunks stuck up splintered in the air.

Daniel stood behind Corns and Willard as they stared up the slopes wide-eyed. Hundreds of bodies lined the face of the mountain. In some places there were clumps of bodies. Corns spoke softly into the radio handset and reported that all was quiet.

Corns looked distraught, ready to cry. Willard looked back at Daniel and shook his head. In a whisper Daniel said "Oh shit" so no one else could hear.

Orders came through to secure the area and dig in, to make ready for the next onslaught. Daniel gazed at the dark image before him, waiting for Corns or Willard to take the next move. His upper lip twitched uncontrollably in a tic several times then subsided.

Corns led the platoon up the slippery mountain. They climbed over uprooted trees and torn dead bodies. They froze as they heard running footsteps coming from behind them on the trail they controlled. It was Sergeant Reese from the company's platoon in the rear, carrying a double-barreled shotgun sawed off to less than a foot long. He ran up to Corns and started speaking very quickly in whispers.

"How'd that honky get a gun like that?" Willard said in an aside to Daniel.

Reese took the lead alone. Corns looked back at Willard with a glance of disgust and bewilderment. The overwhelming quiet of death on the mountain was interrupted only by the sloshy steps of cautious Marines led by a maniac with a shotgun.

Daniel walked up next to Willard, whose slow head movement from side to side never ceased, and touched him on the arm.

"This as bad as it seems, Willard?"

"Don't know, Doc. Never been here before... Seems bad to me... That wild man with the double-barrel ain't a good sign."

Corns moved up without making a sound and stuck his face next to Daniel's ear.

"Shut the fuck up, Doc," he whispered.

Corns looked at Willard then moved ahead, behind Reese.

"Fuck that nigger," Willard whispered to Daniel as they moved forward.

"A graveyard, Willard," Daniel whispered.

An hour later they saw daylight up ahead, through the mingling of tree stumps and misty rain. The top of the mountain was before them yet there was no firefight. Corns signalled for the squad to dig in then begin preparing an LZ. All of them tried to act as cool as the veterans, but the veterans of the bush more than the newbies, hacked widly at the ground, determined to get cover as quickly as possible. Reese came back out of the mist and hissed at Corns face-to-face.

"Wait a goddamn minute, Corporal. I rank here. I say we're going on, over the ridge!"

"Forget that, Sarg," said Corns in a whisper. "The Cutter says dig in, ready an LZ... You go on if you want."

"Spineless coward," Reese said, spit to his side, then dropped his gear and continued up the hill wearing only flak-jacket and pointing the shotgun forward.

Corns watched the mist where Reese had gone as the men dug in. Daniel helped Willard hack out a deep hole for the three of them.

"I found 'em! I found 'em!" they heard Reese shout.

Reese discovered two wounded NVA in a foxhole waiting to be given first aid treatment by their captors. Reese raised the gun and fired point-blank, then spit and laughed. He walked back down the mountainside wiping flecks of blood from his face and neck.

"What the hell you looking at!" Reese said to Corns.

Tears filled Corns' eyes as he stared the sergeant back down the hill. Corns lit a cigarette and cupped it, standing by himself looking into the mist.

By twilight the other two companies of the battalion moved on to other rises and gullies of the mountain, setting a trap, while Charlie Company took the high ground. Dusk settled in and Daniel dreaded the darkness of night. He stopped digging then looked down the mountain and shuddered.

"I feel 'em, Doc. I feel 'em down there," Willard said then eyed the M-14. "The gooks are gonna be pissed tonight."

Daniel, feeling like his nerves were coming through his skin, started stripping, cleaning and oiling the .45. He oiled the holster too. Willard stomped on the bottom of the new foxhole then pushed frags into the loose soil of the foxhole lip. The world suddenly gave way, into a huge explosion. Thirty feet behind them a napalmlike mortar round burst open. Daniel discovered himself curled into a fetal position whimpering like a scared puppy in the mud. No one seemed to know where the round came from or whose tube it was popped from. Two men were dead from the explosion, their bodies covered in horrible burns that bubbled even after life was snuffed from the bodies. Daniel tried to get up but his legs wouldn't work. He got up, wobbled for a step, then sank to his knees again, crying in fear and frustration. He folded into a fetal position again and sucked in the warmth of the mud through his skin. His own urine running down his own leg felt good to him.

Minutes later flares began popping in the sky and lighting the terrible ground from little parachutes. Daniel moved about treating the victims of the mortar blast. Then he watched as the last one was carried on a makeshift poncho-stretcher to the unsecured LZ atop the mountain. He got back to the foxhole to find his personal gear and some medical supplies sizzling in the light rain from the willie-peter of the mortar round. Corns and Willard were already in the foxhole staring forward. Daniel slid in next to them.

"Another Charlie Blood Ridge, Corns?" Daniel asked, still staring ahead with Corns.

Corns didn't answer.

"I sure hope not," Willard said to Daniel. "But I can feel it, Doc. Any minute now, I just bet ya... Motherfuckers!" and he spit onto the foxhole lip.

NVA mortar rounds began tearing open patches of earth starting at the bottom of the mountain and weaving into gulches and across rises. The pounding went on for fifteen minutes, using up a large amount of the enemy's ammo.

Five minutes into the barrage Daniel crawled from the hole to the sound of "Corpsman up!" He slid away, his body tracks squiggled on the mud. He made it to a tree stump and insculpted himself into the mud of the tree's bole. He looked up between explosions and saw Reese light up a cigarette between cupped hands. The jungle below Reese flared with tracers and Reese lay suddenly silent, a gamy target slumped over the edge of his foxhole, the shotgun laid across his pack with several extra rounds next to it. Daniel slid down to the foxhole and jumped in, then grabbed the pistol-length shotgun and the extra rounds. He pulled the .45 from the shoulder holster and threw it in the mud, then stuffed the stubby shotgun into the holster.

His muscles felt like electrified rubber as he fumbled across the muddy hillside. While illuminating flares popped in the sky, a new salvo of mortar rounds exploded at the base of the mountain and began moving up.

"Corpsman up!"

He got up and trotted down the hill toward the call. He noticed that few grunts were firing. Then he noticed that all of them were dead. The hill was relined in bodies from both sides. Unable to find the source of the scream for help, he belly-crawled back up the hillside. He still saw no one alive. He crawled on, past a pile of bodies. A little higher up the hill he saw Corns and Willard staring out from the foxhole in a daze. He watched as Corns handed Willard the flask, then Willard taking a swig and gagging.

"Nice work, Willard," Corns whispered while staring down the breathless hillside.

"Two niggers left. Come on, slopeheads," Willard said.

"Hey asshole!" Daniel whispered.

Corns and Willard whipped around with dead-eye glances then acknowledged Daniel's presence. They all opened their mouths as if laughing, without sound, and Daniel crawled along on his stomach with elbows and knees. He slid into the foxhole and they all stared forward, waiting. The last flare died out and the heavy silence continued in the smoky mist of the air.

"Getting your luck, eh, Doc?" Willard whispered.

"Better than medals, Doc," Corns said and snickered.

"That ain't luck in front of me," Daniel said. "Gimme that flask you're so proud of, Corns."

They heard rustlings on the trail below. They waited with guns up for the final send-off. Then a new batch of flares lit the mountain sky and a Marine walking point for another battalion came into view. The stealthy point man looked up at the mountain and stopped, then signalled with his M-16 for others to move forward.

"About time," Corns said in a normal voice, the first time he'd spoken above a whisper in many hours.

"Thanks for stopping by, you white puke," Willard said, still in a whisper.

The point man seemed to acknowledge Willard with a nod of

the head, looking up through the smoke and mist at the trio in the foxhole. More flares popped in the air and floated down in little parachutes. As the men of the new battalion crawled up the mountain the trio jumped out of the foxhole and stood watching, dumbfounded, in a daze. Lockwood came stomping down the hill and out of a cloud of smoky mist with the same, calm predatory expression on his face. His eyes were bloodshot with the approach of dawn, but he grinned.

"We're what's left of Charlie," he said to Corns while looking around at the dead ground, then at the fresh troops.

Daniel turned away from them to flip a cigarette butt behind him into the mud. A lone NVA jumped out of a foxhole with a long knife hefted over his head and ready to come down on Willard with a vengeance. In one quick pivot Daniel raised the stubby shotgun and fired point-blank. The heavy thunder and flash in front of him snapped his wrist. The barrel shot out a flame a short distance into the oriental face, then tore off the head.

The headless creature stretched out at Daniel's feet, twitching in the mud and spurting blood. Daniel watched, standing motionless. The smoky air puffed up around him like swirls of fog.

Corns and Willard slapped him on the back in thanks and congratulations, then they turned back to watch the arriving troops. He didn't hear them. He only gazed at the body that stretched in front of him like his shadow, watching the fleeting rhythm of life. His gut tightened up and he started to retch.

"We're brothers... blood brothers," he mumbled as he stared at the slain enemy.

"You got it right that time," Corns said and grinned at Daniel.

• • •

The world of the jungle continued to supply the leeches of war like a medieval doctor-butcher. More moments and more mountains moved by like dark clouds in a sky composed of unrelenting and bizarre strangeness. Dreary days of body bending drudgery punctuated by violent firefights embellished the grand still hunt.

Daniel lost his bearings during this slow chaotic grind that was thick with fear and fighting. He awakened and carried both medical supplies and the shotgun.

"Doc likes that shotgun," Corns said to Willard in a whisper as they checked a perimeter post one dark evening.

"No shit. Even sleeps with it."

"I think he's changed some since that first firefight," Corns said then smiled to himself.

"No shit."

The Grotto

Daniel sat on the ground with his back propped up against a bamboo hut, cigarette smoke drifting up past his face in the murky air. The interior of the hut lit up briefly as a rare breeze flipped open the doorway flap. He sipped from a bottle of South Vietnamese gutter whiskey and looked about with eyes that seemed to ache in irony as he sat at the corner of the Ville.

A day after arriving in the rear, Charlie Company was sent to guard a pro-American village in a relatively secure zone. It was a good time for the men to freshen up for the next foray into the DMZ. Except for one squad, the company holed up in an old French garrison that was thick-walled and safe. From there guards looked out over a hundred yards of mud and road to the Ville. The Ville consisted of dozens of bamboo huts roofed in palm leaves, each containing a family of displaced South Vietnamese souls.

Corns' squad occupied the line of huts that served as a security fence next to the paddock, a grassy patch separating their friendly village from a suspected pro-Viet Cong village. At the end of the paddock line, at the northern corner of the Ville, was Corns' hut. Inside that hovel, four souls pulled up the cover of security. Corns was still bright-eyed and strong, but growing weary. Willard was weary but smiling. Daniel was stoned and very tired. And Forbes, a newby, a lanky laconic redhead from Portland Oregon, was now in charge of the field radio that was attached to the squad in the Ville.

Daniel crumpled a resinous marijuana bud into the emptied end of his cigarette, then took a slug of the foul firewater before lighting the cigarette. Willard brushed through the scraggly burlap doorway and propped the M-14 against the hut's center post.

"What's happening, Doc?"

Daniel just looked up at Willard in a momentary stare.

"Hell of an explanation, Doc. Hell of an explanation... Let me have some of that," he said and propped himself up against the flimsy wall next to Daniel.

"They got some dog-ugly women in this Ville," Willard said with a smile.

Daniel stared ahead with a smirk.

Willard took a hit on Daniel's cigarette, drawing in a maximum breath of smoke. After a few seconds he exhaled, blinking.

"Good shit, Doc."

He got up slowly and pulled back the door flap.

"Hey, Doc," he said and chuckled. "Water buffalo tied up out in our front yard by the VC fence," he said as he stretched, then pointed.

Daniel scribbled big letters on a cardboard box top with a piece of charcoal then got up as if his whole body ached with soreness. He hung the sign above the doorway on the outside. It read, "THE GROTTO."

He sat back down inside against the flimsy bamboo wall, his shoulders hunched forward and stared in a daze at the new morning air. His upper torso muscles always bulged now, after months of moving through the jungle with pack and gear like a pack animal. As he stared forward, images of boyhood shot into his mind.

HE'D GRAB HIS AIR-RIFLE AND CANTEEN AND WANDER INTO THE DRY FOOTHILLS, ACTING OUT MILITARY COMMANDS AND HOLDING OFF HORDES OF INDIANS, OR WWII JAPANESE, OR GERMANS WITH FEROCITY AND NEVER-ENDING AMMO FROM BEHIND A LONE BOULDER OR OAK TREE. OLD OAK TREES BECAME ARTILLERY EXPLOSIONS.

The sun made slits in the air like uneven blinds. He lit a cigarette and grinned into the air. He re-read a letter from Francine that ended with a brief but very explicit P.S. He imagined her on the mud-packed floor of the Grotto, flower dress torn up and away. He thought about the Vietnamese peasant women bartering and smiling through black teeth, sitting on their haunches in black pajamalike pants. The image made him even more listless. But the image of Francine aroused him.

Threads of light filtered through the strung bamboo walls. Daniel heard the field radio crackle as Forbes brushed through the doorway then sat on his spot.

"How's it going, Doc?" Forbes asked, glancing at Daniel.

The lieutenant's voice came through between electronic screeches on the radio.

"Is your squad leader there?" the radio squawked in military lingo.

"What should I say, Doc?"

"Corns is doing PR with the village headman."

"When the corporal is done," the lieutenant barked, "have him return message."

"You'd think you guys weren't fighting a war," Forbes quipped and smiled wryly.

"We've been fighting it, Forbes. It's your turn," Daniel said as he walked to the hut next door, the home of an old man who used to be a property owner but who now only owned a large jug of rice firewater.

"Corns?" Daniel said at the doorway.

"Come in, bak-si," the old man called.

Daniel flipped up the silk door flap and walked in. Corns and the elderly man sat cross-legged on opposite sides of a low red-lacquered table. A demi-john of rice liquor sat at the old man's side.

"You ought to try this stuff, Doc. Real nice."

"No thanks, Corns. The lieuy was just on the hook for you."

Corns sprang up then thanked the gray-haired man and exited.

"Cupful?" the old man asked Daniel in Vietnamese.

"Sure, why not?" Daniel said in Vietnamese then chugged a large cupful.

He walked out gagging, thanking the old man in Vietnamese.

When Daniel entered the Grotto Corns was finished receiving orders from the lieutenant. They were going out on patrol to check out a suspected VC village 1500 yards away.

"We hump a klick and a half, check it out, then get our asses back here as quick as possible," Corns said to Daniel. "If we hit any shit, we'll blow the place."

In a few minutes the ten-man troop moved single file down the hard mud road, passing a clapboard restaurant, an Army compound, then slowly across rice paddy ridges, looking for trip-wires.

They came within sight of the village then stopped to study the location on the map before going in. There was a sudden pop-pop-pop in the air and they all hugged the ground. They got up to find a nine-year-old boy playing with firecrackers. Corns lead the squad on toward the village as Willard took the boy behind a tree and crushed his hand with the butt of the M-14. The boy screamed and Willard gagged him with a large field dressing. He motioned for the boy to be quiet or be dead and the boy stopped, sobbing as he rocked back and forth holding his maimed hand.

"Simple justice," Willard said as he caught up with the rest of the squad.

He chuckled as an old woman came out of a hut and began sweeping the entrance to her hut with a rice-stalk broom.

"No VC in there, Doc," Willard said as they approached and began encircling the village. "Ain't it a shame?"

"Sometimes I think you like this shit," Daniel said.

"I know you like it, white boy. It's called preventative medicine."

"Fuck you, Willard."

"Slow down, Doc... Just joking. Seein' if you're still smiling."

Daniel glanced at Willard.

Everyone in the squad began tearing apart wooden beds at the joints and overturning earthen cruses, searching for weapons.

"Corporal Hovington!" a newby whispered to Corns as the newby passed a hut entrance. "Someone's hiding in there. Behind that back panel."

Corns directed the squad with hand signals to surround the hut while Willard and Daniel guarded a nexus of paths at the perimeter of the village.

"Do it!" Corns said matter-of-factly.

The air was stabbed by the percussions of several automatic

rifles and .45s. A cloud of rice stalk and flour dust enveloped the quaking hut. They waited a few seconds then entered and tore down a false wall. In a bamboo cubbyhole they found the bullet-mangled body of a twelve-year-old girl. Daniel came up to see, then walked away alone, rubbing his forehead and temples. Corns came up to Daniel.

"What is with you, Doc?"

"I'm just so goddamn tired of this shit."

"Listen to me. I'm telling you. I'm sick of it too. But we got no choice, Doc. Listen to me," he said, then put a hand on Daniel's shoulder. "You okay? You're starting to act freaked out. Like you're out on the edge."

"We just blew the shit out of an innocent girl."

"It was a mistake, Doc, that's all... Don't get squeamish on us now."

"Okay, okay... Enough."

"They're just animals, Doc... Meat... Listen to me. I had a dream last night. I had a dream and I've got a new way for us to play the game. You listening?"

"What, you want a bull horn?"

"Smartass honky."

"Gee, thanks."

"Are you listening?"

"Yeh. Go ahead."

"We don't have to do much while we're guarding the friendlies. A patrol once in a while is about all. A little search and destroy to keep the old blood perking. Know what I mean?" Corns said and turned to check on the men, who were tearing apart and starting to burn other huts. "We're all a little flippo, Doc. So what? It's a game. It's a game and we got to start acting like it. Like it's a movie and we're actors."

Daniel looked into Corns' eyes.

"Dig it?" Corns said and grinned. "We'll be like gunfighters in a movie. Let's see what Willard thinks... Willard!" Corns yelled. "Come here!"

Willard sauntered from the ransacked village toward Corns and Daniel.

"From now on, Willard," Corns began, "we're like gunfighters in an old Western movie. Just for the hell of it."

"Okay," Willard said and chuckled

" Listen to me," Corns said. "From now on, Willard, you'll be Jesse for Jesse James, I'll be Wyatt for Wyatt Earp, and Doc... hmm, what should be call him?"

Willard thought for a few moments.

"I've got it," he said. "Let's call him Doc Holliday... The meanest medical man the East ever did see."

"Yeh! That's it," Corns said. "And don't tell anybody about the nicknames but us."

"Sounds good!" Willard said. "What say, Doc?"

"Sounds okay to me, Jesse. But what'll we call Forbes?"

"Forbes?" said Corns. "Forget it. He's too new. He hasn't earned it yet."

Corns signalled for the squad to form into a patrol formation, then left the dead body inside the burning hut. The squad moved along dirt paths and roads in a haphazard but wary line. They approached an open air marketplace and saw women of all ages selling vegetables, plastic goods and cigarettes. The men bantered with the women and eyed the goods. Corns sent a point man up ahead fifty paces as a precaution. Huddled clusters of men talked with the women, who were all dressed in long black pajamalike pants.

The trio walked in a huddle telling jokes. They looked around as they talked, watching windows and roofs and trees.

"Hey, Holliday," Willard said, "remember the time you jumped through your tent?"

"What happened, anyway?" Corns said.

"It was a black night. Absolutely black," Daniel said. "I set up my tent low to the ground, smoked part of joint to go to sleep, then started dozing off. I thought I felt something on my stomach, but I couldn't even see my belt buckle, it was so dark. I didn't see anything so I closed my eyes. Then, all of a sudden, I felt something crawling on my chest. I opened my eyes quick and a huge scorpion was headed toward my chin, its tail curled and ready to strike at my face. I jumped up through my poncho and screamed, brushing my chest like a madman."

Corns and Willard chuckled.

A violent crack-boom shook the air ahead of them. The point man walked up to a bamboo church window and lifted it. He looked down rows of empty pews and saw nothing in through the dank air. A VC stuck a rifle barrel through the wall to his chest and fired.

They searched for the culprit but he vanished. Daniel checked the newby for life and felt none. Corns called for a medical chopper. Within minutes it landed in the wide roadway. They watched the body loaded on board and the chopper lift off, then resumed their trek in the heavy sunshine. They were quiet and serious, intent on getting back to the safety of the Ville.

That afternoon there was an extra bottle of whiskey in the Grotto to blot out the day's fright. Forbes sat hunched over a letter to his girlfriend in Portland, trying to describe his first patrol. Daniel lit a cigarette and stared at the center post as if in a recurrent dream.

Willard and Corns ducked into the Grotto from the neighbor's hut in the twilight air.

"Hey, Holliday," he said, forgetting Forbes. "Gimme one of those cigarettes you're so proud of."

Daniel flicked Corns a long filtered cigarette without looking.

"Thanks, Holliday."

A pink and purple sunset streaked the sky outside the Grotto. Inside the Grotto Daniel lit a candle he'd bartered for while on patrol. He grabbed the whiskey bottle and chugged on it, then gasped. Corns looked at Daniel and Daniel looked at Corns. The silent look spoke to each of them. Their eyes seemed to ask questions and provide answers at the same time: "Can I take any more of this shit?"

"Of course you can. It might even get worse."

Forbes left then came back from the garrison with fresh batteries for the radio. Daniel saw the bottom of a frosted bottle of gin Forbes hid in a pouch.

Corns and Willard soon slept in a corner of the Grotto. When Forbes saw them passed out, he pulled the gin from the pouch. He looked at Daniel and smiled.

"My girl sent me some good gin, Doc. Want a snort?"

"Sure. But why not Corns and Willard?"

"I don't know... A pint doesn't go very far, I guess... So what's new these days, Doc?" Forbes asked while unscrewing the lid, then passed the bottle and stared at Daniel.

"Here's to Wyatt and Jesse," Daniel said, then tilted the bottle for a long slug of gin. "Thanks, Forbes," and handed it back. "No pain, Forbes. Only sleep. Adios."

As Daniel fell asleep Forbes watched the occasional tic of the medic's lip jerk up. He scratched a note on a second page to his girlfriend: "I learn more about this war from the three guys I live with than from my own experience. Into the Great Jungle I walk, my love."

Just after sunup Daniel walked warily down the old French garrison road toward the Army compound. He walked through the calm clear morning air holding the stubby shotgun tightly and pointed in front of him. He passed the small open air restaurant and several wooden shanties, looking in every doorway and crawl space. He passed the shacks and then a large grassy area and relaxed only when he spotted the massive molehill bunkers of the Army compound set inside barbed wire. At the gate he met a thickset sergeant with shaving cream on one side of his face.

"Hi, Sarg. I'm a medic with Charlie Company, just down the road from here. I'm low on some basic med supplies and we're not getting resupplied for a while... Okay if I look around?"

"Sure. Help yourself."

The sergeant wiped away the remaining shave cream and grinned as he turned to walk away. "We've got more than we'll ever use," he said over his shoulder.

"Thanks," Daniel said as he descended in a large sandbagged room covered by a tent. "Like giving candy to a..." He picked up a large plastic jar and read the label: "Aspirin and amphetamine — use for shell shock, special maneuvers..." His eyes opened wide and he grabbed some gauze bandages, stuffing them on top of the large jar already in his medical bag.

He walked out into the sun trying to remain calm. The sergeant sat atop a bunker a short distance away, eating C-rats and looking out over the land.

"Thanks! Got everything I need," Daniel shouted and waved across the compound.

"Keep those jar-heads going," he said and grinned, then turned back to watch the sultry land.

Walking past the shanties with shotgun drawn and ready, he was like watching yin and yang. Between buildings the sun would shine on his face and it seemed to light up with expected pleasure. In the shade and checking out openings, the shadows brought out the grimness of death in his face. He was soon near the garrison and walked through the grassy paddock the Grotto.

He flipped up the door flap and saw Corns and Willard eating crackers and jam and trying to wake up.

"Where you been?" Corns asked Daniel.

Daniel pulled out the plastic jar.

"A thousand uppers, while you slept!"

"What?" Willard said, reading the label.

"Christ, Holliday, you just made my day," said Corns. "These things got to be worth some bucks."

"I'd say about a buck apiece, wouldn't you?" Daniel said to both of them.

Forbes turned over and pulled up his poncho liner for more sleep.

They all fingered the jar. Willard lit the candle stub and held it up to the jar. The amber jar sent off flickering reflections across their faces.

"This stuff is probably eighty percent aspirin and twenty percent upper," Daniel said. "But I'm the medical guy here. I say they're fifty-fifty... We'll sell 'em for a buck each, use the money to buy smoke and sell it and... We just hit it big!"

"Wow," Willard said in a sigh. "We've got to find a good smoke woman quick... I talked to a girl yesterday said she might be able to get some. But she wants a buck a smoke."

"It'll happen," Daniel boasted to Corns. "I can feel it. Like luck. Like luck. It'll just happen! This whole company is going on a speed blitz... Beginning with us. Let's drop fifteen or twenty each."

They chuckled and hooted in whispers. They gulped down pills and canteen water, then Willard and Corns left for the garrison to begin bartering. On the way Willard stopped by a hut, snuck in the door, then reappeared with ten joints.

"How'd you do that?" Corns asked.

Willard just smiled, and they walked on.

Inside the grotto, Daniel counted out piles of pills by candle light. The sun came up above the neighbor's hut and filtered sunlight filled the Grotto in vertical slits.

An hour later Corns and Willard returned talking rapidly.

"We got people want to buy fifty for cash, right now," Willard said, snapping his fingers in delight. "Not bad, eh?"

"And top this, Holliday," Corns said. "Willard found out the joint lady will give us ten joints for one upper."

By late afternoon the Grotto was stocked with dozens of hard-to-get objects like cologne, a bowie knife, an infrared scope, and more. There were even cartons of Marlboros and Winstons.

In the late afternoon Daniel walked swiftly through the knee-high grass of the paddock to the shitter, a deep hole in the ground with two boards to squat on. He hunched down with his back to the suspected VC village and studied the dusky image of the Ville. Fred Harckbud, a thin hunch-shouldered hillbilly, walked slowly through the grass toward Daniel. He stopped about twenty feet from the shitter.

"Doc?" he said with deference.

"Yeh, Fred. I'm sitting right here."

"Well, Doc," he said then smiled as a swarm of flies came up through Daniel's legs. "I heard you want to buy some marijuana cheap. Right?"

"Why, Fred?"

"I found this here family that's darn near turned me into a son. The mama-san says she can get 'em real cheap."

"Okay. What's cheap?"

"A nickel apiece, Doc... As many as you want."

"I'll be damned, Fred. You're something."

"How much money do you have, Doc?"

He handed Fred sixty dollars.

"Fifty bucks is for a thousand joints, Fred. Ten is for you... I need you to keep it between us how many I'm getting, okay?"

"Sure. But you need a thousand? Really?"

"Yeh, to start. We've got to take advantage of this situation, Fred."

Daniel headed back through the grass with the mighty strides of amphetamines. He entered the Grotto with his head abuzz and lit half a dozen candles, then stood tall and stretched his fingers into the grass roof.

"This shit's a lot better than my first firefight," Daniel said and sat down by Corns and Willard.

"What'd Fred want?" Willard asked.

Daniel thumbed off the cap on a fifth of Wild Turkey and sipped on it.

"Found a gook chick that'll get smoke at five cents apiece."

"You're shitting me," Corns said as he lit a cigarette.

"No. But I'm paying him more... People don't need to know how much we're dealing."

"Good thinking, Holliday," Willard said. "You're getting more like a black man every day."

"Thanks," Daniel said, then lunged across the small space and wrestled Willard over.

Corns grabbed Willard and they both held him down as Daniel forced Wild Turkey into his mouth.

"Willard," Corns said and laughed, "you quit messin' with Holliday or Wyatt's going to kick your nigger ass."

Daniel got up and took a deep breath in, only to be tackled by Corns and pinned by Willard.

• • •

No one ever discovered who snuck into Charlie's hilltop camp during Daniel's first night with the company, before the firefight in the river, and slit Captain Murwood's throat. But Clay Brown had raised so much racial trouble in his company, he was transferred into Charlie. He now lived behind the garrison's thick walls.

Forbes walked into the Grotto and gasped.

"My god Doc this is incredible... Is this a war or an auction?"

"Both," Daniel said. "Help yourself. You're one of us now," and handed Forbes the bottle of Wild Turkey.

"Okay, Doc. I've got nothing but time to kill."

Daniel stopped and studied Forbes.

"You are one strange guy, Forbes."

"Thanks, Doc. I get by."

Willard and Corns walked in talking. Willard handed Daniel a new pair of argyle socks. Corns handed Daniel a lump of U.S. dollars and piaster notes. Willard plopped a bag of joints on the floor.

They stood by the center post in the light of many candles and jabbered about luck. They wiped sweat from their foreheads and kept talking, passing a bottle of whiskey. They heard a knock on the bamboo doorway and stopped.

"Corns!" a hoarse voice whispered. "You in there?"

"Clay Brown," Corns said in recognition then gave Daniel a quick glance. He pushed back the door flap and said, "Come on in, bro'. Make yourself at home."

After introductions the five chums chugged whiskey in the Grotto.

"Looks like you got a good thing going, Doc," Clay said. "I can work my old company for you if you want."

"How you going to do that, Clay," Willard said. "They're miles from here."

"I'll work that out. It'll just take a little work, that's all... Besides," he said and grinned at Daniel, "I can use some free smoke."

Clay left the Grotto after exchanging the intricate black handshake with Willard and Corns. Forbes swallowed some uppers while sitting inside by his radio. The trio went outside by a foxhole near the Grotto. Daniel jumped over the foxhole in light-headed confusion and walked to the shitter in the dark.

"Don't fall in, white boy," Willard said after him.

Fred walked up to the shitter from the VC-fence and startled Daniel.

"Hi, Doc," he said.

"Jeez! Fred! I thought you were a gook!... Be careful."

"Sorry... Here's the stuff," he said, handing Daniel a large bundle wrapped in newspaper.

"Thanks, Fred," Daniel said, staring in rapt attention at the bundle. "Oh... and here, Fred. Here's a hundred bucks. Get me a couple thousand more tomorrow or the next day. And here's fifty for you... We're partners."

"Sounds good, Doc," Fred said, then turned and walked away through the grass.

Daniel came back to the foxhole with the bundle. Corns guessed at the contents and gasped.

"We've got to celebrate."

Corns went inside and got three flares he traded for an upper. He stumbled by Forbes and back out of the Grotto. Corns stopped and stuck his head back inside the Grotto.

"What do you think of the rotten old veterans now, Red?"

"Fine. Just fine," Forbes said with pursed lips. "I like it real fine."

Corns turned and handed a flare to Willard and one to Daniel, then swung his arm to show Daniel how to pop the flare. He pointed the flare up in his left hand and hit the butt of the flare with his upswinging right palm. It popped and shot into the sky, where it exploded into white light. They laughed and Willard popped his, and the sky was lit in red. Then Daniel shot his, but he held it forward and not up. The flare shot across a large field and landed on the grass roof of a villager's hut a hundred yards away. They watched the family scamper out of the ignited hut and dance around it in dismay. The trio laughed until the radio exploded with noise from the garrison.

Corns told the lieutenant that he had no idea what was happening or where the flare bursts originated.

In two minutes The Cutter strode up alone, carrying only his M-16 and a bandolier of banana clips.

"I don't care if you party, you idiots," he said to the trio with harshness in his voice. "But keep it cool enough the lieutenant don't know about it, see?"

The Cutter turned and left.

The trio stared after Lockwood as if they could see him through the dark.

Inside the Grotto the four took final gulps of whiskey and fell into sleep. But the pills were too active in Forbes system. He raised up, lit a candle, and scribbled notes to his girlfriend, looking into the candlelight between words and imagining misty mountains east of Portland.

● ● ●

Forbes sat staring out at the VC village as dawn began lighting the air. The radio screeched. The trio awoke with aching hangovers as they heard the lieutenant's voice blaring from the radio, telling Corns to take his squad out on patrol.

"You've got to be joking," Willard said.

"Back to reality," Corns said as he stood, stretched, then went out to wake and ready his men for a patrol. He moved from hut to hut on the line, telling the men to be ready to hump in ten minutes.

Fifteen minutes later Corns led his squad on a two-mile course that would eat up six hours. They passed the women with betelnut black teeth setting out their wares at the marketplace. The women chomped on their leaf-wrapped betelnut and joked about the manhood of the GIs. Only Daniel understood them, but his head ached too much for response. They humped on and on, through rice paddies and villages and clumps of jungle. After three hours, Corns halted the weary squad and turned it around for the walk back home to the Ville. A boy walked suddenly from between two huts toward Corns. He touched Corns' side before anyone could react. He started to speak then halted in fear as Corns stuck the barrel of a .45 at the boy's throat. Willard aimed the M-14 from five yards away as Daniel walked up with the cocked shotgun.

"Gotcha, Tarzan," Willard said to Corns and snickered.

"Real funny, Jesse," Corns said. "Doc, what's this little gook jabbering about?"

"'Bak-si.' The kid wants a doctor. Somebody's sick in his village." Daniel grinned. "That's me, boss."

Corns used hand signals to send two grunts as guards for Daniel. The small group moved along a curving path. Still within earshot of Corns, they walked to a large hut. The boy pointed then walked away.

"Grab the kid!" Daniel said.

A grunt tripped the boy then sat on him, still looking around.

"Doc, we better get out of here," the grunt said.

"Okay, just a minute," Daniel replied. "Let's see what's inside this hut first," he said as he pushed open the door flap with the shotgun barrel. Daniel moved up to the body slowly, then felt the listless shoulder of a woman lying under a thin cover. He nudged her jaw with the gun. He flinched at the sound of a baby's whimper. It was wrapped in an old poncho liner and tucked into a C-ration box. Daniel focused on the woman. He raised her eyelids and saw that she was dying of pernicious anemia. The sensation of death rushed into his mind from his fingertips like capillary attraction. He knew he could not help, that she would soon die, and with her, the baby. The thought pierced his combat crust. He bit his hand and tears leaked out of squinted eyes as he backed away. He wiped the tears away then exited the hut.

"Generation to generation," he mumbled as he signalled for the two grunts to go with him back to the squad. The boy ran away.

"What's wrong, Doc?" Willard said.

"Nothing... They're being left to die... No one can help... No one will help," he said and rubbed his eyes. "Let's just get out of here. They're just meat anyway."

Three hours later they dragged themselves by the outdoor restaurant near the garrison. The patrol was finished. Corns sent the squad on to the Ville but kept Willard, Daniel and Forbes.

"Doc's going to buy us a beer here," Corns said and sat down at a rickety table.

"This place is filthy," Forbes said.

"Not good enough for you, newby?" Willard said and pushed Forbes down onto the bench. "Corns says we're having a beer. And Doc's paying for it, so shut your face up and enjoy, enjoy."

"We'll just have a couple of beers on Doc then scurry back to the Ville, Forbes," Corns said. "What's with you, Doc? You act like you saw a ghost back there."

A little old man ran out from a back pantry and bowed. Daniel talked to him in broken Vietnamese. The man nodded and went to prepare his service.

"Let's hope it's just beer we get," Daniel said.

The old man brought beers in tall dark bottles and fried crusts with dipping sauce. They sipped beers and joked about the NVA being scared of Forbes' red hair but that the VC wanted to scalp him and wear it as a charm.

Suddenly an ARVN officer walked out from between two huts with a drawn pistol. Another soldier, an ARVN non-com, fired at the officer with an M-16. Corns and the others dove for the ground under the table and watched. The officer ran in front of the restaurant and shot at the other ARVN.

"What is going on?" Willard said.

"I have no idea," Corns said. "But the damn fools made me spill my beer."

The man with the M-16 jumped out from a different set of huts and pumped a full clip into the officer. The man looked around then walked away slowly, over a ridge and across a rice paddy.

"A gook OK Corral," Daniel said as he got up and turned to walk with the others toward the Grotto. He tossed several piaster notes in the street by the restaurant and shouted for the old man to pick them up. They looked back over their shoulders at the dead officer.

•   •   •

Back in the Grotto, Daniel opened a new bottle of whiskey and took a long swig.

"Like your first firefight, Forbes?" Daniel asked.

"Very strange," Forbes said, fiddling with knobs on his field radio.

"Stick tight, Forbes," Corns said, taking the bottle from Daniel. "We help each other."

"Grotto?" Clay yelled outside their doorway. He staggered in stinking of too much whiskey. "White man's cave, that's what it is," he said, shaking in the doorway.

"What's happening?" Corns said

"Not much, Uncle Tom," Clay said.

"Cut that bullshit... Doc's my buddy."

"Don't fuck with me, white boy," Clay said to Daniel.

Daniel looked to Willard for advice.

"Don't look at him, asshole!" Clay shouted at Daniel. "Look at me!"

Corns rose and grabbed Clay's arm. Clay swung at Corns but missed. Willard and Daniel jumped in, wrestling then pinning Clay inside the Grotto.

"Get the lieuy on the hook, Forbes," Corns said. "Tell him we got one very drunk monkey over here."

Clay went limp and smiled.

"You mean, Corns... you're helping this honky hold down a brother?"

"Doc's my brother. You're a monkey."

Two grunts ran up from the garrison and escorted Clay away from the Ville.

The trio walked back into the Grotto breathing heavily and trying to shake off the bad spell.

"Will someone watch the radio while I go over to the garrison?" Forbes asked.

"Forget that!" Corns snapped. "You're the goddamn radioman. You watch it!"

Forbes walked out with the radio slung on an arm and joined another newby four huts down the row.

"I got to get some air," Willard said and walked off into the Ville carrying the M-14 across his arms like a baby.

"What the fuck's happening around this place!" he said and spit on the hard mud floor, then put his head between his knees, sitting with arms wrapped around his legs.

Daniel rubbed the tic from his upper lip and looked out the raised door flap at the grassy paddock and VC village.

"Don't sweat it," he said and pulled his hand away. "Like you told me the first time we talked... on that dirt road, remember?... 'Don't mean a thing, Doc,' you said. Remember?"

"That's a bad guy to mess with," Corns said and raised his head from between his knees. He lit a cigarette for Daniel, then one for himself. "He's crazy... Just as soon kill you as look at you... The black and white thing's just a symptom."

They stared out the doorway quietly, smoking cigarette after cigarette.

An hour later they began mellowing into relaxation. They heard footsteps at the side of the hut. Someone was creeping up to the doorway.

"Willard?" Corns said softly.

Clay's image suddenly filled the doorway, with a .45 cocked and pointed at Daniel's face.

"You made a big mistake, Doc," Clay said, the Adam's apple jerking up with each of Clay's remarks.

"Why me, man? I'm just trying to help people."

"Bullshit!" Clay said then blinked and looked at Corns.

Corns spoke and it was as if his words purged the air of violence and filled it with rock-hard calm.

"Doc didn't do shit, man. Who are you trying to fool?"

Clay looked at Corns as if struck in the face.

"Get out of here, Clay," Corns said. "You've stretched this thing way out."

Clay eased his grip on the pistol. He relaxed his arm until the weapon was at his side, then backed out of the hut and into the sunshine.

As Clay walked away Daniel and Corns stared quickly at each other, unsure what to do. Corns started to speak when they heard the crack-boom! of Clay's .45. He'd shot the old man next door in the face, ripping away the backside of the old man's head. Clay walked on. Daniel pulled out the shotgun and Corns his .45 and exited the Grotto. Just as they caught sight of Clay, Clay saw Fred walking on a path between two huts and shot him in the chest. Clay seemed sobered by the deed and walked away with the gun hanging by his side.

Corns aimed at Clay from behind.

"You fucking nigger! Killed one of my men, nigger... Turn and face me!"

"Don't!" Daniel yelled at Corns. "Corns! Don't! Stop! He isn't worth it!"

"This guy deserves to die!" Corns shouted, shaking from anger and walking slowly toward Clay.

"Corns. Please, listen to me," Daniel said, coming up next to Corns. "They'll throw you in the brig... Please. It ain't worth it."

The words broke Corns' spell. He let up on the hammer then lowered the pistol.

"Get out of here!" Daniel yelled at the throng of villagers who came up to watch. "You're like flies on shit! Get away!" He fired a round from the shotgun into the air and they scurried.

The rest of Corns' squad aimed weapons at Clay and escorted

him back to the garrison.

Willard ran up and stood with Corns as Daniel worked on Fred.

"He's alive but just barely," Daniel said. "We need a chopper ASAP, Corns."

They lifted Fred onto a makeshift stretcher and carried him to the roadway in front of the garrison.

"Doc," Corns came up and said. "Bad news. Only choppers available are Army... Some lieutenant colonel is headed here now to run things."

As the gunship approached, so did the sub-colonel. He barked out orders and shoved Daniel out of the way.

The chopper lifted off with Fred and the officer asked for Daniel's name, rank, and outfit.

Daniel gave it to him, then spit in the road before turning and walking back into the Ville.

The lieutenant colonel ordered Daniel to stop but Daniel kept walking. A Jeep drove up, the officer hopped in, then sped away, staring after Daniel.

●　●　●

"It all just turns up shit no matter what we do," Corns said to Daniel and Willard in the Grotto.

Corns saw Daniel's lip pop up in a twitch and laughed. Daniel held his lip in embarrassment, then burst out laughing too. All three squirmed on the floor laughing, breathless.

"Did I ever tell you what 'bak-si' means?... It means witch doctor," then he laughed again.

"You're one very wicked witch doctor," Willard said and they laughed more.

"Know what else?" Daniel said, grabbing a bottle of whiskey and chugging on it. 'Tet' is a Vietnamese variation of a Chinese word. Means 'festival.' Just think, the Tet Offensive was a festival... We celebrate, don't we?"

Corns sat up and wiped tears from his eyes.

"Hey, honky. We tell you we're going to Singapore for R&R?"

"Well, thanks for inviting me, you racist pigs!" Daniel said and lit a joint.

"You can come too if you want, Holliday," Willard said seriously.

"Yeh. Come with us, Doc," Corns said. "We'll tear the place up."

Daniel took a drag from the joint and passed it to Willard.

"No thanks. I'm going to Japan later on."

They stopped laughing and caught their breaths, but lay on the hard floor and looked up through the grass roof.

"Doc," Willard said, remember that time you and The Cutter captured that gook? Then we all had to take him back to the last LZ?"

"Yeh," Daniel said as he lifted his head to drink from the bottle, "one of the freakiest experiences ever."

"What happened, Jesse," Corns said.

"Captured the gook. Decided to quiz him for info, so they sent Lockwood, me," Willard said, "Doc and some other guys back to our last LZ. I don't know what you were doin', Wyatt. Probably sleeping."

Corns rose up on an elbow and smashed a fist into Willard's thigh, gaving him a charley horse.

"You cold-hearted bastard," Willard said and sighed. "Anyway, we set out, quiet as cod. The gook was tied up. But he was already starting to act up, so The Cutter throws him up on a shoulder like a bag of potatoes. Me and Holliday here were behind The Cutter and the gook, checking out the bush real thorough like. I tell you. We were so scared. The bush just seemed to be crawlin' with gooks. Ambush city. And old Doc here, still trying to be Pacifist numero uno, puts his hand on the gook's shoulder, trying to make him feel at home or some kind of shit." Willard took a swig of whiskey then continued. "So this gook, see... he lifts his head off The Cutter's back and hisses, then spits in old Doc's face. Bigger than shit... A few minutes later The Cutter says it's time to put the gook down for some rest. Asks Doc where to put the gook. Old Doc here sees an old exploded tree trunk sticking up in splinters and points to it. The Cutter swung the gook off his shoulder and right onto that stump. Snap! Broke the fucker's back. Sent a shiver right up my spine."

"So what happened then?" Corns demanded.

"We got back somehow, without the gook."

"You guys never told me that," Corns said and lit a cigarette. Forbes walked in with the radio.

"Where you been?" Corns asked.

"Talking to the guys in the garrison... Clay's in handcuffs waiting for a chopper. Going directly to the brig in DaNang... How did this whole thing get loose?"

"A long time ago," Corns said. "Before you were born... before there was fire."

Forbes snorted a laugh then took a joint from Willard.

Without warning a barrage of mortar rounds began exploding in the VC village in sets of six. Wave after wave hit until everything was afire across from the Ville. Corns' squad watched from foxholes. When it was over, The Cutter ran up. He told Corns the Army had made a mistake, had gotten incorrect grid co-ordinates.

"Doc," he said, "you've got to go in. An Army medical team is being choppered in now. You hook up with them, clean up, then report back here."

The air was full of smoke and wailing from the VC village. Daniel met the Army team and went into the smoldering huts to help. Inside one hut he saw a woman bleeding from several shrapnel wounds, whimpering and looking over her shoulder at her two small boys. The boys were sprawled on the floor like rag dolls, with arms and legs minced by the explosions. Daniel imagined the entire exploded and smoldering village as a burst temescal. He wanted out, immediately. Within an hour they put the mother and youngsters on choppers, then left in a hyper kind of stupor. Daniel walked back to the Grotto and collapsed on his spot.

"Doc," Lockwood's whisper came through the flimsy wall fifteen minutes later. "Come here."

Daniel stood up and walked outside. Corns and Willard waited inside and listened.

"You're all right, Doc," The Cutter said. "Kind of an idealistic asshole sometimes... But you do good work."

"Oh good," Daniel said. "Thanks."

The Cutter laughed in a snort.

"We're pacifying the land, Doc... The whole country... Cutting out the bad parts, right?"

"Like surgeons. Like ace surgeons," Daniel said.

Lockwood gave a rare smile and chuckled, then turned and loped back to the garrison.

• • •

The trio stood in the garrison roadway sweating under the noon's next sun. Daniel handed Corns and Willard an extra roll of bills.

"Bring back some goodies," he said to Willard.

Corns and Willard entered the garrison gates and vanished from sight without good-byes. Daniel stared at the empty gate then walked back toward the Grotto rubbing his new paunch.

A heavy jungle rain came with evening and lasted for days. Daniel smoked and sipped and stared at the center post. One morning while the other guys were still in Singapore, Daniel awoke with his head throbbing thunderously. Forbes put a thermometer into his mouth then checked it.

"Goddamn, Doc," Forbes said, "it reads one-o-five. You'd better get out of here before your head explodes."

Daniel stared with bloodshot eyes at the palm leaves above, then used the field radio to ask The Cutter to order him a chopper. Meanwhile he had Forbes hand out his goods and gear to the other squad members. Then Daniel motioned everyone away but Forbes. Once alone with the radioman, Daniel handed him a thick roll of U.S. bills that was hidden in his medical bag. Forbes unrolled the bill and gasped.

"There's twenty-eight thousand here, Doc."

"No shit, Red... Tell Willard and Corns to party. I'm out but I'll be back."

"Okay. Sure, Doc. Whatever you say."

Daniel heard the tornadolike whir of the medical chopper coming for him.

"Something else, Forbes."

"Yeh. What, Doc?"

"Here's an extra five grand... I want that Army colonel snuffed... in broad daylight."

Forbes balked, then took the money.

"Okay, Doc. Somebody'll do it."

The Marines of the squad walked the stretcher through the Ville. The villagers looked on from the alleys between the huts as another prone victim whisked by on a stretcher.

Daniel stared up at the hot sky. Each heartbeat was an explosion in his head as ruinous cerebral malaria ate deeper and deeper at his brain. He began laughing in a hoarse series of fits of wailing, then he was quiet. The only thing that moved was his twitching lip.

"Brisling!" he said into the whir of the chopper blades. "I'll get you. I'm going to hurt you where it hurts the most!"

Afterworld

Daniel's skin burned as he was lowered into a bathtub full of ice cubes on the medical ship SANCTUARY. He screamed at the new waves of throbbing. At the same time his mind seemed to explode, Corns and Willard jumped in a cattle truck headed for Phu-bai from DaNang.

"Goddamn that Suzie chick was something," Corns said and slapped Willard's thigh.

"I could tell," Willard said and sighed. "And her friend.... .

While Willard was in mid-sentence the truck tripped a wire and twenty enemy claymore's simultaneously crushed and exploded the truck.

● ● ●

Daniel was taken off the SANCTUARY and quickly released from active duty, into his mother's care.

A week later he received a letter from Forbes, telling of Corns and Willard.

Three days later he arrived at Brisling's house under a full moon, armed for combat. It was the house of the enemy, even though Brisling was still in Vietnam. He decided to go after what mattered most to Brisling, his family.

"Just another temescal," he said with a smirk on his face as he broke the glass to throw in the Chi-Com grenades.